Green Six Sigma

A Lean Approach to Sustainable Climate Change Initiatives

Ron Basu

WILEY

Library of Congress Cataloging-in-Publication Data is Available:

ISBN 978-1-119-86123-2 (hardback)
ISBN 978-1-119-86125-6 (ePub)
ISBN 978-1-119-86124-9 (ePDF)

Cover Design: Wiley
Cover Images: © Mendelex/Shutterstock; © NPeter/Shutterstock;
Courtesy of Ron Basu
Printed and bound by CPI Group (UK) Ltd, Croydon, CR0 4YY

C9781119861232_120122

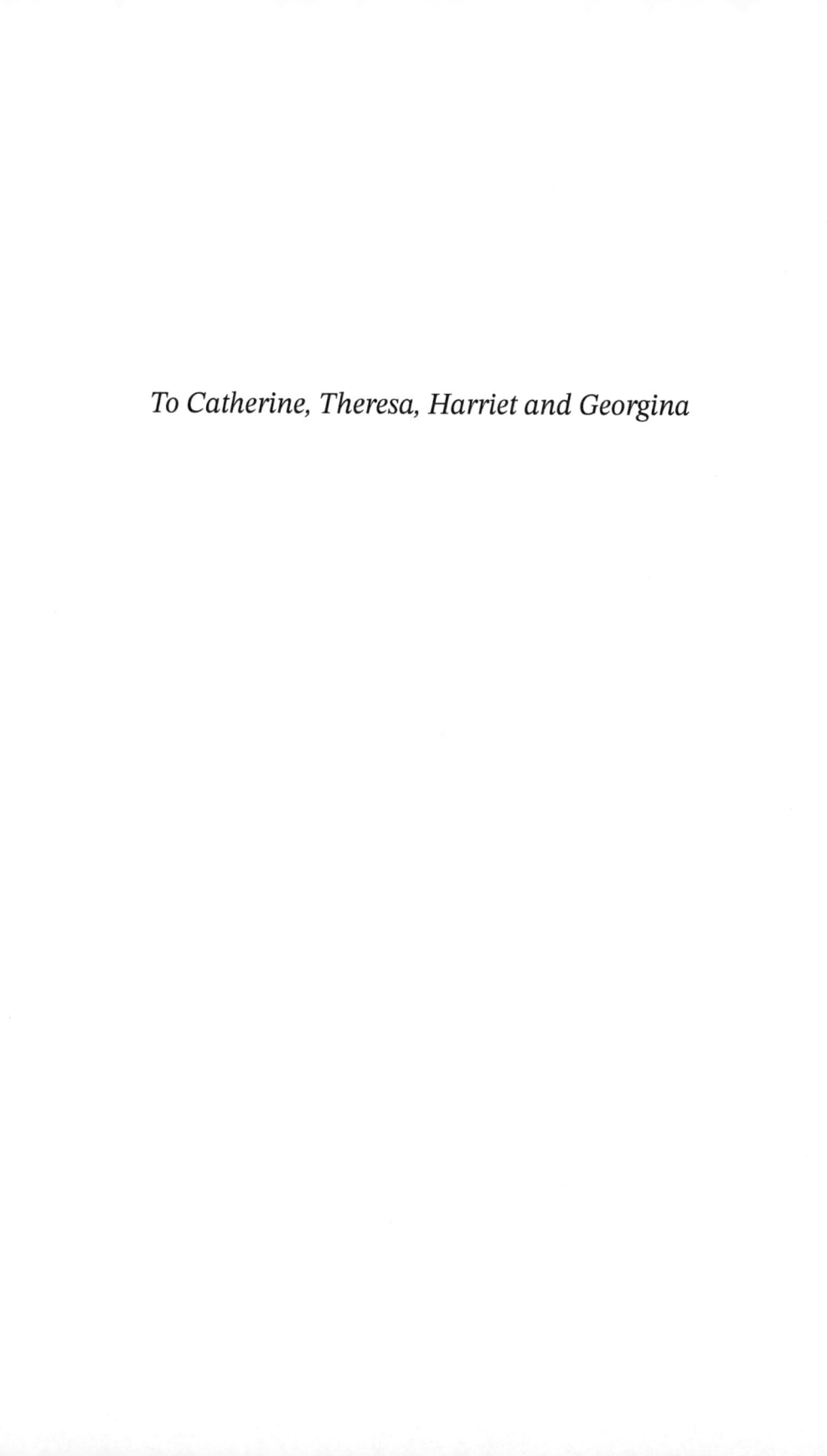

To Catherine, Theresa, Harriet and Georgina

Contents

Preface   ix
Acknowledgements   xiii
About the Author   xv

Chapter 1: Climate Change Challenges   1

Chapter 2: International and National Climate Change
                Initiatives   13

Chapter 3: The Evolution of Six Sigma, Lean Six Sigma
                and Green Six Sigma   27

Chapter 4: More of Green Six Sigma   53

Chapter 5: Green Six Sigma Tools   95

Chapter 6: The Digital Revolution and Climate Change   197

Chapter 7: Green Six Sigma and Clean Energy   219

Chapter 8: Green Six Sigma and Green Supply Chain   235

Chapter 9: Green Six Sigma and Green Transport 259

Chapter 10: Green Six Sigma and Retrofitting Buildings 275

Chapter 11: Green Six Sigma and Climate Adaptation 291

Chapter 12: Implementation: Making It Happen 311

Appendix 1: Carbon Footprint Factsheet 345

Appendix 2: Yield Conversion Table 351

References 353
Glossary 361
Index 377

Preface

Background

While sailing on a Princess Cruise a few years back I had the privilege to listen to a lecture by Mary Robinson, previously President of Ireland and also UN High Commissioner of Human Rights. She spoke for half an hour on how to avoid climate change disaster. The idea of writing a book to address these issues was conceived then in my mind. Before Mrs Robinson's lecture I was also influenced by the 'Blue Planet II' documentary on plastics pollution by David Attenborough and the movie 'An Inconvenient Truth' by Al Gore. Then, on the eve of COP26 in Glasgow there were climate-related disasters in Western Europe, North America, China and South Asia. I decided that it was now the time to write a book on climate change so that I can look into the eyes of my grandchildren and say that I have tried to do my bit.

I am not an environmental scientist but have some expertise in Six Sigma applications in achieving operations excellence in organisations. My research revealed that there were many publications on climate change and also on Six Sigma and its hybrids (e.g. Lean Six Sigma) but there was no bridge between the two. Thus, the concept of Green Six Sigma, which is basically the adaptation of Lean Six Sigma for climate change initiatives, was developed.

About This Book

There are 12 chapters in this book. Three chapters are devoted to the concept of Green Six Sigma with its tools and techniques. The other nine chapters deal with the causes of climate change and how we can mitigate and adapt to its consequences, assisted by Green Six Sigma. Green Six Sigma is not a silver bullet. It is a catalyst to accelerate climate change initiatives leading to sustainable processes and environmental standards.

Who Should Use This Book?

This book is aimed at a broad cross-section of readership including:

- Leaders of the global community with the responsibility for climate change initiatives will find this book informative to sponsor the training and applications of Green Six Sigma in the current and future projects of climate change.
- Functional managers, participants and practitioners in Six Sigma and Operational Excellence will find that this book will provide them with a comprehensive insight into the tools and techniques of sustainable improvement in a single package for climate change initiatives.
  - Senior executives, both in the manufacturing and service industries, will find that this book gives them a better understanding of basic tools and techniques and helps them to support climate change initiatives and sustain a strong competitive position.
- Professional management and training consultants will find the comprehensive approach of tools and techniques as an essential

handbook for Six Sigma related climate change assignments and seminars.

- Universities, management schools, academies and research associations will find this book valuable to fill the visible gap in the basics of operational excellence especially focused on climate change.

The readership will be global and particularly cover North America, the UK, Continental Europe, Australia and the Asia Pacific countries.

I have made an effort to furnish you with both simple and more complex concepts that are nonetheless easy to understand. At the end of each chapter some simple tips named 'Green Tips' are included. Mahatma Gandhi once said, 'Be the change you want to be in the world'. I hope this book will in some way help you to bring about that change in climate change that we urgently need.

Ron Basu
Gerrards Cross, England

Acknowledgements

I am grateful to the many contributors for the case examples and research papers on climate change included in the book with special mentions to Dr Michael Cross and Dr Avik Basu.

Every effort has been made to credit the authors, publishers and websites for materials used in this book. I apologise if inadvertently any sources remain unacknowledged and if known I shall be pleased to credit them in the next edition.

My sincere thanks go to the staff of my publisher John Wiley & Sons Ltd, especially to Gemma Valler and Purvi Patel for getting this project off the ground.

Finally, the project could not have been completed without the encouragement and help of my family, especially my wife Moira, sister-in-law Reena, son Robi and daughter Bonnie. Bonnie's contributions to edit draft chapters have been invaluable.

Ron Basu

About the Author

Ron Basu is director of RB Consultants and a visiting fellow at Henley Business School, England. He is also a visiting professor at SKEMA Business School, France. He specialises in operational excellence and supply chain management and has research interests in performance management and project management.

Previously he held senior management roles in blue-chip companies like GSK, GlaxoWellcome and Unilever and led global initiatives and projects in Six Sigma, ERP/MRPII, Supply Chain Re-engineering and Total Productive Maintenance. Prior to this he worked as management consultant with A.T. Kearney.

He is the co-author of *Total Manufacturing Solutions, Quality Beyond Six Sigma, Total Operations Solutions* and *Total Supply Chain Management* and the author of books with titles *Measuring e-Business Performance, Implementing Quality, Implementing Six Sigma and Lean, FIT SIGMA, Managing Project Supply Chains, Managing Quality in Projects, Managing Global Supply Chains* and *Managing Projects in Research and Development.* He has authored a number of peer reviewed papers in the operational excellence and project management fields.

After graduating in manufacturing engineering from UMIST, Manchester, Ron obtained an MSc in Operational Research from Strathclyde University, Glasgow. He has also completed a PhD at Reading University. He is a fellow of the Institution of Mechanical Engineers, the Institute of Business Consultancy and the Chartered Quality Institute. He is also the winner of the APM Project Management Award.

Chapter 1
Climate Change Challenges

'What humans do over the next 50 years will determine the fate of all life on the planet.'

– David Attenborough

1.1.   Introduction

'Climate change' as a scientific term may well sound quite tame and vernacular, and possibly does not convey a sufficient sense of urgency. It becomes confusing when scientists additionally talk about ice ages and other natural changes to the climate that have occurred throughout the history of our planet. The term 'global warming' has also been used as another phrase for the same thing, but, by contrast, this expression clearly imparts an unambiguous message concerning the imminent danger posed to humans and other living objects on earth.

What is beyond dispute is that the earth's temperature is rising, and even growth of two degrees centigrade would melt the ice sheets of the Polar Regions, resulting in a sea level increase of many metres. I have to admit that in the context of discussions regarding our future well-being I do prefer the term 'global warming'. However, as 'climate change' is the official term being used by the United Nations (e.g. UNF-CCC: United Nations Framework Convention of Climate Change and IPCC: Intergovernmental Panel of Climate Change), I shall also use this phrase primarily to express the impact of global warming.

The world is producing 51 Gigatons or 51 billion tons of greenhouse gases every year. These greenhouse gases include carbon dioxide (CO_2), methane (CH_4), nitrous oxide (N_2O), water vapour (H_2O) and ozone (O_3), as shown in Table 1.1.

Carbon dioxide has been found to be the most important greenhouse gas related to global warming. It constitutes 82% of all greenhouse gases and stays in the atmosphere for a long time. Recent studies have shown that 75% of carbon will not disappear for a time calculated to be between centuries to thousands of years while the other 25% will stay with us forever. Methane causes many times more warming, molecule for molecule, than carbon dioxide when it reaches the atmosphere, but methane does not stay in the atmosphere as long as carbon dioxide. In addition, man-made (anthropogenic) activities are creating a serious global warming crisis that could last far longer than we ever thought possible – unless we act immediately.

Let us consider the basic principle involved here. A greenhouse is made of glass to allow sunlight to pass through and warm the air inside. The heat is trapped by the glass and the interior becomes warmer and warmer. We experience this so-called 'greenhouse effect' when our cars are parked in the sun and their interiors can become much hotter than the external temperature. Greenhouse gases work in a similar fashion but on a massive scale to increase the earth's temperature; hence this familiar term. Carbon dioxide, methane and other greenhouse gases stay in the atmosphere for

Table 1.1   Greenhouse gases

Greenhouse Gases	Percentages
Carbon dioxide	82
Methane	10
Nitrous oxide	6
Others	2

SOURCE: US EPA (2019).

a long time and trap the heat that would otherwise escape to the atmosphere, thus causing the earth's temperature to climb.

Let us now examine how much the earth's temperature is rising and why this is causing serious concern.

As carbon dioxide commands the lion's share of greenhouse gases, the emission of all gases is expressed as a carbon dioxide equivalent (CO_2 e).

1.2. The Earth's Temperature Is Rising

Greenhouse gas emissions, especially carbon dioxide, have increased gradually since 1840 and dramatically since 1950, as shown in Figure 1.1.

Sunlight passes through the thick layer of greenhouse gases without getting absorbed to reach the earth's surface and therefore warms up the planet. The earth radiates some of the heat energy back towards space and this hits the greenhouse gas molecules. This in turn makes the molecules vibrate faster, thus

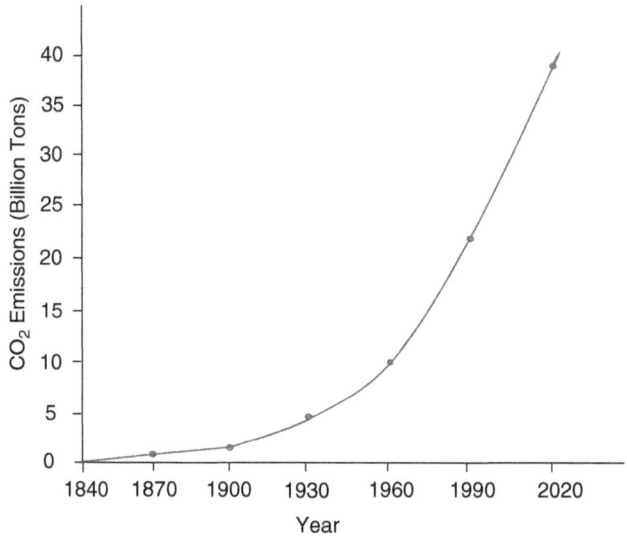

Figure 1.1 The rise of CO_2 emissions since 1840
SOURCE: Global Carbon Project Report (2019).

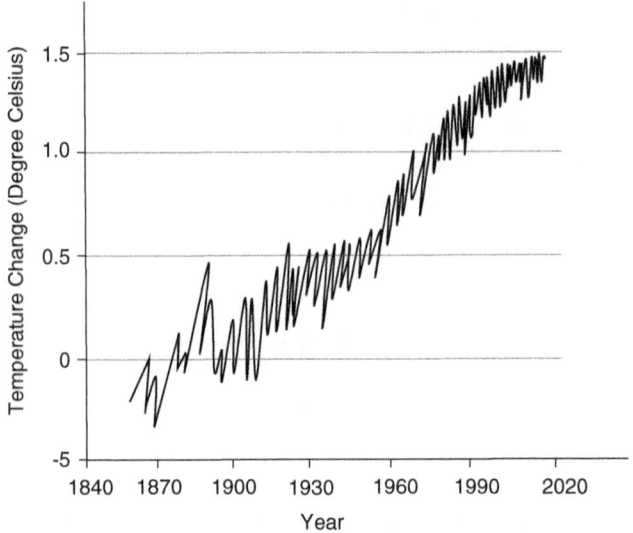

Figure 1.2 The rise of global temperatures since 1840
SOURCE: Global Carbon Project Report (2019).

heating up the atmosphere. Only molecules of greenhouse gases, such as carbon dioxide, have the right structure to absorb radiation and thus to heat up the earth's temperature. Therefore, it is not surprising that the average global temperature since 1840 has also risen almost at the same rate as the increase of carbon dioxide (see Figure 1.2).

The significant correlation between global temperatures and CO_2 emissions is clearly visible in Figure 1.3.

Scientists acknowledge (IPCC, 2021) that there is uncertainty about how much or how quickly the temperature will increase and exactly what effect these higher figures will have. The jury is out regarding the accuracy of the numbers, but there is no doubt that the earth is warming and that this is occurring as a direct result of human activities.

Scientists are debating the direct impact of global warming. However, IPCC reports are clear that global warming *is* the major factor involved in causing the harmful effects of climate change.

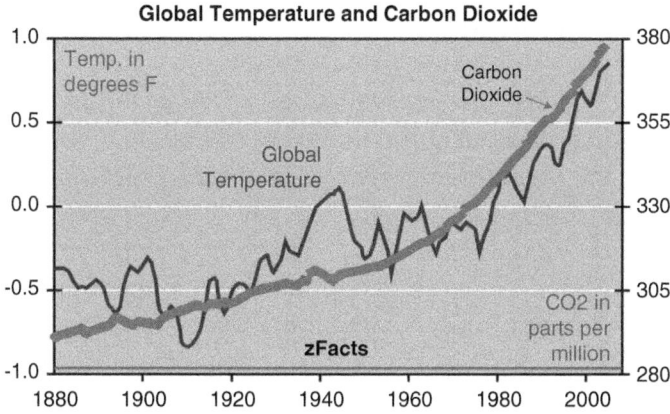

Figure 1.3 The rise of global temperatures and carbon dioxide emissions

SOURCE: Global Carbon Project Report (2019).

There is growing evidence that global warming is making storms wetter and the occurrence of severe cyclones more frequent. A hotter climate also means that there will be more frequent wildfires. An alarming effect of global warming is that sea levels will rise mainly because the polar icebergs are melting. Rising sea levels will be even worse for the poorer people in the world such as those living in Bangladesh and the Pacific Islands.

The potential impacts on plants and animals also make for very bleak reading. The prediction in IPCC reports is that a rise of two degrees centigrade could destroy the geographic range of animals by 8%, plants by 16% and insects by 18%. There were 7,300 major disasters in the 10 years between 2009 and 2019, resulting in 1.2 million deaths and wiping out $3 trillion (3.7%) from the global economy (IPCC, 2021). The scientific evidence would lead us to believe that, although the impact is gradual, at some point it will become catastrophic and irreversible. Even if the 'best case' scenario of that point is 50 years away, the inevitable conclusion from the data is that we must act now.

Let us start by exploring the root causes of global warming in more detail.

1.3.   Greenhouse Gas Emissions by Country

The rate of greenhouse gas emissions from a country, especially carbon dioxide, depends upon many considerations. The two main factors are the generation and consumption of electricity and the population of the country. David Mackay of Cambridge University has produced a graph (Gates, 2021, page 6) which shows that the income per person of a country is proportional to the energy used per head. It was evident from the graph that richer countries (for example, the USA, Canada, Qatar) consume many times more energy per person than the poorer countries (such as Niger, Ethiopia, Haiti). Greater energy consumption means more carbon dioxide emissions. However, it is not the richer nations alone who are causing the higher emission rates of carbon dioxide. Standards of living are going up in emerging economies with a rising demand for energy, cars, buildings and refrigerators. In addition, the global population is also rising.

Figure 1.4 shows the emission rate over the last two decades for populous countries and regions. It is evident that emissions

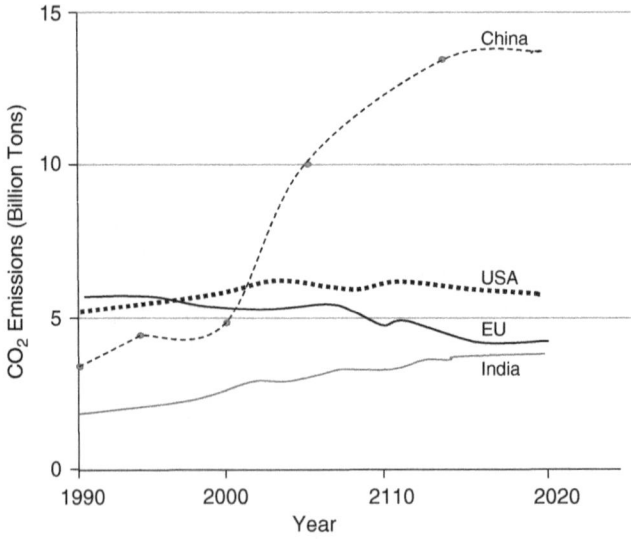

Figure 1.4   The CO_2 emission rates for countries and regions
SOURCE: Gates (2021, page 41).

from advanced economies like the USA and European Union have stayed fairly flat, but if we look at emerging economies, especially China, they are growing rapidly. Of course, undoubtedly it is good news that people are improving their standards of living thanks to globalisation, but the unfortunate consequence is that this is bad news for the planet we all live on. As standards of living are accelerating rapidly in developing countries like China, India, Brazil and Nigeria, both energy consumption and carbon emissions are also increasing at a commensurate rate. It is important to note that in the future there will be an even faster growth in carbon dioxide emissions from these emerging economies.

Each country, depending on its power generation process, power consumption and population, emits differing amounts of greenhouse gases into the atmosphere. Table 1.2 shows data that

Table 1.2   Top 20 countries emitting CO_2 in 2020

Rank	Countries	CO_2 emissions (Giga tonnes)	Percentage (%)
1	China	10.06	28
2	USA	5.41	15
3	India	2.65	7
4	Russian Federation	1.71	5
5	Japan	1.16	3
6	Germany	0.75	2
7	Iran	0.72	2
8	South Korea	0.65	2
9	Saudi Arabia	0.62	2
10	Indonesia	0.61	2
11	Canada	0.56	2
12	Mexico	0.47	1
13	South Africa	0.46	1
14	Brazil	0.45	1
15	Turkey	0.42	1
16	Australia	0.42	1
17	United Kingdom	0.37	1
18	Poland	0.34	1
19	France	0.33	1
20	Italy	0.33	1

SOURCE: Earth Systems Science Data (2020).

estimates carbon dioxide (CO_2) emissions (the main component of greenhouse gases) from the combustion of coal, natural gas, oil and other fuels, including industrial waste and non-renewable munici-pal waste. It shows the ranking of the top 20 countries as the high-est emitters of carbon dioxide in 2020.

The top 20 carbon dioxide emitting countries account for 79% of the total CO_2 emissions of the world and the top 5 countries (China, USA, India, Russia and Japan) are responsible for 58% of the total emissions.

A very useful way to show the impact of CO_2 in the atmosphere is by ppm, or parts per million. This number tells us how many parts of carbon dioxide there are in one million parts of air. Figure 1.5 shows the rapid rise of CO_2 ppm levels along with the rise in CO_2 emissions in the atmosphere over the last 100 years.

Carbon dioxide concentrations are rising mostly because of the fossil fuels that people are burning for energy. Fossil fuels like coal and oil contain carbon that plants pulled out of the atmosphere through photosynthesis over the span of many millions of years; however, now we are returning that carbon to the atmosphere within a timespan of just a few hundred years. The current level of

CO_2 in the atmosphere and annual emissions (1750-2019)

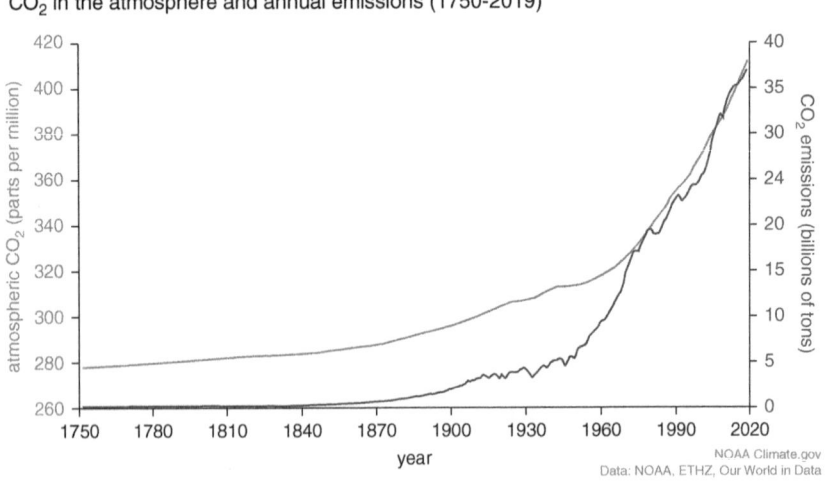

NOAA Climate.gov
Data: NOAA, ETHZ, Our World in Data

Figure 1.5   The CO_2 emission rates and CO_2 ppm

ppm in 2020 is 410, but this figure is growing. The danger level of CO_2 could occur when we are exposed to levels above 5,000 ppm for a number of hours. A further critical point is that even higher levels of CO_2 can cause asphyxiation as carbon dioxide replaces oxygen in the blood. We do know that exposure to concentrations of around 40,000 PPM is immediately dangerous to life and health.

1.4. Greenhouse Gas Emissions by Economic Sector

It is disturbing to learn that greenhouse gas emissions are anthropogenic, which means that these environmental changes are caused mainly by human behaviour, that is everything that humans do to live and prosper in a society. The share of emissions depends on the various sectors of the economy contributing to our lifestyle, such as how we make things, how we grow our foods, how we are plugging into electricity and how we are getting around.

We can see that there are some paradoxes involved. For example, while we would all agree that we need both cement and steel to build our infrastructures, however making steel and cement alone accounts for approximately 10% of all emissions. There are some variations in the proportion of data for greenhouse gas emissions by economic sector depending on the sources and their chosen categories. I have chosen the categories and data from IPCC (2014a) as shown in Table 1.3.

From this table, we can note that electricity and energy account for just over a third of all greenhouse gas emissions. Indeed, the

Table 1.3 Greenhouse gas emissions by economic sector

Economic Sector	Percentages
Electricity and other energy	35
Agriculture and land	24
Industry	21
Transports	14
Buildings	6

SOURCE: IPCC (2014a).

burning of coal, natural gas and oil for electricity and heat is the largest single source of global greenhouse gas emissions.

Greenhouse gas emissions from the agriculture and land sector come mostly from agriculture (the cultivation of crops and livestock) and the practice of deforestation. The gas emissions from cattle and sheep are also a significant source in this sector.

Greenhouse gas emissions from industry primarily involve fossil fuels burned on site at facilities for energy. This sector also includes emissions from chemical, metallurgical and mineral transformation processes not associated with energy consumption and emissions from waste management activities.

If we consider the transportation sector, greenhouse gas emissions primarily involve fossil fuels burned for road, rail, air and marine transportation. Almost all (95%) of the world's transportation energy comes from petroleum-based fuels, largely gasoline and diesel.

Greenhouse gas emissions from the energy sector arise from onsite energy generation and burning fuels for heat in buildings or cooking in homes. Emissions from the electricity and other sectors are covered in Chapter 7.

1.5. Summary

From the evidence-based analysis in this chapter some key points can be summarised:

- The global warming debate is over. There is incontrovertible evidence now that over the last 50 years our planet is warming between 0.5 degrees centigrade and 1.5 degrees centigrade. If no action is taken, the temperature will continue to rise and consequently sea levels will increase, with impacts on our weather cycle, including more frequent cyclones, wildfires and incidences of flooding.
- The world is producing 51 billion tonnes of greenhouse gases every year; the biggest contributor is carbon dioxide (82%)

generated mainly from the combustion of coal, natural gas, oil and other fuels.

- The world's most advanced economies (e.g. USA, Japan, EU, UK and Canada) have been producing greenhouse gases. However, the growth in emissions will come from the emerging and populous economies (e.g. China, India, Brazil, Russia, Nigeria and Indonesia).
  - The largest economic sector of CO_2 emissions is the generations and consumption of energy (35%). Fossil fuels (e.g. coal, gas and oil) are the major sources of power plants and energy consumption in industries and houses.
  - To avoid the climate disaster we must act now. We need to invest in future research for breakthrough solutions, but we have to deploy the tools we already have, such as solar and wind.

If we have a breakthrough process solution now we must apply it immediately. We should also aim for a sustainable outcome. The United Nations (United Nations Foundation, 2020) projected 17 sustainable development goals (SDGs) to be achieved by 2030, of which climate change is the 13th goal. Sustainability focuses on meeting the requirements of the present without compromising the ability of future generations to meet their own needs.

Green Six Sigma (a hybrid of Six Sigma) is designed to provide both breakthrough process solutions and sustainable outcomes.

Green Tips

- Remember three numbers: 51 billion, zero and 2050: 51 billion tonnes of greenhouse gases are added to the atmosphere every year and our target is net-zero emission by 2050.
- Carbon dioxide is the biggest contributor (82%) of greenhouse gases.
- We must act now with urgency to avoid a climate disaster.

Chapter 2

International and National Climate Change Initiatives

'We must now agree on a binding review mechanism under international law, so that this century can be called the century of decarbonisation'

– Angela Merkel

2.1. Introduction

It was not until 1972 that environmental issues received serious attention from any national or international organisations. In June 1972 the first Earth Summit held in Stockholm adopted a declaration that set out principles for the preservation and enhancement of the human environment. The conference also proposed the establishment of stations to monitor long-term trends in atmospheric properties; however, at this stage, climate change was not the central preoccupation. Over the next two decades concerns for the global climate slowly gained traction and garnered international interest. From around the late 1980s global warming and the depletion of the ozone layer became increasingly prominent in the sphere of international public debate and a fixture on the political agenda, with the formation of the IPCC (Intergovernmental Panel on Climate Change) in 1988.

As a sense of urgency gained momentum and demands increased for stronger international action on climate change, the United Nations General Assembly decided to convene the United Nations Conference on Environment and Development. This summit was held in Rio de Janeiro in 1992. The most significant event during the conference was the agreement of the United Nations Framework Convention on Climate Change (UNFCCC), which was signed by 158 States.

2.2.   International Climate Change Initiatives

Against this backdrop, a number of international initiatives on climate change were established including:

- The United Nations Framework Convention on Climate Change (UNFCCC)
- Kyoto Protocol
- International Carbon Action Partnership (ICAP)
- The Paris Climate Agreement
- The Conference of Parties (COP)
- IPCC

2.2.1.   *The United Nations Framework Convention on Climate Change (UNFCCC)*

The UNFCCC is an international environmental treaty addressing climate change signed by 158 states at Rio de Janeiro in 1992. The United Nations established a Secretariat headquartered in Bonn to implement the Rio de Janeiro agreement.

The treaty established three categories of signatory states with differential responsibilities. The categories are: developed countries (Annex 1), developed countries with special financial responsibilities (Annex 2) and developing countries. Annex 1 countries are members of the EU and thirteen Eastern European states in transition to market economies. This group is called upon to adopt national policies to limit greenhouse gas emissions. Annex 2 countries include all Annex 1 countries except the thirteen East European states. This group is asked to provide financial resources to meet the costs of developing countries to reduce greenhouse gas emissions. Finally, the developing countries of the third category are required to submit progress reports of their individual commitments on climate change and emission targets for greenhouse gases.

The UNFCCC has been criticised for its apparent ineffectiveness in reducing levels of emissions of greenhouse gases since its creation. However, it should take the credit for being the major international forum of climate change and the source of other international climate change initiatives such as the Kyoto Protocol, ICAP, COP and IPCC, which will be discussed below.

2.2.2.   The Kyoto Protocol

The Kyoto Protocol was adopted in Kyoto in December 1997 by 192 countries. It extends the 1992 UNFCCC objective to reduce greenhouse gas emissions based on the scientific consensus that global warming is occurring and that CO_2 emissions as a result of human activity are causing this. The Kyoto Protocol applies to the six components of greenhouse gases, including carbon dioxide (CO_2), methane (CH_4) and nitrous oxide (N_2O) as the main contributors.

The Protocol acknowledges that developed and developing countries have different capabilities in combating climate change and places the obligation more heavily on developed countries. The Protocol's first commitment period started in 2008 and 36 countries fully complied with it. The second commitment period, known as the Doha Amendment, commenced in 2012, under which

37 countries, including EU and Australia, have binding targets. However, there have been stumbling blocks along the way. Japan, New Zealand and Russia have participated in Kyoto but have not committed to the second-round targets. Other developed countries without second-round goals are Canada (which ceremonially withdrew from the Protocol in 2012) and the United States (which has not ratified). Of the 37 countries with binding commitments, 34 have ratified and 147 states have accepted the Doha Amendment in principle.

Following the much-publicised departure of Canada in 2012 and the lack of ratification by many countries including the USA, the Kyoto Protocol is considered to have failed to deliver. This resulted in the adoption of the Paris Agreement in 2015 as a separate instrument under the UNFCCC.

2.2.3. *International Carbon Action Partnership (ICAP)*

The International Carbon Action Partnership (ICAP) was founded in Lisbon in 2007 by more than fifteen government representatives as an international cooperative forum. From its Secretariat based in Berlin, ICAP coordinates the sharing of best practices and monitors the progress of the ETS (Emission Trading Scheme). ETS is an incentive-based approach for reducing emission pollutants, also known as 'cap and trade'. A maximum 'cap' or limit is set on the total amount of greenhouse gases that can be emitted by all participating members.

ICAP regularly publishes the status report of emission trading worldwide (ICAP, 2021). The partnership currently counts 32 full members and five observers. The UK launched its own domestic ETS following its departure from the European Union while the Chinese government officially announced the start of the first compliance cycle of its domestic ETS in January 2021, ending in December 2021.

ICAP advocates for a Paris Agreement that supports countries in using market mechanisms on a voluntary basis to help achieve their intended nationally determined contributions.

2.2.4. The Paris Climate Agreement

The Paris Climate Agreement (also known as the Paris Accord) is an international treaty on the climate crisis. Its stated aim is to radically reduce global carbon emissions and restrict the rise in the Earth's temperature to less than 2 degrees centigrade. This treaty was signed by all 189 participating countries in Paris in December 2015 at COP 21.

There are four guiding principles for the Agreement:

- To support Parties in transferring part of their mitigation outcomes to other Parties for compliance, leading to greater emissions reductions than can be achieved individually.
- To provide for a sound and transparent accounting framework for internationally transferred mitigation outcomes and build trust among Parties.
- To encourage the development and use of robust monitoring, reporting and verification (MRV) standards and ensure that the environmental integrity of Parties' mitigation commitments is not undermined.
- To build upon the knowledge and institutions developed by countries and the UNFCCC.

The participating countries are also required to report every two years on how much greenhouse gas is being produced within their geographical boundaries. These reports are called 'greenhouse gas inventories'. Countries must also provide feedback on their efforts regarding climate change adaptation responses.

The treaty is bound by international laws. Although the participating countries are not bound by law to aim towards one universal goal, they are required to establish and review their own climate targets and plans every five years. These objectives must be set on a consistent basis. The plans and targets are known as NDCs or nationally determined contributions. With 189 nations having ratified the landmark accord since 2015, the USA is the only country in the world to have formally withdrawn from it in June 2017. However, the succeeding US administration of President Biden re-joined the Paris Climate Agreement in February 2021.

Notwithstanding the fact that, inevitably, some doubts arose when President Trump began the process of extracting the USA from the Paris Agreement, the treaty has proved to be remarkably resilient. The key axis of the EU and China has remained intact. There are other successes such as the inclusion of 1 degree centigrade as the aspirational target, a powerful movement towards 'net-zero emissions' as well as a multiplicity of successful actions on climate by large businesses. However, even with all these positive steps, emissions have continued to rise globally. The UN Environment Programme (UNEP) reported that releases escalated from 50 billion tonnes in 2015 to 55 billion tonnes in 2019.

Despite the evident challenges, there is once again a sense of optimism around what can be achieved with President Joe Biden re-joining the Paris Agreement on his first day in office, and China's President Xi Jinping committing the world's largest emitter to a zero emissions target by 2060.

2.2.5.   The Conference of Parties (COP)

The COP is the decision-making body of the UNFCCC and can produce some very important outcomes. For example, the Paris Climate Agreement was signed at the COP 21 in 2015. All States that are Parties to the Convention are represented and work together to make the relevant decisions that safeguard the successful implementation of the Convention. The COP meets annually and reviews the national communications and emission inventories submitted by Parties. The COP dates back to March 1995 when the first COP meeting was held in Berlin, Germany, while the most recent, COP 25, took place at Madrid in 2019.

COP 26 was to be held in Glasgow in 2020 but was rescheduled as a result of the Covid-19 pandemic and is due to occur in November 2021. It will take place in an atmosphere of anticipation, and expectations are high as President Biden has prioritised climate change, promising to convene a climate summit of the world's major economies within 100 days of taking office. All eyes will be on those countries who have not yet committed to long-term net-zero targets. There will also be an appetite to see progress from those nations who have already dedicated themselves and who have already offered detailed plans for cutting emissions by 2030.

2.2.6.   The Intergovernmental Panel on Climate Change (IPCC)

The IPCC or Intergovernmental Panel on Climate Change is a highly respected body of the United Nations and was established in 1988. In conjunction with former US Vice-President Al Gore, the IPCC won the Nobel Prize in 2007.

The group works to produce reports on climate change which are commonly held to be the official consensus of scientists, experts and global governments. These documents allow the IPCC to assess, summarise and provide an overview of knowledge, progress, impacts and the future risks of climate change. The reports are drafted and reviewed by the scientific community at various stages, thus guaranteeing objectivity and authenticity.

2.2.7.   Other International Initiatives

There are other international bodies involved in climate change initiatives, albeit with lower *profiles, including GEF and GCP.*

The Global Environment Facility (GEF) was set up in 1992 at the Rio Earth Summit. GEF supports 184 countries in partnership with some private sector groups and civil society organisations to address global environmental issues. GEF also provides financial support for projects related to climate change, international waters, the ozone layer and environmental pollutions. The organisation has financed or co-financed more than 4,800 projects in 170 countries.

The Global Carbon Project (GCP) was established in 2001 as a global research project of Future Earth, a network of the international science community. Based in Canberra, its aim is to decelerate the escalation of greenhouse gases in the atmosphere. The primary focus of GCP research is carbon management and the group regularly publishes Global Carbon Project reports in English, Chinese, Japanese and Russian.

2.3.   National Climate Change Initiatives

Both developed and developing countries, as part of UNFCCC and the Paris Climate Agreement, are contributing to climate change initiatives as well as submitting reports on greenhouse gas inventories. In addition, many states are proactively following national climate change strategies. In this section, some of these national and regional initiatives are discussed.

2.3.1.   European Union Emissions Trading System (EU ETS)

The European Union Emissions Trading System (EU ETS) was launched in 2005 as the first large greenhouse trading scheme.

All installations must monitor and report their greenhouse gas emissions. A maximum cap is set on the total quantity of greenhouse gases that can be emitted by all participating installations. EU allowances for emissions are then auctioned off and can subsequently be traded. If emissions exceed the amount permitted by allowances, an installation must purchase allowances from others. Conversely, if an installation has performed well and has demonstrated success at reducing its emissions, it can sell its leftover credits. This is known as 'the cap and trade principle'.

In 2013 the EU ETS covered more than 11,000 installations of the power stations and factories of all 27 EU member countries. Subsequently, the EU ETS was also extended to EU airports.

We will now examine in more detail how some key global economies are performing in terms of climate change, with a focus upon some of the worst 'sinners' in this area.

2.3.2.   UK Climate Change Initiatives

British climate change initiatives are ambitious. The UK aims not just to meet the tenets of the Kyoto Protocol to reduce all greenhouse emissions by 12.5% from 1990 levels by 2012. In fact, new commitments will set the UK on a path to slash its carbon emissions by 78% by the year 2035. Furthermore, the 2008 Climate Change Act commits the UK government to cut national greenhouse gas emissions by at least 100% of 1990 levels (net zero) by 2050.

Achieving these targets would require more widespread use of electric cars, low-carbon heating and renewable electricity as well as cultural changes to food purchasing habits by a reduction in the consumption of meat and dairy products. Following Brexit, the UK entered its own UK-only ETS, although this is broadly similar to the EU ETS described above and the same ethos applies. Industries and power plants receive permits to emit greenhouse gases and can trade them at the market rate. Increasing renewable energy production, by wind, solar and nuclear power is one fundamental way that will allow the UK to meet its binding net-zero target by 2050.

At the COP 21 meeting held in Paris, Britain joined 'Mission Innovation' with a group of twenty countries, pledging to 'double spending on clean tech R and D'.

2.3.3.   USA Climate Change Initiatives

The United States of America is the second highest polluter of greenhouse gases but arguably holds maximum power and influence in global climate change initiatives. A look at the varying policies of US administrations towards green initiatives in this century reveals rather a 'swing of the pendulum' effect. It is evident that recent Republican presidents (viz. George W. Bush and Donald Trump) have sought to protect fossil fuel industries while their Democrat counterparts (Barack Obama and Joe Biden) are more proactive supporters of global and national climate change initiatives.

The USA, although a signatory to the Kyoto Protocol, has neither ratified nor withdrawn from this agreement. President Clinton in 1993 committed the United States to reducing their greenhouse gas emissions to 1990 levels by 2020. However, in 2001 George W. Bush announced that the United States would not implement the Kyoto Protocol.

Bush's successor adopted a different and more proactive approach to the pressing problem of climate change. In 2009 President Obama announced that the USA would enter a 'cap and trade' system to limit global warming. He also established a new office, the White House Office of Energy and Climate Change, and appointed Todd Stern as the Special Envoy for Climate Change. In 2013 President Obama and Chinese President Xi Jinping formulated a landmark agreement to reduce CO_2 and two years later, in 2015, President Obama became a signatory of the Paris Climate Agreement. In the same year the United States committed to reducing emissions to 26–28% below 2005 levels by the year 2025, a reflection of the US goal to convert the national economy into one of low-carbon reliance.

However, 2017 saw another reversal of attitudes with a change of administration, when President Trump withdrew the US from the Paris Climate Agreement and appointed Scott Pruitt, a climate change denialist, as his director of the Environmental Protection Agency (EPA).

Since taking office in 2021, the Biden administration has re-joined the Paris Climate Agreement and created a National Climate Task Force. President Biden has also proposed spending on climate change in his infrastructure bill, including $174 billion for electric cars and $35 billion for research and development into climate change initiatives.

2.3.4. China Climate Change Initiatives

China accounts for 28% of global greenhouse gas emissions and is the world's number one polluter due to an energy infrastructure heavily reliant upon the use of fossil fuels and coal. Furthermore, major industries including the construction and manufacturing sectors contribute heavily to the country's enormous levels of carbon dioxide emissions. China is already experiencing the severe impacts of global warming upon its agriculture, water resources and the environment.

However, as a signatory to the Paris Climate Agreement, the nation appears to be committed to climate change initiatives. President Xi Jinping announced in 2020 at the UN General Assembly that his country would hit peak carbon emissions before 2030, aiming towards attaining carbon neutral status by 2060. The National Leading Group on Climate Change (NLGCC) was established by the Chinese government in June 2007. It was created in response to international pressure and constitutes a ministerial 'super group' designed to coordinate complex decision-making processes related to the key areas of climate change, emissions reductions and the conservation of energy. Furthermore, in terms of clean technology, China is a major world producer and exporter of solar panels, wind turbines and electric cars.

2.3.5. India Climate Change Initiatives

Another major problem area is India, the third largest global polluter of greenhouse gas emissions (7%). If India is to achieve an economic growth rate of over 8% then the country should also focus on its energy constraints. India is highly dependent on imported oil, which constitutes 70% of its requirements.

The nation was on track to achieve its NDCs (nationally determined contributions) from 2015, but it is also one of the fastest growing economies in the world, with a rapidly expanding climate footprint. The country's emissions have risen by a staggering 184% since 1990 – in fact, China is the only nation whose emissions have increased by a larger rate. Prime Minister Modi played a prominent role in COP 21 in Paris and has said that he also expects developed countries to support international financing to India's climate change initiatives.

2.3.6. Russia Climate Change Initiatives

Russia ranks fourth in the greenhouse gas emission table (5%) and also has a high profile on the international political stage. The country has signed all UN climate treaties including the Paris Climate Agreement and thus agrees to aim to reach net-zero carbon emissions by 2050.

In 2020, a long-term strategy was presented by Russia on how to reduce greenhouse gas emissions by 2050. An internal review also claims that Russia's greenhouse gas emissions decreased by an encouraging 30% between 1990 and 2018.

However, Russia's energy strategy is not clear. The country enjoys a major advantage, being fortunate in possessing one of the largest stores of solar, wind, geothermal and biofuels in the world. However, the nation's 'Energy Strategy 2035' has also projected a substantial increase of Russian fossil fuel production, combustion and exports within the next fifteen years.

2.3.7.   Japan Climate Change Initiatives

Japan is fifth in the list of global polluters with its 3% share. The country is in many ways synonymous with key climate initiatives, as Japan acted as the host of COP 3 in Kyoto in 1997 when the Kyoto Protocol was adopted. However, the country's performance in emissions control prior to 2013 was less than satisfactory. Since the East Japan earthquake of 11th March 2011 Japan's dependence on coal-fired power has increased. The country's policy decision to continue the new construction of coal-fired power plants domestically and to support them financially abroad was criticised by the international community.

Matsushita (2020) recommends three key measures that Japan should adopt:

1. Set ambitious greenhouse gas reduction targets such as a 40–50% reduction by 2030 and net-zero emissions by 2050;
2. Radically reform current coal-fired power policy, including stopping construction of new coal-fired power plants and discontinue providing financial assistance for the construction of coal-fired power plants abroad; and
3. Introduce full-fledged carbon pricing.

2.4.   Summary

Despite the variety of records and achievements and discrepancies in these status updates, there is no doubt that, notwithstanding some pauses due to geopolitical factors, all major economies at least in theory are committed to international climate change initiatives. In addition, the major economies have signed all UN climate treaties including the Paris Climate Agreement.

The international community generally agrees on the science behind climate change and how to set greenhouse emissions reduction targets. However, many experts have diverged on whether the Paris Climate Agreement will be enough to prevent the average global temperature from rising 1.5 degrees centigrade. The IPCC regularly assesses the latest climate science and produces consensus-based reports for countries. Its Green Strategy has become a positive force both in geopolitics and international businesses.

However, the actual results achieved so far are not very encouraging. Current policies could result in a 2.9 degree rise by 2100 (IPCC, 2021). In spite of a drop in greenhouse gas emissions in 2020 due the 'lockdown effect' of the Covid-19 pandemic, overall releases are rising, from 50 billion tonnes in 2015 to 55 billion tonnes in 2019 (UNEP, 2019). Regardless of the growth in renewables and clean technology, countries are on track to produce more than double the amount of fossil fuels by 2030.

Looking ahead, we must be optimistic in order to harness energy and expertise. It is encouraging that the desire for change is evident. We can expect a plethora of new announcements and initiatives on climate action and we are beginning to witness the political momentum necessary to solve global warming problems. There is a new sense of optimism following the mobilisation of global efforts during the Covid-19 pandemic. In the immediate future, it is essential that we see concrete action including international and government plans and funding regarding climate change initiatives. However, we need to make it happen at the sources of greenhouse emissions by taking grassroots action at power plants, factories, service centres, transport infrastructures and buildings.

The good news is that we have the technology and holistic processes to mitigate these climate change outcomes at source. Let us now examine also how Green Six Sigma aims to address these key issues for our times.

Green Tips

- In the Paris Climate Agreement, signed by 189 countries, the aim is to restrict the rise in the Earth's temperature to less than 2 degrees centigrade by 2050.
- Three top polluters of greenhouse gases are China, USA, and India.
- IPCC (Intergovernmental Panel of Climate Change) is the most respected body for climate change reporting.

Chapter 3

The Evolution of Six Sigma, Lean Six Sigma and Green Six Sigma

'Quality is not something you install like a new carpet. You implant it. Quality is something you work at. It is a learning process.'
– Edward Deming

3.1. Introduction

'Today, depending on who you listen to, Six Sigma is either a revolution slashing trillions of dollars from corporate inefficiency, or it is the most maddening management fad yet devised to keep front-line workers too busy collecting data to do their jobs.' (*USA Today*, 21 July 1998)

At the time of writing, it has been 23 years since the above statement was made. During this time the 'Six Sigma revolution' has created a huge impact in the field of operational excellence, yet conflicting views are still prevalent.

27

Let us evaluate the arguments for both sides. On a positive note, the success of 'Six Sigma' in General Electric under the leadership of Jack Welch is undisputed. In the GE company report of 2000, their CEO was unstinting in his praise: 'Six Sigma has galvanized our company with an intensity the likes of which I have never seen in my 40 years of GE.' Even financial analysts and investment bankers compliment the success of Six Sigma at GE. An analyst at Morgan Stanley, Dean Witter, recently estimated that GE's gross annual benefit from Six Sigma could reach 5% of sales and that share values might increase by between 10 and 15%.

However, the situation is more complex than such predictions would suggest. In spite of the demonstrated benefits of many improvement techniques, such as Total Quality Management, Business Process Re-Engineering and Six Sigma, most attempts by companies to use them have ended in failure (Easton and Jarrell, 1998). Sterman et al. (1997) conclude that firms have found it extremely difficult to sustain even initially successful process improvement initiatives. Yet more puzzling is the fact that successful improvement programmes have sometimes led to declining business performance, causing lay-offs and low employee morale. Motorola, the originator of Six Sigma, announced in 1998 that its second quarter profit was almost nonexistent and that consequently it was cutting 15,000 of its 150,000 jobs.

To counter heavyweight enthusiasts like Jack Welch (GE) and Larry Bossidy (Allied Signal), it must be said in the interests of balance that there are sharp critics of Six Sigma. In fact, while Six Sigma may sound new, its critics say that it is really just Statistical Process Control in fresh clothing. Others dismiss it as another transitory management fad that will soon pass.

It is evident that, like any good product, 'Six Sigma' should also have a finite life cycle. In addition, business managers can be forgiven if they are often confused by the grey areas of distinction between quality initiatives such as TQM, Six Sigma and Lean Sigma.

Against this background, let us examine the evolution of total quality improvement processes (or in a broader sense operational excellence) from ad-hoc upgrading, working up to TQM and then to Six Sigma and finally to Lean Sigma. Building on the success factors of these processes the vital question is: How do we sustain the results? The author has named this sustainable process FIT SIGMA™ (see Basu, 2011).

So, what is FIT SIGMA? Firstly, take the key ingredient of quality and then add accuracy in the order of 3.4 defects in 1,000,000. Now implement this across your business with an intensive education and training programme. The result is Six Sigma. Now let us look at Lean Enterprise, an updated version of classical industrial engineering. It focuses on delivered value from a customer's perspective and strives to eliminate all non-value-added activities ('waste') for each product or service along a value chain. The integration of the complementary approaches of Six Sigma and Lean Enterprise is known as Lean Sigma. FIT SIGMA is simply the next wave. If Lean Sigma provides agility and efficiency, then FIT SIGMA allows a sustainable fitness. In addition, the control of variation from the mean (small Sigma 'σ') in the Six Sigma process is transformed to company-wide integration (capital Sigma 'Σ') in the FIT SIGMA process. Furthermore, the philosophy of FIT SIGMA should ensure that it is indeed fit for the organisation.

The road map to FIT SIGMA (see Figure 3.1) contains three waves and it should be noted that the entry point of each organisation will vary:

First Wave	:	As Is to TQM
Second Wave	:	TQM to Lean Six Sigma
Third Wave	:	Lean Six Sigma to FIT SIGMA and Green Six Sigma

3.2.   First Wave: As Is to TQM

The organised division of labour to improve operations may have started with Adam Smith in 1776. However, it is often the Industrial Engineering approach, which has roots in F.W. Taylor's 'Scientific Management', that is credited with the formal initiation of the first wave of operational excellence. This industrial engineering approach was sharpened by operational research and complemented by operational tools such as management accounting.

During the years following the Second World War, the 'first wave' saw through the rapid growth of industrialisation, but in the short term the focus seemed to be upon both increasing volume and reducing the cost. In general, improvement processes were 'ad-hoc', factory centric and conducive to 'pockets of excellence'. Then in the 1970s the holistic approach of Total Quality Management initiated the 'second wave' of operational excellence. The traditional factors of quality control and quality assurance are aimed at achieving an agreed and consistent level of quality. However, TQM goes far beyond mere conformity to standard. TQM is a company-wide programme and requires a culture in which every member of the organisation believes that not a single day should go by within that organisation without in some way improving the quality of its goods and services.

3.3.   Second Wave: TQM to Lean Six Sigma

Learning the basics from W.E. Deming and J.M. Juran, Japanese companies extended and customised the integrated approach and culture of TQM (Basu and Wright, 1997; Oakland, 2003). Arguably the economic growth and manufacturing dominance of Japanese industries in the 1980s can be attributed to the successful application of TQM in Japan. The three fundamental tenets of Juran's TQM process are, firstly, upper management leadership of quality; secondly, continuous education on quality for all; and, finally, an annual plan for quality improvement and cost reduction. These foundations are still valid today and embedded within the Six Sigma/ Lean Sigma philosophies. Philip Crosby and other leading TQM consultants incorporated customer focus and Deming's SPC tools and propagated the TQM philosophy both to the USA and the industrialised world. The Malcolm Baldridge Quality Award, ISO 9000 and the Deming Quality Award have enhanced the popularity of

TQM throughout the world, while in Europe the EFQM (European Foundation of Quality Management) was formed. During the 1980s TQM seemed to be everywhere and some of its definitions such as 'fitness for the purpose', 'quality is what the customer wants' and 'getting it right first time' became so overused that they were almost clichés. Thus the impact of TQM began to diminish.

In order to complement the gaps to be found in TQM in specific areas of Operation Excellence, high profile consultants marketed mostly Japanese practices in the form of a host of three letter acronyms such as JIT, TPM, BPR and MRPII. Total Productive Maintenance (TPM) has demonstrated successes outside Japan by focusing on increasing the capacity of individual processes. TQM was the buzzword of the 1980s but it is viewed by many, especially in the US quality field, as an embarrassing failure – a quality concept that promised more than it could deliver. Philip Crosby pinpoints the cause of TQM 'failures' as 'TQM never did anything to define quality, which is conformance to standards'. Perhaps the pendulum swung too far towards the concept of quality as 'goodness' and the employee culture. It was against this background that the scene for Six Sigma appeared to establish itself.

Six Sigma began back in 1985 when Bill Smith, an engineer at Motorola, came up with the idea of inserting hardnosed statistics into the blurred philosophy of quality. In statistical terms, Sigma (σ) is a measure of variation from the mean; thus the greater the value of Sigma, the fewer the defects. Most companies produce results that are at best around four Sigma or more than 6,000 defects. By contrast at the Six Sigma level, the expectation is only 3.4 defects per million as companies move towards attaining this far higher level of performance.

Although invented at Motorola, Six Sigma has been experimented with by Allied Signal and perfected at General Electric. Following the recent merger of these two companies, GE is truly the home of Six Sigma. During the last five years, Six Sigma has taken the quantum leap into operational excellence in many blue chip companies including DuPont, Raytheon, Ivensys, Marconi, Bombardier Shorts, Seagate Technology and GlaxoSmithKline.

The key success factors differentiating Six Sigma from TQM are:

- The emphasis on statistical science and measurement.
- A rigorous and structured training deployment plan (Champion, Master Black Belt, Black Belt and Green Belt).
- A project focused approach with a single set of problem-solving techniques such as DMAIC (Define, Measure, Analyse, Improve, Control).
- Reinforcement of the Juran tenets (Top management leadership, continuous education and annual savings plan).

Following their recent application in companies like Glaxo-SmithKline, Raytheon, Ivensys and Seagate, the Six Sigma programmes have moved towards the Lean Sigma philosophy, which integrates Six Sigma with the complementary approach of Lean Enterprise. Lean focuses the company's resources and its suppliers on the delivered value from the customer's perspective. Lean Enterprise begins with Lean production, the concept of waste reduction developed from industrial engineering principles and refined by Toyota. It expands upon these principles to engage all support partners and customers along the value stream. Common goals to both Six Sigma and Lean Sigma are the elimination of waste and improvement of process capability. The industrial engineering tools of Lean Enterprise complement the science of the statistical processes of Six Sigma. It is the integration of these tools in Lean Sigma that provides an operational excellence methodology capable of addressing the entire value delivery system.

3.4. Third Wave: Lean Six Sigma to FIT SIGMA and Green Six Sigma

Lean Six Sigma is the beginning of the 'third wave' (see Figure 3.1). The predictable Six Sigma precisions combined with the speed and agility of Lean produces definitive solutions for better, faster and cheaper business processes. Through the systematic identification

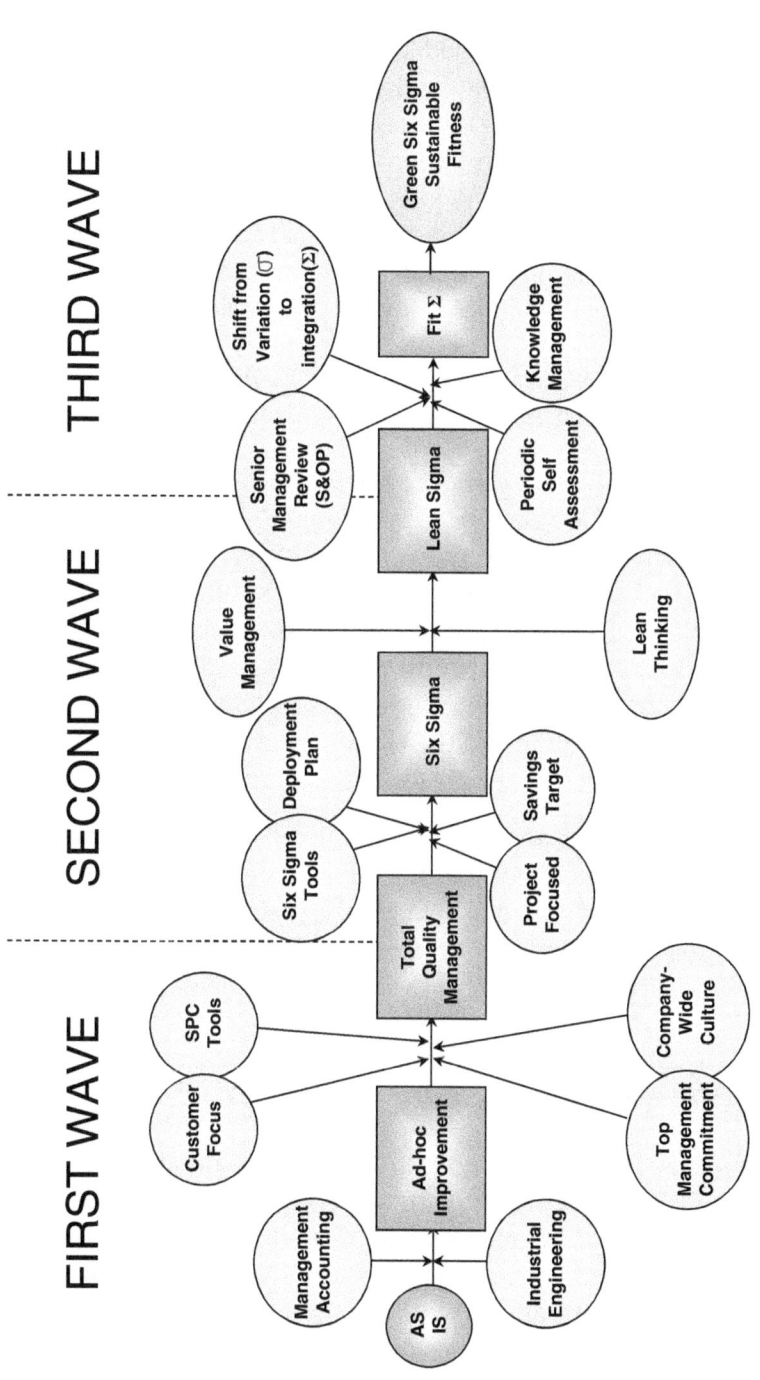

Figure 3.1 Road map to operational excellence
© Ron Basu

and eradication of non-value-added activities, optimum value flow is achieved, cycle times are reduced and defects eliminated.

The dramatic bottom line results and extensive training deployment of Six Sigma and Lean Sigma must be sustained with additional features for securing the longer-term competitive advantage of a company. The process to do just that is FIT SIGMA. The best practices of Six Sigma, Lean Sigma as well as other proven operational excellence best practices underpin the basic building blocks of FIT SIGMA.

Four additional features are embedded in the Lean Sigma philosophy to create FIT SIGMA. These are:

- A formal senior management review process at regular intervals, similar to the Sales and Operational Planning process.
- Periodic self-assessment with a structured checklist, which is formalised by a certification or award, similar to the EFQM award but with more emphasis on self-assessment.
- A continuous learning and knowledge management programme.
- The extension of the programme across the whole business with the shifting of the theme of the variation control (σ) of Six Sigma to the integration of a seamless organisation (Σ).

Green Six Sigma is an adaptation of Six Sigma, Lean Six Sigma and FIT SIGMA to the specific applications for climate change initiatives. A new feature of Green Six Sigma is the extension of DMAIC (Define, Measure, Analyse, Improve and Control) to DMAICS (Define, Measure, Analyse, Improve, Control and Sustain).

3.5.   More About Six Sigma

Six Sigma is an approach that takes a whole system attitude to the improvement of quality and customer service so as to enhance the bottom line. The Six Sigma concept matured between 1985 and 1986 and grew out of various quality initiatives at Motorola. Like most such quality initiatives since the days of Dr Deming in the sixties and in particular the concept of Total Quality Management

(TQM), Six Sigma requires a total culture throughout an organisation. This means that everyone at all levels should possess a passion for continuous improvement with the ultimate aim of achieving virtual perfection. The difference with Six Sigma is the setting of a performance level that equates to 3.4 defects per 1 million opportunities. To ascertain whether Six Sigma has been achieved requires a common language throughout the organisation (at all levels and within each function) and standardised, uniform measurement techniques of quality. The overall Six Sigma philosophy has a goal of total customer satisfaction.

A survey (Basu and Wright, 2003) was conducted with the following leading companies in the UK who had adopted the Six Sigma approach to quality:

Motorola

Allied Signal (Honeywell)

General Electric

Raytheon

DuPont Teijn

Bombadier Shorts

Seagate Technology

Foxboro (Invensys)

Norando

Ericson

The results indicated that the main driver leading to the application of Six Sigma within a company is cost savings rather than customer satisfaction! In coming to this conclusion the firms benefited from informal networking with members of the above companies as well as leading consulting groups such as Air Academy Associates, Rath and Strong, Price Waterhouse Cooper, Iomega and Cambridge Management Consulting. The surveyed companies reported between them a long list of intangible and indirect benefits. However, these plus points did not seem to be supported by any employee or customer surveys.

Nonetheless, very real results from the adoption of Six Sigma continue to be noted. For example, in 1997 Citibank undertook a Six Sigma initiative and after just three years it was reported that defects had reduced by ten times (see Erwin and Douglas, 2000, for details). Likewise, General Electric state that the initial $300 million invested in 1997 in Six Sigma will deliver between $400 million and $500 million savings with additional incremental margins of $100 to $200 million. Wipro Corporation in India says that from a start in 1999, after just two years defects were reduced to such an extent as to realise a gain of eight times over their initial investment in Six Sigma.

The application of operational excellence concepts are now extended to non-manufacturing processes. 'Firms such as Motorola and General Electric . . . successfully implemented Six Sigma. Motorola saved $15 billion in an 11 year period. General Electric saved $2 billion in 1999 alone. . . . Although Six Sigma initiatives have focused primarily on improving the performance of manufacturing processes, the concepts are widely applied in non-manufacturing, administrative and service functions' (Weinstein et al., 2008).

3.6.   What Is Six Sigma?

So just what is the enigma of Six Sigma? Sigma is a classical Greek letter (σ) that is used in mathematical and statistical models to signify the standard deviation from the mean. This might sound like statistical mumbo jumbo, but in reality is a very simple concept. The mean (more correctly referred to as the arithmetic mean) is what most of us would call the average. For example, if a player in cricket batted 10 times and the total of his or her 10 scores is 650, then the average is 65 (even though s/he might have 'scored' nil on one occasion and 250 off another ball). This is because mathematically, each turn at bat contributes to the average. In statistical terms the arithmetic mean of the total score of 650 is 65, arrived at by dividing the total number of runs by the number of bats (650/10).

Table 3.1   Results of tossing 10 coins 100 times

Number of heads	0	1	2	3	4	5	6	7	8	9	10
Frequency		1	2	5	12	18	23	16	10	9	3	1

The next basic concept in statistics is frequency distribution. An often quoted example in statistical textbooks is the tossing of 10 coins 100 times. The result of each throw of the 10 coins could range from 10 heads and no tails, to 10 tails and no heads, or any combination in between, i.e. one head and nine tails, two heads and eight tails and so on. We would expect that if the coins are evenly balanced that we are more likely to have a probability of five heads and five tails than we are to get ten heads and no tails!

Table 3.1 shows the result of tossing 10 coins 100 times. This can be shown as a histogram as in Figure 3.2 and also as a distribution curve: see Figure 3.3.

The curve shown in Figure 3.3 is an example of a normal distribution curve. The curve is bell shaped (that is, it is symmetrical from the midpoint). Of course not all distributions will provide this outline, but under normal circumstances and given a large enough population, in our example concerning 100 throws of 10 coins, it is very likely that the distribution curve will be similar to that shown in Figure 3.2. The midpoint is shown on our curve as 'x'. In statistical language, x represents the measure of central dispersion but in everyday English the term 'midpoint' indicates the same thing and is good enough for us!

If we assume a normal distribution curve as shown in Figure 3.3, one standard deviation from both sides of the midpoint (midpoint plus or minus one sigma) will include 68.27% of the total and two standard deviations (two sigma) from both sides of the midpoint will include 95.45% of the total. Thus three standard deviations (three sigma) will cover 99.73%. If we extend out to six standard deviations (six sigma) from each side of the midpoint, we cover 99.99966% of the total!

Now let us look at the quality program known as Six Sigma, our subject. Regarding this, we can observe that, for a process, the

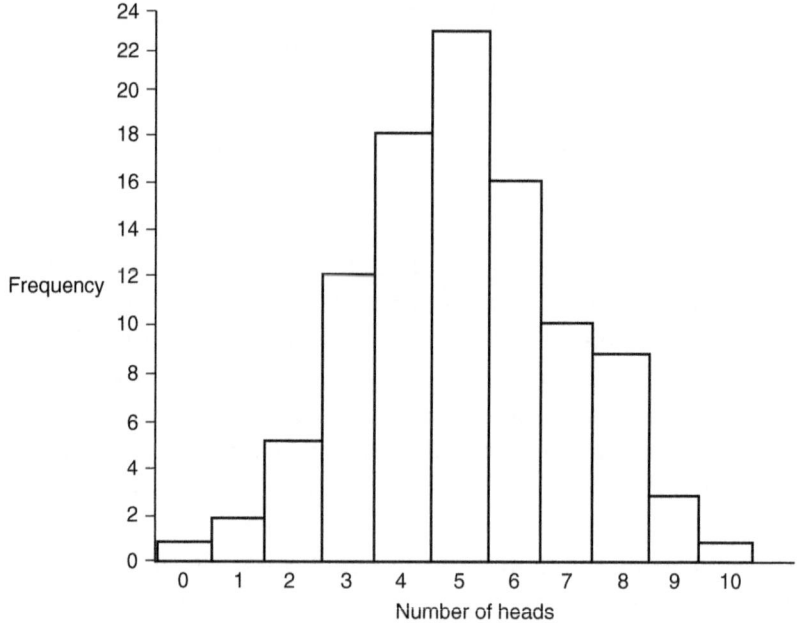

Figure 3.2   A histogram of tossing 10 coins

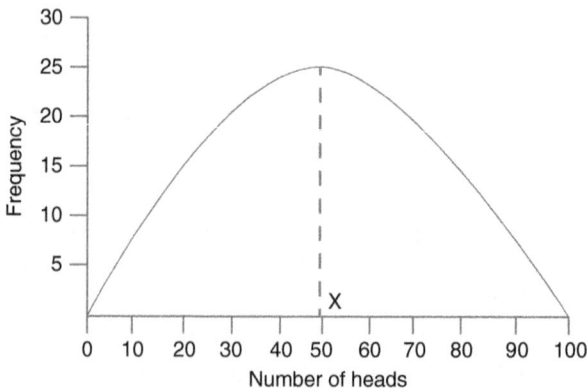

Figure 3.3   Normal distribution curve

higher the Sigma the more the outputs of the process (be they products or services) and the closer they will be to always meeting the customer requirements. In other words, the higher the Sigma the fewer the defects. It should be noted that the higher multiple Sigma does not increase the 'variation', it only increases the area covered under the distribution curve. For example:

With one sigma, 68.27% of products or services will meet customer requirements and there will be 317,300 defects per million opportunities.

Whereas with three sigma, 99.73% of products or services will meet customer requirements and there will be 2,700 defects per million opportunities.

But, with Six Sigma, 99.99966% of products or services will meet customer requirements and there will be 3.4 defects per million opportunities.

Thus, in effect, Six Sigma is a theoretical statistical measurement allowing the assessment of the quality of products and services to a position where there exist practically zero defects for any product or process in an organisation.

The key success factors differentiating Six Sigma from TQM are:

- Emphasis on statistical science and measurement.
- Structured training plans at different levels (Champion, Master Black Belt, Black Belt and Green Belt).
- Project focused approach with a single set of problem-solving techniques such as DMAIC (Define, Measure, Analyze, Improve and Control).
- Reinforcement of Juran's tenets such as top management leadership, continuous education and an annual savings plan.
- Effects quantified in tangible savings (as opposed to TQM where it was often said that we cannot measure the benefits, but if we did not have TQM who knows what losses might have occurred?).

This last point concerning the quantification of tangible savings is a major selling point for Six Sigma.

It is usually possible to measure the cost of poor quality (COPQ) with the sigma level at which the process consistently performs. The COPQ if the performance level is at Six Sigma will be less than 1% of cost of sales, whereas at three sigma (three sigma is regarded by many organisations as a very acceptable level of process quality) the corresponding COPQ will range from 25 to 30% of cost of sales. These figures are explained/justified later in this book.

3.7. The Structured Approach of Six Sigma

Following the rigorous application of Six Sigma in many organisations, including Motorola, Allied Signal, General Electric, Bombardier, ABB, American Express, Wipro, GSK and others, a proven structured approach has emerged for product and process improvement. This structured and hierarchical process is shown below:

EXECUTIVE LEADERS/SPONSORS

↓

MASTER BLACK BELTS
(also known as Champions)
Owners of Critical Projects

↓

BLACK BELTS
(also known as Experts)
Change agents assigned to Masters
to tackle critical projects

↓

GREEN BELTS
(also known as Agent Advocates)
Grass root support to implement changes

The top management must have a total commitment to the implementation of Six Sigma and accomplish the following tasks:

1. Establish a Six Sigma leadership team.
2. Develop and roll out a deployment plan for the training of Master Black Belts, Black Belts and Green Belts.
3. Assign Master Black Belts to identify and own critical projects related to key business issues.
4. Provide support for Black Belts to make breakthrough improvements in critical projects.
5. Encourage Green Belts to identify and implement 'just do it' projects.
6. Set aggressive Six Sigma Targets. This is done by the Six Sigma leadership team.
7. Continuously evaluate the Six Sigma implementation and deployment programmes and make changes if necessary.

3.7.1. Six Sigma Deployment

A critical piece of successful Six Sigma experience is the Six Sigma Deployment Plan. A typical plan includes four parts.

1. Business alignment planning.
2. First wave of Black Belt training.
3. Second wave (and subsequent waves as required) of Black and Green Belt training.
4. Infrastructure development to deliver results and sustain culture.

Business alignment planning ensures that Six Sigma projects align with business strategy and drive results. Preliminary project selection criteria start with projects having potential substantial savings (1 million US dollars or more). During the leadership education programme, which usually lasts for five days, Master Black Belts are selected and Masters are assigned to key business issues and projects. Intensive Master Black Belt instruction takes three to four weeks. Concurrently, while the Masters are being trained, the selection process for those to be qualified as Black Belts is also carried out.

Master Black Belts (MBBs) have a thorough understanding of the improvement process, DMAIC, Six Sigma associated statistics and change management.

An MBB is competent to lead and manage significant end to end projects. They are also capable of coaching Green Belts.

Black Belt training is a combination of formal classroom education and onsite project work. Teaching is spread over four to five months, and includes four or five weeks of classroom work with the balance being onsite project experience.

Green Belts (GB) have an awareness of Six Sigma principles and in particular apply the DMAIC cycle to work with and support Black Belts in end-to-end projects. Green Belt training is usually distributed over six or perhaps seven weeks including five days of formal classroom work.

External consultants and experienced trainers are usually needed to manage and train the first deployment wave. For the second and third waves of the deployment plan, in-house Master Black Belts take charge of both the training and the management of specific projects.

3.8.   Certification of Black Belts and Master Black Belts

The certification authority is the Six Sigma Academy. They have set standards and guidelines as follows:

Black Belts are awarded a certificate after completing:

Three weeks of formal classroom Black Belt training.

One week of change management and project management training.

Completion, as a team leader, of an end-to-end $1 million Black Belt project.

Demonstrated Six Sigma commitment evidenced by mentoring Green Belts and the preparation of Green Belt training material.

Master Black Belts are awarded a Masters certificate after:

Black Belt certification.

Completion of five end-to-end Black Belt projects as team leader.

Delivery of three Green Belt training sessions.

Demonstrated commitment to the Six Sigma philosophy through mentoring Black Belt and/or Green Belt projects.

An example of a black belt training schedule is shown in Table 3.2.

Table 3.2   Sample of Black Belt training

Week 1	Week 2	Week 3	Week 4
Define and measure	Analyse advanced statistics	Improve and control	Advanced statistical techniques
Variation		Generating improvement	Design of experiments
Data collection	Analyse and SPC tools	Change management	Process capability
Basic statistics			Quality function deployment
Cost of poor quality		Improve and control tools	Multivariance analysis
Define and measure tools			Design for Six Sigma

3.9.   What Is Lean Six Sigma?

Lean Six Sigma (also known as Lean Sigma) is the combination of two world class approaches (viz. Six Sigma and Lean Manufacturing) to organisational performance improvement. You have been introduced to Six Sigma in the preceding section. Let us now explain Lean Manufacturing and then show how these two approaches are combined in Lean Six Sigma.

The term 'lean manufacturing' was first employed by Womack and Jones in 1998 as a description of the way in which manufacturing was carried out at Toyota. Toyota called their manufacturing process the Toyota Production System (TPS). Ohno (1988), who is said to be the founder of the TPS system, noted that the basis of this TPS method is the elimination of waste. In order to achieve this, two pillars are used:

- Just in Time
- Automation with a human touch

'Just in Time' in a production means that the right parts reach the assembly line at the time they are needed and only in the amount required. The basic tool for achieving Just in Time is the Kanban system. 'Automation with a human touch' goes back to Sakichi Toyoda, the founder of Toyota, who invented the automatic loom. This loom would automatically stop if a thread broke, thereby preventing any work being carried out after the defect had occurred. According to Ohno (1988), an important part of the TPS system is the ability to prevent mistakes from happening again. This is achieved by solving the cause of the problem rather than the actual mistake. Examples of tools for problem solving and finding root causes of difficulties are Genshi Genbutso, which means going to the source to directly observe the problem, cause effect diagrams (also known as fish bone diagrams) and the '5 Whys' , or asking questions five times.

Ohno (1988) identified seven types of waste or 'mudas':

1. Waste of overproduction
2. Waste of time on hand (waiting)
3. Waste in transportation
4. Waste of processing itself (processing too much)
5. Waste of stock on hand (inventory)
6. Waste of movement
7. Waste of making defective products

According to Ohno, the biggest source of waste is overproduction as it leads to many of the other types of squandering and misuse.

Liker (2004) has written several books about Toyota and he describes 14 management principles garnered from the company. Liker writes in his book that Lean is not just about implementing tools such as 5S and Just in Time. It also concerns applying a complete system of Lean Thinking and culture. This view is supported by Womack and Jones (1998) in a concept for Lean Thinking described as: 'Lean Thinking is lean because it provides a way to do more and more with less and less'. Their five principles of Lean Thinking are Value, Value Stream, Flow, Pull and Perfection.

However, the application of Lean Thinking has moved with time and the experience of organisations in both the manufacturing and service sectors. Basu and Wright (2017) have extended Lean Thinking to supply chain management. The competition for gaining and retaining customers and market share is between supply chains rather than other functions of companies. A supply chain therefore has to be lean with four interrelated key characteristics or objectives:

1. Elimination of waste
2. Smooth operation flow
3. High level of efficiency
4. Quality assurance

3.9.1. *Elimination of Waste*

The lean methodology as laid out by Womack and Jones (1998) is sharply focused on the identification and elimination of 'mudas' or waste. Indeed, their first two principles (i.e. Value and Value Stream) are centered around the elimination of waste. Their motto has been 'banish waste and create wealth in your organisation'. It starts with Value Stream Mapping to identify value and then pinpoints waste with the Process Mapping of valued processes, followed by systematically eliminating them. This emphasis on waste abolition has probably made 'lean' synonymous with the absence of waste. Waste reduction is often a good place to start in the overall effort to create a lean supply chain because it can often be achieved with little or no capital investment.

3.9.2. Smooth Operational Flow

The well-publicised Just in Time (JIT) approach is a key driver of a lean supply chain and, as we have indicated earlier, it requires materials and products to flow 'like water' from the supplier through the production process on to the customer. The capacity bottlenecks are eliminated, the process times of work stations are balanced and there are few buffer inventories between operations. Smooth operation flow requires the applications of appropriate approaches. Three of the most frequently applied methods are:

- Cellular manufacturing
- Kanban pull system
- Theory of constraints

In the cellular manufacturing concept, the traditional batch production area is transformed into flow line layouts so that ideally a single piece flows through the line at any time. In practice, an optimum batch size is calculated starting with the most critical work centers and the largest inventory carrying costs. Action is taken for improvement both at these work centres and concerning methods that have the greatest impact on the throughput, customer satisfaction, operating cost and inventory carrying charges. Secondly, Kanban (literally meaning 'card') is a way of pulling parts and products through the manufacturing or logistics sequence as needed. It is therefore sometimes referred to as the 'pull system'. Finally, 'the theory of constraints' is a management philosophy developed by E.M. Goldratt (1999). It enables the managers of a system to achieve more of the goal that system is designed to produce. However, the concept or the objective is not new. Nonetheless, in service operations where it is often difficult to quantify the capacity constraint, the theory of constraints (TOC) could be very useful.

3.9.3. High Level of Efficiency

The more popular concepts of lean operations tend to be the principles of mudas, flow and the pull system. However, a preliminary analysis of all these methods, as we have described earlier, high-lights the fact that all assume sufficient machine availability as a prerequisite. In our experience, for many companies attempting a lean transformation, this assumption is just not true. Machine availability depends on maximising the machine up time by eliminating the root causes of down time. The ratio of up time and planned operation time is the efficiency of the operation. Therefore, in order to make lean concepts work it is vital that the precondition of running the operations at a high level of efficiency should be met.

3.9.4.   Quality Assurance

Womack and Jones (1998) propose 'Perfection' as the fifth Lean principle. According to this tenet, a lean manufacturer sets his/her targets for perfection in an incremental (Kaizen) path. The idea of Total Quality Management (TQM) also is to systematically and continuously remove the root causes of poor quality from the production processes so that the organisation as a whole and its products are kept moving towards perfection. This relentless pursuit of the faultless has to be a key attitude of an organisation that is 'going for lean'.

3.10.   More on Lean Six Sigma

If the objective of Six Sigma is the reduction of variation, then Lean Six Sigma aims to accomplish the mission of the organisation better, faster and cheaper. To put it another way, Lean Six Sigma combines the focus on efficiency by Lean and the emphasis on quality by Six Sigma. There is a tradeoff between quality (better), faster (delivery time) and cheaper (cost). The key is to leverage Lean Six Sigma to enable the organisation to get better, faster and cheaper – all at the same time. In general, Six Sigma is used to reduce defects and errors, thus making products or processes better. However, Six Sigma also reduces waste and streamlines processes like Lean. In fact, although Lean is primarily used to remove waste, in doing so it also reduces rework. When you reduce rework you also reduce defects. Therefore it is more sensible to combine the two methodologies of Lean and Six Sigma to make one approach of Lean Six Sigma. For example, consider a problem of lead time that varies between 20 and 12 weeks with an average of 16 weeks. With a Six Sigma approach it now fluctuates between 18 and 17 weeks with a mean value of 16 weeks. When Lean Six Sigma is applied the lead time is reduced to 10 weeks, varying between 11 and 9 weeks.

There appear to be two approaches of Lean Six Sigma (De Carlo, 2007). One is to follow the DMAIC methodology of Six Sigma, to focus on the business objective of value creation and to apply additional Lean tools such as Value Stream Mapping and Rapid Changeover. The second approach is centred on Kaizen Event (SCORE) rather than DMAIC. It is argued that the DMAIC process often takes longer when root causes are not known. On the other hand, you may employ a Kaizen event when the root causes are known (e.g. for cycle time reduction). This may follow a war-room-like environment for a short period (also called the Kaizen Blitz). However, a drawback of this process is that it may not bring the rigour of data-driven measurement and analysis of DMAIC. As shown in Table 3.3, although there are similarities between DMAIC and SCORE, the former is more related to project management and the latter is more linked to industrial engineering.

Table 3.3   DMAIC and SCORE

Six Sigma (DMAIC)	Lean Kaizen (SCORE)
Define	Select
Measure	Clarify
Analyse	Organise
Improve	Run
Control	Evaluate

3.11.   Why FIT SIGMA?

We live in a competitive world. The pace of change is increasing and businesses and national economies are continuously being disrupted. In recent times the biggest external factors have been the collapse of banking and the finance market, causing job losses and a sharp decline of gross domestic products, followed by the Covid pandemic. We have also experienced the impact of the Internet and e-business. The spectacular rise in 1999 and fall in 2000 of so many so-called dot.com companies showed that without substance businesses are not sustainable. When the huge bubble bursts it is the innocent consumers who will feel the effect. Added to this, we need to factor in large scale mergers, and acquisitions are continuously taking place in all sectors of manufacturing and service industries.

Globalisation and the economic growth, particularly in China, are reshaping the economic power balance and consequent business strategies. We can conclude that change is here to stay, and it often comes quickly from unexpected quarters. The challenge for all businesses is to find the benefits of change with an appropriate value adding a change programme.

The failed dot.com companies of the last two decades and the more current problems of the banking industry have demonstrated that their early apparent success was not sustainable. There are similar stories of unsustainable improvements in traditional businesses in the 'old economy' (pre–e-business). In spite of the demonstrated benefits of many improvement techniques such as Total Quality Management, Business Process Re-engineering and Six Sigma/Lean Sigma, many attempts to implement and uphold improvements have fizzled out, not with a bang but with a whimper. What is more puzzling is that some companies (such as Motorola and Ford) who successfully implemented a quality initiative (such as Six Sigma) have subsequently experienced overall drops in business performance, resulting in layoffs and lower employee morale. Therefore we need a sustainable continuous improvement programme.

The well-publicised results of Six Sigma were first exhibited by Motorola, General Electric and Allied Signal and then by Ford and Dow Chemical. This created an image of Six Sigma as a process primarily for large manufacturing multinationals who can sanction a huge budget for consultants to train hundreds of Black Belts. In addition to the apparent misconceptions of high start-up costs and the process being only suitable for manufacturing, an aversion to sophisticated statistical techniques also discouraged the service sector and small and medium enterprises from applying Six Sigma. Therefore there is a need for a 'fit for purpose' improvement programme suitable for all types or sizes of organisations.

As described in the following chapters, the holistic and appropriate methodology of FIT SIGMA aim to address these gaps by focusing on three fundamentals:

- Fitness for purpose
- Fitness for integration
- Fitness for sustainability

3.12.   What Is Green Six Sigma?

Green Six Sigma is the updated version of FIT SIGMA tailored to climate change initiatives. As explained further in the following chapters, Green Six Sigma includes three additional tenets over FIT SIGMA, which are:

- More emphasis on Lean and moving towards the circular economy.
- In addition to the sustainability of the process and performance there is the sustainability of the environment.
- Extension of DMAIC (Define, Measure, Analyse, Improve and Control) to DMAICS (Define, Measure, Analyse, Improve, Control and Sustain).

A circular economy is aimed at eliminating waste and the continual use of resources. The approach is to reuse resources, repair defects, refurbish facilities, rebuild products to original specifications, and recycle wastes to create a closed-loop system. The outcome is minimising the use of resource input, wastes, pollution and carbon emissions.

The measuring and monitoring of carbon emissions, carbon reduction and carbon offsetting is a major component of the sustainability of the environment. A carbon offset is a reduction in emissions of greenhouse gases made in order to compensate for emissions made elsewhere. The offsetting is done by planting trees or buying carbon offsets from emission trading companies. Carbon reduction is done by direct actions such as energy economy, changing the energy sources to renewables, reducing travel and reducing wastes.

3.13. Summary

Quality management has evolved over the years through various stages, from inspection to control to assurance to TQM. The new waves of Six Sigma, Lean Processes and FIT SIGMA are embedded in the holistic programmes of operational excellence. Our belief is that quality is not a new or separate discipline, but rather that it pervades all management actions. Our philosophy is that quality is too important to be left to the managers and that, in fact, quality is everybody's concern, not only in the organisation, but is also in the interest of customers and suppliers as well as any other stakeholder.

Quality has two main aspects. It can be measured from the customer's perspective – customer satisfaction – and it can be viewed from the standpoint of the efficient use of resources. These two seemingly separate objectives are in fact inseparable when quality is considered. An organisation that wishes to compete in the global market must be efficient and provide a high level of customer satisfaction. No organisation will be able to afford to provide a world class service unless its use of resources is efficient and non-value-adding activities have been minimized, and no organisation can afford not to be world class.

With the above logic and the application of a Six Sigma or Lean Sigma, practitioners should address both customer service and resource utilization in a cost-effective way. Quality has three dimensions – product quality, process quality and organisation quality (Basu, 2012). The results should also be sustainable and underpinned by people related organisation quality. Results should also be focused towards the sustainability of the environment of net-zero carbon emissions. As explained in the following chapters, this is where the value of Green Six Sigma lies.

Green Tips

- TQM (Total Quality Management) is the company-wide programmer in improving products, processes, services and culture.
- Six Sigma is the data driven TQM to achieve zero defects underpinned by assessed training deployment, structured project cycle and project driven improvements.
- Lean Six Sigma is a combined approach of Six Sigma and Lean Thinking to systematically eliminate wastes and reduce variation in processes.
- Green Six Sigma is the adaptation of Lean Six Sigma for climate change initiatives with an additional project cycle of Sustain.

Chapter 4
More of Green Six Sigma

'The golden rule is that there is no golden rule.'
— *George Bernard Shaw*

4.1.   Introduction

The success of Six Sigma and Lean Six Sigma cannot be faulted. The rigorous Six Sigma process combined with the speed and agility of Lean Six Sigma has produced definitive solutions for better, faster and cheaper business processes. Through the systematic identification and eradication of non-value-added activities an optimum value flow is achieved, cycle times are reduced and defects eliminated. However, business managers do understand the grey areas of distinction between different quality initiatives and justifiably are expressing concerns, including raising the question 'How do we sustain these results?' Thus, we need FIT SIGMA. The next question is 'How do we sustain the environment?' Thus, we need Green Six Sigma. It follows that as Green Six Sigma is based on FIT SIGMA, any reference to FIT SIGMA will also apply to Green Six Sigma.

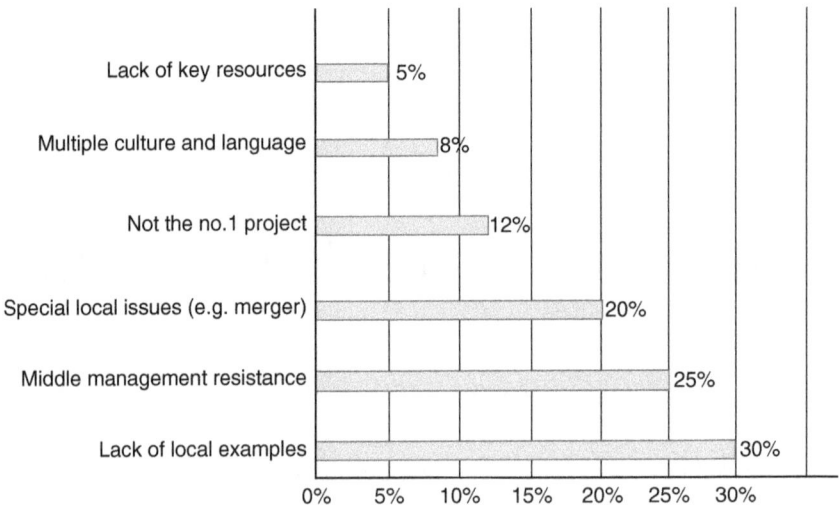

Figure 4.1 Main barriers to quality movement

A survey by Basu (2001)[1] has shown that there are considerable barriers to achieving and sustaining results in quality initiatives. These are illustrated in Figure 4.1.

The biggest obstacle appears to be the packaged approach of the programme, causing a paucity of customised local solutions. Furthermore, due to the 'top-down' directive, middle managers are often not 'on board'. The initiative is not owned by employees. We can identify additional and complementary areas of concern including:

- 'Some star performers of Six Sigma have shown poor business results' (e.g. site closures by Motorola)
- 'Incomplete initiatives' (e.g. Marconi abandoned Six Sigma during the economic downturn of 2001)
- 'Change of management and loss of sponsors' (e.g. the decline of Six Sigma at Allied Signal after the departure of Larry Bossidy)
- 'External push by high powered consultants' (e.g. the dominance of the Air Academy consortium in the GSK programme)

---

[1] Unpublished GSK survey, January 2001.

- 'Excellent early results not sustained' (e.g. Raytheon relaunched Lean Sigma after a drop in performance)
- 'High start-up costs impede small and medium enterprises' (the initial training start-up cost for Six Sigma is reported to be over $1 million)
- 'Still regarded as tools for manufacturing' (in spite of the success of Six Sigma in GE Capital)

The dramatic bottom-line results and extensive training deployment of Six Sigma and Lean Sigma must be sustained with additional features in order to secure the long-term competitive advantage of a company. If Lean Sigma provides agility and efficiency, then measures must be in place to develop a sustainable fitness. The process to do just that is FIT SIGMA[2]. In addition, the control of variation from the mean in the Six Sigma process (σ) is transformed to company-wide integration in the FIT SIGMA process (Σ). 'FIT SIGMA' is therefore synonymous with 'FIT Σ'. Furthermore, the philosophy of FIT Σ should ensure that it is indeed fit for all organisations – whether large or small, manufacturing or service. In this book both FIT SIGMA and FIT Σ should be treated as identical terms.

FIT Σ is a solution for sustainable excellence in all operations. It is a quality process beyond Six Sigma. The fundamentals of FIT Σ are underpinned by the three cornerstones, as shown in Figure 4.2.

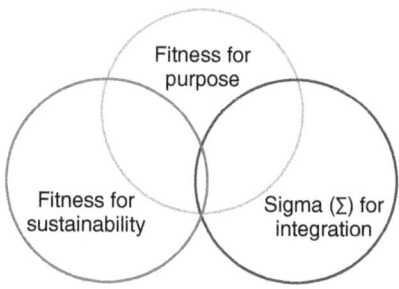

Figure 4.2 FIT Σ fundamentals

[2] FIT SIGMA is a registered trademark of Performance Excellence Ltd.

Taken individually, the main components of these cornerstones are not new, but they do constitute proven processes. However, the combination of these components is both novel and unique to create the total process called FIT Σ. These elements are:

FITNESS FOR THE PURPOSE
- Initial assessment
- All functions
- Any size of organisation
- Aligning with business strategy

SIGMA (Σ) FOR IMPROVEMENT AND INTEGRATION
- Appropriate Six Sigma tools
- Appropriate DMAIC methodology
- Learning deployment
- Project plan and delivery
- Shift from variation (σ) to integration (Σ)

FITNESS FOR SUSTAINABILITY
- Performance management
- Self-assessment and certification
- Senior management review (S&OP)
- Knowledge management

4.2.   Fitness for the Purpose

It was Joseph Juran who coined the phrase 'fitness for the purpose' relating to the basic requirements for quality. In the context of FIT Σ, 'fitness for the purpose' has wider implications. Here, 'fitness' means that the FIT Σ methodology is tailored to 'fit' all types of operations (whether manufacturing, service or transport) as well as all sizes of organisations (whether a multi-billion dollar global operation or a small local enterprise). The customisation of the improvement programme to identify the right fit appropriate to the type and size of operation is determined by a formalised initial assessment process.

Treacy and Wiersema (1993) described three value disciplines in a business strategy:

Operational excellence

Customer intimacy

Product leadership

They suggested that in a business context, organisations must select and excel at one of these value disciplines as a core operating model, while remaining adept at the other two. Regardless of an organisation's specific core competence or the sector in which it operates (e.g. manufacturing, retail, service, or technology), the value discipline shapes the choices made by managers on a day-to-day basis. Applying the same logic in FIT SIGMA, each organisation must align the objectives and scope of the programme with the value disciplines of the business strategy.

It is advantageous, although not essential, to apply the initial assessment process based on a set of questions that could be applied later for the periodic self-assessment or certification process. This certification process, which will be described in more detail later, may be adapted either from international quality awards (such as the European Foundation of Quality Management or America's Malcolm Baldridge Quality Award) or a holistic, published checklist such as Basu and Wright's Total Solutions 200 Questions (Basu and Wright, 1997), or even the company's own inventory. Regardless of the scheme, it is essential that the checklist is customised and that the key players of the company believe in it. As part of the Six Sigma or Lean Sigma programme, a 'baseline analysis' is carried out to identify areas of improvement, but this is performed at a later stage after committing the company to a rigorous deployment programme. The initial assessment is similar to that of a 'baseline analysis', but it is carried out right at the onset before the start of the deployment plan.

We believe that there are substantial benefits to be gained from designing your own assessment process rather than following a consulting firm's standards. However, it is imperative that the company is aware of the requirements and criteria of the assessment. The initial evaluation requires a good understanding of one's own processes while an objective training to international standards is necessary for the certification. In both cases, the assessor is a trained expert.

Case Example 4.1   Six Sigma in an SME (Small and Medium Enterprise)

The Solectron factory in Ostersund, Sweden, where AXE switchboards are manufactured, employs approximately 1,000 people. The site was formerly part of the Ericsson Network of core products AB. Solectron as an independent company was experiencing tough competition, even at the crest of the 'telecom boom'. With the downturn in the market from 2000, the competition became increasingly fierce. The management were toying with the idea of launching a Six Sigma initiative, but their initial enquiry revealed that they would be set back by at least $1 million if they began a formal Black Belt training programme with the Six Sigma Academy at Scottsdale, Arizona.

Ericsson, the parent company of previous years, had already embarked upon a Six Sigma initiative. The Black Belt training programme was also in full swing. Solectron decided to send a promising manager to a Black Belt training course via the Ericsson deployment plan. The young manager duly returned to Ostersund with great enthusiasm and applied a preliminary 'base line analysis' rooted in a simple checklist. The results were then presented to the management and a customised programme was drafted. The training programme was extensive, but Solectron relied on the Black Belts from Ericsson and also retained the same consultants as and when required.

Ten members of the top management team attended a one-day course on Six Sigma, fourteen people were trained as

'Black Belts' on a seven-month part-time programme and twenty more attended a two-day course. Six Sigma applications at this factory saved US $0.5 million during the first year of the project. This amounted to about $500 per employee, but was actually closer to a huge $36,000 per employee trained in Six Sigma methods. A modest start in terms of savings per Black Belt perhaps, but the investment was also a fraction of a 'pure play' Six Sigma initiative. More significantly, this customised approach enabled Solectron to have a launch pad to gain a much-needed competitive advantage.

Solectron applied the FIT Σ methodology – 'Fitness for the purpose' – albeit not consciously under any label.

Many organisations have dived into a Six Sigma programme without going through the earlier crucial stages of identifying the real requirements. Arguably, a significant number of companies that initiated a Six Sigma programme did so because they felt threatened in terms of their very survival or they became victims of management fads. The 'GE factor' was too strong to ignore. However, we should not interpret this 'GE factor' as a licence to blindly copy General Electric, but rather an exhortation to 'Get Effective' by applying the FIT Σ methodology. The starting point is an initial assessment as illustrated in Figure 4.3.

The initial assessment process can benefit from the application of a rating scale to each criterion or question on a ladder of, say, 1 to 5, with 1 being marked as 'poor' and 5 ranked as 'excellent'. A spider diagram can be constructed from the scores of each criterion to highlight the gaps.

The 'fitness for the purpose' philosophy also applies to the type of business, whether it is manufacturing operations in a factory or a service procedure in an office. The success of GE Capital after the application of Six Sigma is well documented. However, Jack Welch has often been quoted as the success factor rather than the

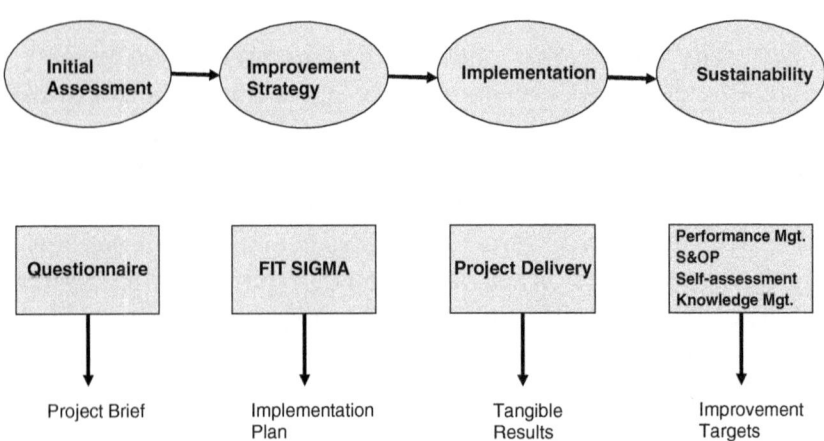

Figure 4.3   Fitness for the purpose

application of the principles of Six Sigma and, after all, GE Capital is a huge operation of billions of dollars.

4.3.   Sigma (Σ) for Improvement and Integration

The key cornerstone of FIT Σ methodology is 'Sigma (Σ) for improvement and integration'. The 'improvement' aspect is essentially based upon the proven tools and processes of Six Sigma/Lean Sigma initiatives. While the contents of Six Sigma or Lean Sigma approaches vary according to a company, a consultant or an author, the common features with FIT Σ are:

- Appropriate Six Sigma tools
- Appropriate DMAIC methodology
- Learning deployment
- Project plan and delivery
- Shift from variation (σ) to integration (Σ)

4.3.1.   The Appropriate Green Six Sigma Tools

When subjected to rigorous and more detailed analysis, it is true that Six Sigma or Lean Sigma tools are not original and we should

Table 4.1   The Six Sigma tools

Basic Tools:
Pareto Diagram
- Flow Process Chart
- UCL/LCL Control Chart
- Cause and Effect Diagram
- Input-Process-Output (IPO) Diagram
- Brainstorming
- Scatter Diagram
- Histogram
- The Seven Wastes
- The Five Ss
Advanced Tools:
Failure Mode and Effect Analysis (FMEA)
- Design of Experiments (DOE)
- Design for Six Sigma (DFSS)

acknowledge their antecedents. For example, the focus on variation is historically known as the control chart devised by Deming and Schewhart. Design of Experiments can be linked to Taguchi's methods. The proactive use of Pareto and 'fishbone' diagrams in Six Sigma may seem laudable, but these are really 'old hat', being the clothing of TQM and tools originally developed by Pareto and Ishikawa. The flow process chart of Lean Sigma is also a classic industrial engineering tool. Therefore we do not propose to introduce any new so-called 'FIT Σ tools', but rather to refer to them as 'Six Sigma tools'. Thomas Edison once said, 'Your idea has to be original only in its adaptation to the problem you are currently working on'. The adaptation of the existing apparatus constitutes the 'appropriate Six Sigma' tools, as shown in Table 4.1.

Some of the tools outlined above have been described in previous chapters and further details can be found in Appendix 1. We recommend that the Learning Deployment of FIT Σ should ensure both the understanding and application of these 'appropriate tools'.

Chapter 5 describes in more detail some suitable Green Six Sigma tools.

4.3.2. Appropriate DMAIC Methodology

- The basic framework of DMAIC cannot be doubted and it is also a core requirement of FIT SIGMA. However, the time and cost of using DMAIC should be weighed against the complexity and potential benefits of each project. Depending on the requirements of an individual undertaking, three levels of methodology are suggested:
- DMAIC Full
- DMAIC Lite
- KAIZEN Event

DMAIC Full is the pure play data-driven Six Sigma framework in five stages of Define, Measure, Analyse, Improve and Control.

DMAIC Lite is the modified framework of FIT SIGMA for small and medium enterprises (SMEs) comprising three stages (Define, Measure and Analyse and Improve and Control).

A KAIZEN Event is a structured continuous improvement process constituting a small group of people to improve a specific aspect of the business process in a rapid and focused manner. This method is applicable to all types and sizes of organisations and is usually employed when the root causes of the problem are known.

4.3.3. Learning Deployment

In order to use tools 'appropriate for Six Sigma' to achieve longer-term benefits, it is essential that an extensive learning deployment programme is dedicated to the education and training of employees at all levels. This learning deployment plan should be formulated after the 'initial assessment' and details will vary according to the 'quality level' and size of the organisation. It is recommended that the proven paths of previous Six Sigma and Lean Sigma programmes should be treated with respect and a deployment plan can then be built around the following outline shown in Table 4.2.

Through a rigorous training deployment programme, Six Sigma has contributed to the creation of a people infrastructure within an organisation to enable the rollout of a comprehensive programme.

Table 4.2 Outline of a deployment plan

Programme	Target Audience	Duration	Approximate Number
Leadership Education	Senior Management	2 days	3–5% of employees
Expert Training (Black Belt)	Senior and Middle Management	4–6 weeks (in waves over 6 months)	1% of employees
Advocate Training (Green Belt)	Supervisors and Functional Staff	1 week	10% of employees
Appreciation and Cultural Education	All employees	2 × half days	All

The issue is not who should be trained, but rather who should do the training. The original source of Six Sigma education was the Six Sigma Academy, founded in 1994 in Scottsdale, Arizona. It is run by former Motorola experts Mikel Harry and Richard Schroeder. Their fees have been reported to start at $1 million per corporate client. Although there are many capable consultancy firms offering instruction, such tutoring costs are still running on an average threshold of $40,000 per 'Black Belt'.[3] Thus the initial start-up and training expenses have prevented many small- and medium-sized companies from embracing a Six Sigma programme.

It is essential that high quality input is provided to the training programme. This is usually available from specialist external advisers. At the same time a 'turn key' consultancy support is not only expensive but also contains the risk that 'when consultants leave, expertise leaves as well'. In the FIT Σ Learning Deployment programme, we recommend two options:

Option 1:
- Retain consultants for, say, three months
- Run part of the leadership education and expert training programmes

---

[3] Unpublished GSK survey, January 2001.

- Develop with the assistance of consultants a firm's own trainers and in-house Experts to complete the remaining waves of leadership and expert training
- Coach Advocates (Green Belts) by own Experts
- Cultural education by line managers

Option 2:
- Deploy consultants for one top level leadership education Workshop
- Prepare a small team of Experts (two to five people) as trainers and develop a deployment plan with the assistance of consultants
- Roll out the deployment plan with own Experts
- Ensure that consultants are available if required
- Train Advocates (Green Belts) by own Experts
- Cultural education by line managers

In General Electric, known to be the 'cathedral' of Six Sigma, the Six Sigma programme has been supported globally by a corporate team (known as CLOE – Centre of Learning and Operational Excellence), based at Stanford, Connecticut. Regardless of the type or size of operations, the development of a firm's own training capability is the foundation of sustainable performance.

Case Example 4.2   Six Sigma Training Deployment in Noranda Inc.

Noranda Inc. is a leading international mining and metals company for copper, zinc, magnesium, aluminium and the recycling of metal. With its headquarters in Toronto, the company employs 17,000 people around the world and its annual turnover in 2000 was $6.5 billion.

In August 1999, the board of Noranda decided to embark upon a global Six Sigma project with an initial savings target of $100 million in 2000. There were, however, some specific challenges to overcome. The company business is in a traditional industry with long serving trade. Furthermore, Noranda is a 'de-centralised' organisation with multiple cultures and languages. Senior executives studied the experiences of other companies (GE, Allied Signal, Dupont, Bombardier and Alcoa) and invited the Six Sigma Academy from Arizona to launch the training deployment programme.

The Six Sigma structure at Noranda focused on the training of the following levels:

- Deployment and Project Champions
- Master Black Belts
- Black Belts
- Business Analysts and Validates
- Process Owners
- Green Belts

The Six Sigma Academy was intensely involved for the first three months of the programme and then Noranda started its own education and training. The training accomplishments in 2000 were impressive:

- All 84 top executives followed a two-day workshop.
- 90 Black Belts were certified.
- 31 Champions were trained.
- There were 17 days of Master Black Belt training.
- 3,000 days of Green Belt training.
- More than 3,500 days of training in 2000 – and this has continued.

The Learning Deployment to educate and develop your own Experts or Black Belts provides a successful balance between a well-measured job structuring by a central team of industrial engineers and self-managed work teams. Over the years the principles of industrial engineering and Taylorism became corrupted to the extent where time and motion study found the best method and then imposed that best method upon the worker. Such external control impeded teamwork and created the tedium of repetitive operations. This was followed by the quality circles (mainly in Japan) and self-managed teams (mainly in Scandinavia). The failure of the experimental Volvo factory at Uddevalle in the early 1990s was a wake-up call to realise that planners and team leaders should be trained in analytical tools. The experience of both GM-Toyota joint ventures in California and the Ford-VW factory in Portugal demonstrated that group performance can be improved by training the teams in industrial engineering principles. The collaboration of Expert (or Black Belt) training and the team comprising Advocates (or Green Belts) provides a balance of empowerment, motivation and measured efficiency.

4.3.4.   Project Plan and Delivery

The success of any project is underpinned by management commitment, organisation, resources and formal reviews. A FIT Σ programme is no exception to the basic rules of project management. The process logic of a FIT Σ programme is shown in Figure 4.4, where the positions of a project plan and delivery have been highlighted.

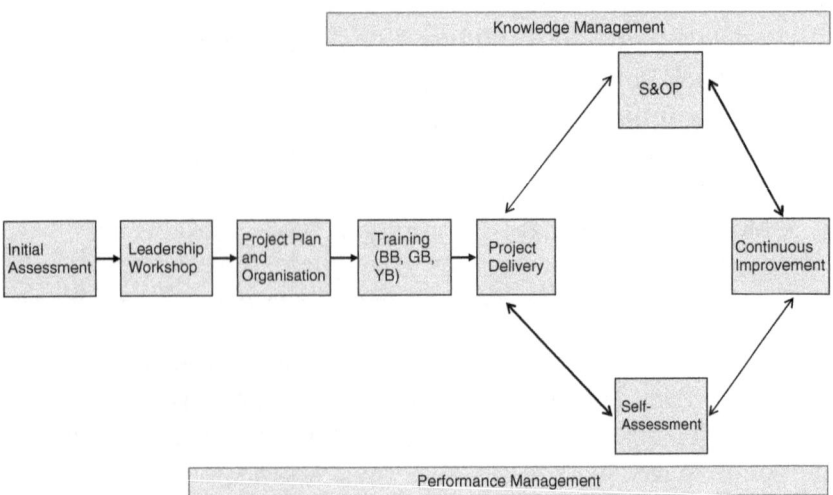

Figure 4.4   FIT Σ process logic

The structure of a project organisation varies according to the operations and culture but it must comprise some essential requirements:

- A sponsor or 'torch bearer' should be at the highest level of the organization
- Project team leaders should be multi-functional and 'Black Belt' trained
- Two-way communication – both top-down and bottom-up
- RACI (Responsibility, Accountability, Consulting and Information) roles should be defined clearly

Figure 4.5 shows an example of a typical project organisation for a FIT Σ programme.

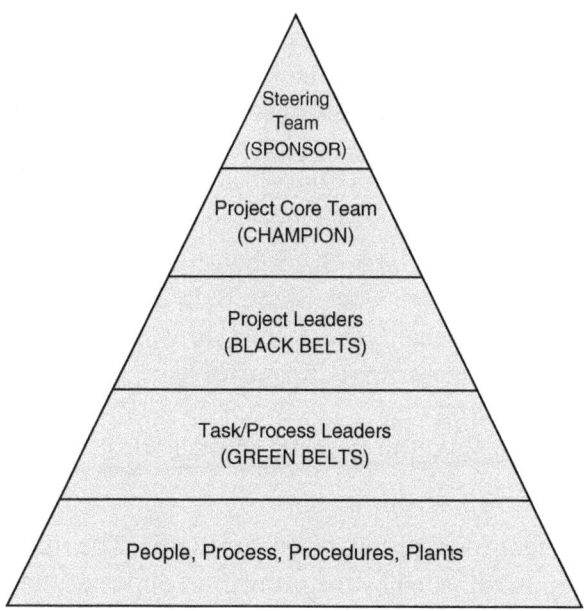

Figure 4.5   Project organisation: a two-way communication process

It is recommended that, at an early stage, following the initial assessment, a project brief or Project Charter is prepared to define clearly:

- Project Organisation
- Time Plan
- Learning Deployment
- Project Selection Criteria
- Key Deliverables and Benefits

The project selection criteria cover two broad categories of ventures within the FIT Σ programme:

(a) Large projects (managed by Black Belts)
(b) Small 'just do it' assignments

Project selection can rely on both the 'top-down' and 'bottom-up' approach. The 'top-down' method usually relates to a large 'Black Belt' project and considers a company's major business issues and performance objectives. Teams identify processes, CTQ (critical to quality) characteristics, process base lining and opportunities for improvement. This tactic has the advantage of aligning FIT Σ projects with strategic, corporate objectives. The 'bottom-up' approach can apply to both large and 'just do it' schemes.

A rule of thumb for large Six Sigma projects was to attain savings of $1 million per year per Black Belt, deriving from between four and six projects each year. A 'just do it' task usually does not incur a significant investment and varies from producing $5,000 to $100,000 savings annually.

Adapted from Oakland five key sources for identifying savings projects are:

1. DPMO (defects per million opportunities) – The number of defects per unit divided by the number of opportunities for defects multiplied by 1,000,000. This number can be converted into a sigma value.
2. COGS (cost of goods sold) – The variance is both fixed and variable costs.

3. COPQ (cost of poor quality) – Comprising internal failure costs, external failure costs, appraisal costs, prevention costs and lost opportunity costs.
4. Capacity (overall equipment effectiveness) – the number of good units a process is able to produce in a given period of time.
5. Cycle time – the length of time it takes to produce a unit of product or service.

It is important that, at the early stage of the programme, both large and 'just do it' projects are straightforward and manageable. These types of ventures are often referred to as 'low hanging fruits' – where improvements can be achieved easily by 'basic tools' (e.g. fishbone diagram, flow process charts, histograms, etc.). A simple selection process for projects is to choose the projects with a high potential for savings and which offer ease of implementation.

However, FIT Σ is far from completing savings projects. Over time, undertakings are selected and implemented to strengthen the company's knowledge base, stabilise processes and procedures and expand the cross-functional boundaries.

Case Example 4.3   A Six Sigma Project in the Dow Chemical Company

Film Tec Corp. is a subsidiary of the Dow Chemical Company in Minneapolis and a manufacturer of water purification membranes. The quality of a membrane is determined by two criteria: flux, or the rate of water that the membrane lets through, and how much impurity is removed from the water. At Film Tec, the practice was that membrane elements were tested prior to shipping to customers. This operation meant that the quality of membranes the customers received was protected but the speed with which they were serviced suffered. Rejected products were costing Film Tec approximately $500,000 a year.

(continued)

70 GREEN SIX SIGMA

(continued)

With a focus on customer needs, the Six Sigma project team required a strategic shift in participation by all employees to analyse systematically the internal manufacturing procedures. A key variable identified for improvement was the inconsistencies in the concentration of a chemical component used in the manufacturing process. The problem stemmed from the interruption to batch feeding the chemical into the manufacturing process. To reduce the variation an inexpensive reservoir was added to feed the chemical while containers were exchanged. Additionally, a level transmitter with an alarm was installed to alert the operators to the low level of this chemical.

The improvements have been significant. The reject rate was reduced from 14.5% down to 2.2%. In addition to these savings for Film Tec, membranes are available to customers faster than before.

4.3.5. *Shift from Variation (σ to Integration Σ)*

The FIT Σ process fully accepts the importance of variation reduction. The risk of an improvement process based upon average values alone has been incontrovertibly proven. Likewise, there is an abundance of real life examples where added values of lower variation or 'span' are well established. It is essential to concentrate on the variation control of sub-systems and individual processes. However, the Six Sigma theme of variation control has often caused the focusing of an improvement plan in a relatively narrow sector or department.

According to web reports, 'Bob Glavin, former CEO of Motorola, has stated that the lack of an initial Six Sigma initiative in non-manufacturing areas was a mistake that cost Motorola $5 billion over a four-year period' (Finkelstein, 2006).

The success of Six Sigma within General Electric was further enhanced by moving from a 'quality focus' to a 'business focus' and extending the initiative to its financial services area (e.g. GE Capital).

It is indicative, though not conclusive, that maximum benefit will be obtained from Six Sigma by integrating it with other proven continuous improvement initiatives and extending the programme to encompass the total business. When that happens, then Six Sigma embraces the FIT Σ philosophy of integration. The shift becomes complete from a small σ (standard deviation) to a capital Σ (summation or integration). In order to ensure that FIT SIGMA spans across all related functions, it is recommended that a Value Stream Mapping is carried out for each key product. This will also help to identify bottlenecks and obvious areas of waste. The road map to sustainable success for the companies engaged in the 'pure play' Six Sigma programme constitutes a great progress towards a company-wide integration of solutions in the FIT Σ process.

Case Example 4.4   Integration of Lean and Supply Chain with Six Sigma at Seagate

Seagate Technology is the world's largest manufacturer of disc drives and HDD recording media. With its headquarters at Scotts Valley, California, the company employs 62,000 people and its turnover in 2000 exceeded $7 billion. The business operates in a market environment with a short product life cycle and quick ramp to high volume. The data storage market is growing 10–20% per year and the technology content doubles every 12 months. Volume products remain in production for only six to nine months.

Seagate Springtown (which is part of Seagate Recording) started a supply chain project to improve materials management and develop a strategic vendor relationship. The fabrication plan at Springtown introduced the Lean Manufacturing philosophy that recognises WASTE as the primary driver of cycle time and product cost. Very soon a change had taken place at Springtown and Lean Manufacturing was wholly integrated with the supply chain initiative.

The corporate office at Scotts Valley was engaged in rolling out a global Six Sigma deployment programme. The Springtown site

(continued)

(continued)

followed the Six Sigma training programme and implemented a number of tools and techniques including the Process Map, Sampling Plan, Cause and Effect Analysis and Control Plans, which identified a 'hidden factory'. The less visible defects of this 'hidden factory' included:

- Repeated measurements (in and out)
- Repeated chains (post- and pre-)
- Transits between manufacturing areas
- Process steps conducted in 'non-standard operating conditions'
- High rework on a process

The Six Sigma methodology proved a key enabler for Supply Chain/Lean Manufacturing and the integrated programme achieved improved process capability and quality as shown by:

- Increased throughput by 31%
- Significant impact on capital expenditure due to increased efficiency of
- existing equipment
- Lower work-in-progress
- 80% pass rate on qualifications for vacuum tools (previously 40%)

4.4.　Fitness for Sustainability

Sustainability, in a general sense, is the capacity to maintain a certain process or state indefinitely. In the context of preserving the environment, it relates to uniting 'the needs of the present without compromising the ability of future generations to meet their own needs' (United Nations, 1987). The sustainability of project outcomes, in the context of FIT SIGMA, is not 'environmental'; rather,

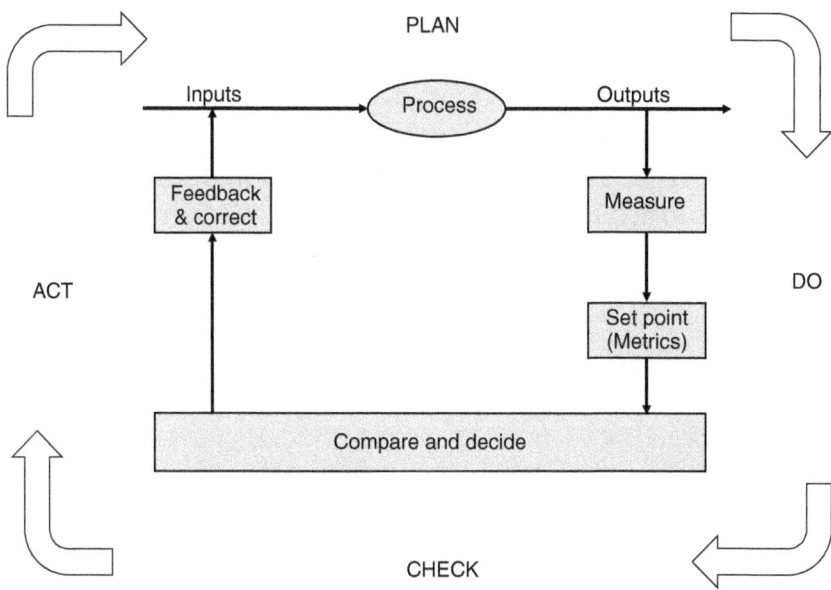

Figure 4.6 A model showing a process towards a longer lasing outcome in project management
SOURCE: Deming (1986).

it is the longer lasting stability of the deliverables and processes as illustrated in Figure 4.6.

The sustainability of FIT SIGMA project outcomes is comparable to the stability of a process. Stability involves attaining consistent and, ultimately, higher process yields defined by a metric or a set point. This is achieved through the application of an improvement methodology and continuous review. Such stability is ensured by minimising the variation of the set point. The approach of the PDCA Cycle (Deming, 1986) enables both temporary and longer-term corrections. The short-term action is aimed at fixing the problem while the permanent corrective steps consist of investigating and eliminating the root causes. This therefore targets the sustainability of the improved process. Thus, a sustainable project is expected to deliver long-lasting outcomes of acceptable quality performance criteria (Mengel, 2008).

The above explanation of sustainable outcome is also in agreement with the following definition of sustained success in British Standards: "The sustained success of an organisation is the result of its ability to achieve and maintain its objectives in the long-term. The achievement of sustained success for any organisation is a complex and demanding challenge in an ever-changing environment" (BSI, 2009).

Having steered your way through the challenges of Six Sigma and Lean Sigma programmes over recent years, you are quite possibly very proud of their achievements in terms of results and the leanness of operations. You certainly deserve to congratulate yourself on attaining your goal, but it must be said that this is just the beginning. Realistically, you have only just embarked upon your path of success.

In a Lean programme, the reduction of overheads and elimination of non-value-added activities are all excellent accomplishments in themselves. However, no Lean practitioner can afford to be complacent. In layman's terms they can be likened to someone who is keen to lose weight with 'crash diets' without incorporating an appropriate fitness programme to back up their new regime. Sure, such a dramatic reduction in caloric intake will produce speedy results, but this will be in the short term only. The target weight, once attained, will be very difficult to uphold without making more far-reaching, holistic changes to nutrition, exercise and lifestyle. Experts always tell us that the only way to achieve and maintain a goal weight in the long term is to completely review every aspect of our lives. We all know that crash diets have an immediate but unsustainable effect – in the end, we are sure to break them, however noble our intentions!

This analogy is one we can all understand and bear in mind when considering how to achieve long-term success and maintain goals that are important to us. Thus in a FIT Σ programme the sustainability of performance is instilled right through the process and not just after the implementation of the deployment plan.

Fitness for the sustainability of performance is underpinned by four key processes:

- Performance Management
- Senior Management Review
- Self-Assessment and Certification
- Knowledge Management

4.4.1. *Performance Management*

The fact that the success of Six Sigma is highly focused on measurements, both statistical and savings, makes performance management a logical and essential component of the programme. In the context of FIT Σ, we address some relevant issues including what we measure, when we measure and how we measure.

There is little doubt, even in the present environment of advanced information technology, that a company's performance is governed by quarterly or annual financial reports. These accounts create an immediate impact on the share value of the company. As the financial reports are linked, an accounting model was developed a long time ago for site-centric activities. The majority of performance measures are still rooted to this traditional accounting practice. The senior managers of a company are usually driven to improve the share values, which affect their personal share options in the firm. Thus we find the traditional accounting model is still being used, even by information age companies.

In addition to reporting basic financial measures (e.g. sales value, net profit, equity, working capital and return on investment), other conventional measures have been extended to assess customer service (market effectives) and resource utilisation (operations efficiency). Wild (2002) argues that the three aspects of customer service – specifications, cost and timing – can be measured against set points or targets. Given many resources as input to a process, resource utilisation can be measured as 'the ratio of useful output to input'. Resource utilisation is cost driven while the objective of customer service is 'value added' to the business.

The models of financial accounting, customer service and resource utilisation may also be applicable to some areas of FIT Σ, but these may not incorporate the key aspect of the programme.

Kaplan and Norton (2004) argued that 'a valuation of intangible assets and company capabilities would be especially helpful since, for information age companies, these assets are more critical to success than traditional physical and tangible assets'. They have created a new model called 'The Balanced Scorecard', as illustrated in Figure 4.7.

The Balanced Scorecard retains traditional financial measures, customer service and resource utilisation (internal business process) and includes additional measures for learning (people) and growth (innovation). This approach complements measures of past performance with drivers for future development. The Balanced Scorecard can be applied to a stable business process following good progress with the FIT Σ programme.

Performance management in FIT Σ should also be 'fit for the purpose' and the appropriate metrics should depend on the stages of the programme. There are three key stages of a FIT Σ initiative in the context of measuring its performance, as shown in Figure 4.8.

As discussed earlier, larger projects in a FIT Σ programme are selected based upon an organisation's strategic goals and requirements. The viability of the project is then established dependent upon certain quantifiable criteria including ROI (return on investment). At the project evaluation stage of a FIT Σ initiative, similar criteria should prevail. Although attempts must be made to show an 'order of magnitude' of ROI data, the emphasis should be focused more on strategic goals and requirements.

The measurement process at the project implementation stage is basically the monitoring of the key factors considered during the project evaluation phase. The following six elements are suggested.

The first factor is to determine the project's value to the business, which can be reflected in the company's overall financial performance. This aspect can be applied by monitoring the savings on a monthly basis.

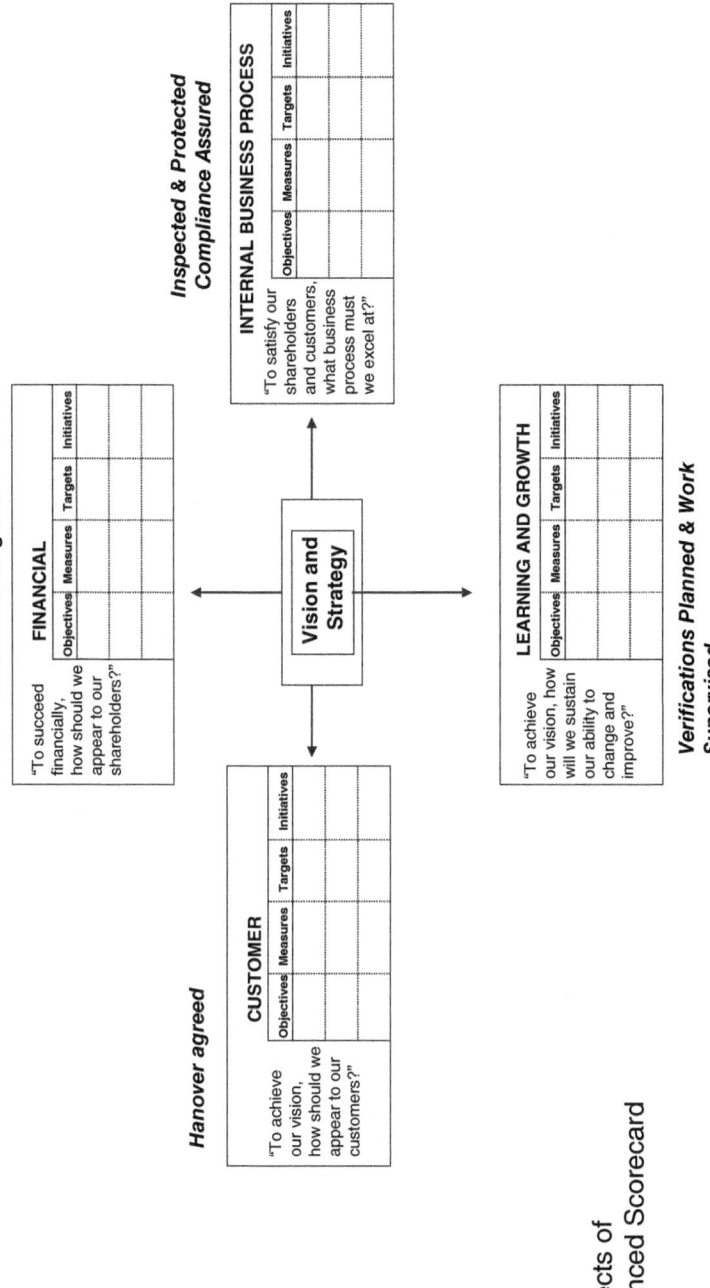

Aspects of
Balanced Scorecard

Figure 4.7 Kaplan and Norton's Balanced Scorecard

SOURCE: Kaplan and Norton (1996).

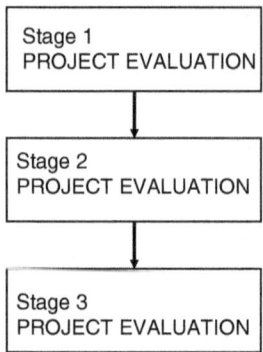

Figure 4.8 The stages of performance management

The second characteristic is the resources required. If resources are outsourced then this cost is measured and monitored. The time-scale of the project is also included in this factor.

The third element is the metrics that may be required to monitor the performance of specific large projects. Examples of this factor are DPMO (defects per million opportunities) and RTY (rolled throughput yield).

Fourthly, it is necessary to monitor the impact of the project on the external market: whether there is an eroding customer service or sales revenue as a result of key company resources deployed in the project.

The fifth phase is to ensure that the FIT Σ initiative continues to align with the overall mission and strategy of the business.

Finally, selective key performance indicators (KPIs) must be established for the next stage of the stable business process.

The transition period of a FIT Σ initiative from the project juncture to a stable business operation is often difficult to pinpoint. The main reasons for contribution to this blurred situation are due to the relatively short project duration and the need for continuous modifications in a dynamic technological environment. Therefore, five of the six factors (excluding the second dynamic) should be monitored for a stable business operation. However, additional emphasis should be given by focusing on the sixth step, the KPIs, and gradually all factors can then be incorporated in selective KPIs. A customised Balanced Scorecard should be appropriate for a stable business process.

Case Example 4.5 Monitoring Performance During a Six Sigma Programme at Dupont Teijin Films

Dupont Teijin Films is a global polyester films business with manufacturing sites in the USA, Europe and Asia. The company was created following the acquisition of Teijin Films of Japan by Dupont. DTF is a market leader but experiencing tough competition from new entrants.

As part of the corporate Six Sigma programme, the Wilton Site of DTF in Middlesbrough, UK, started the deployment plan in 1999. The main objectives of the programme included:

- Increased capacity
- Improved material efficiencies
- Cost reduction
- Increased revenue by higher sales volume

The site project team followed a methodology of 'successful implementation' in three key categories – 'Doing the Right Work' (Process), 'Doing the Work Right' (Efficiency) and 'Creating the Right Environment' (Education and Culture).

Within the category of 'Doing the Work Right' the team introduced:

- Input metrics
- Output metrics
- Tracking profile

The input metrics included the number of Black Belts trained and the total number of people trained. The output metrics covered:

- Money saved
- Number of projects per annum
- Quality index
- CTQ

(continued)

(continued)

- COPQ
- Strategic roadmap

The project team followed an internal self-assessment process every quarter based on a 'Do the Right Work Checklist'. This comprised 24 questions covering Customer Alignment, Business Alignment, Process Baselining and Project Selection.

4.4.2. Senior Management Review (S&OP)

A recurring challenge exists for companies who have invested significant time and resources in implementing proven improvement plans such as Six Sigma. Put simply, this is how to ensure their sustainable performance beyond the duration of a one-off corporate exercise. The annual review of the change programme during the budget planning is ineffective because 12 months is a long time in a competitive marketplace. We can use the analogy of travelling in a car to understand this issue. In order to steer the benefits of the programme and the business objectives to a sustainable future, the senior managers who are in the driving seats must have a clear view of both the front screen and the rear view mirrors. In addition, they must look at them as frequently as possible to decide on their direction and optimum speed.

In recent years the pace of change in technology and marketplace dynamics have been so rapid that the traditional methodology of monitoring actual performance against predetermined budgets set at the beginning of the year may no longer be valid. It is fundamental that businesses are managed based on current conditions and up-to-date assumptions; there is also a vital need to establish an effective communication link, both horizontally across functional divisions and vertically across the management hierarchy, to share common data and decision processes. One such solution to these continuous review requirements is Sales and Operations Planning (S&OP).

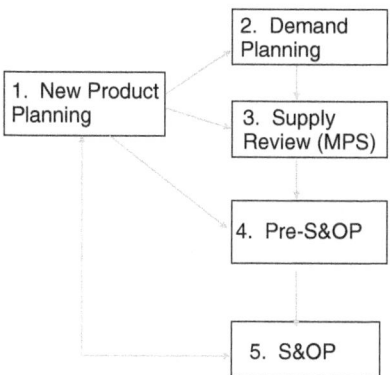

Figure 4.9 Senior management review process (S&OP)

Sales and Operations Planning (S&OP) has become an established company-wide business planning process in the Oliver
Wight MRPII methodology (Ling and Goddard, 1988). The diagram
in Figure 4.9 shows the five steps in the process that will usually be
present. The course of action can be adapted to specific organisational requirements.

New Product Review (Step 1). Many companies follow parallel projects related to the new products in R&D, marketing and operations. The purpose of this review process in Step 1 is to examine
the different objectives of various departments at the beginning
of the month and resolve new product-related assumptions and
concerns. The issues raised will impact upon the demand plan and
the supply chain at a later stage of the process.

Demand Review (Step 2). Demand planning is more of a consensus
art than a forecasting science. Demand may change from month
to month depending on market intelligence, customer confidence,
exchange rates, promotions, product availability and many other
internal and external factors. This review at the end of the first
week of the month, between marketing, sales, IT and logistics,
establishes agreement and accountability for the latest demand
plan identifying changes and issues arising.

Supply Review (Step 3). In the current climate of increasing out-sourcing and supply partnership, the capacity of supply is highly variable and there is a need to ensure the availability and optimisation of supply every month. This review, usually on the second week of the month, between logistics, purchasing and production, establishes the production and procurement plans and raises capacity, inventory and scheduling issues.

Reconciliation Review (Step 4). Problems would have been identified in previous reviews of new products, demand and supply. The reconciliation step goes beyond the balancing of numbers to assess the business advantage and risk for each area of conflict. This review looks at issues from the business point of view rather than departmental objectives. This is also known as the Pre-S&OP Review and its aim is to minimise issues for the final S&OP stage.

Senior Management Review (Step 5). Senior managers or board members, with an MD or CEO in the chair, will approve the plan that will provide clear visibility for a single set of members driving the total business forward. The agenda includes the review of key performance indicators, business trends of operational and financial performance, issues arising from previous reviews and corporate initiatives. This is a powerful forum to adjust business direction and priorities. This is also known as the Sales and Operations Planning (S&OP) Review.

At each process step the reviews must address a planning horizon of 18–36 months in order to make a decision for both operational and strategic objectives. There may be a perceived view that S&OP is a process of aggregate/volume planning for the supply chain. However, it is also a top level forum to provide a link between business plan and strategy. The continuous improvement and sustainability of company performance by a FIT Σ programme can only be ensured in the longer term by a well-structured S&OP or senior management review process. The results and issues related to FIT Σ should be a regular item in the S&OP agenda. Figure 4.10 illustrates how a hierarchy of key performance indictors can be applied and cascaded across the review processes.

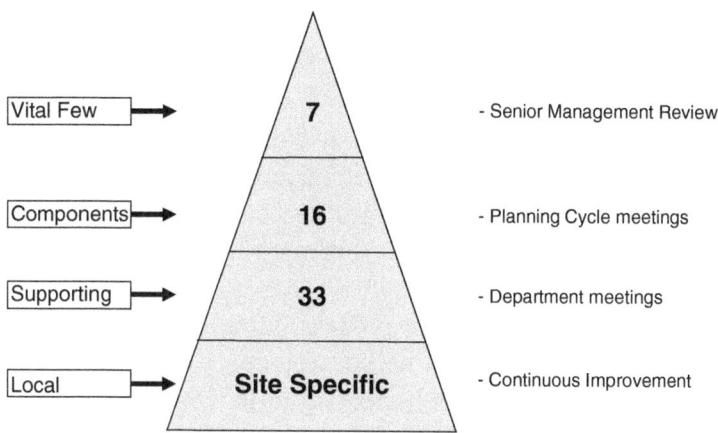

Figure 4.10   Balanced Scorecard hierarchy

Case Example 4.6   S&OP Ensures Sustainable Performance at GSK Turkey

GlaxoSmithKline Turkey (GSK Turkey, previously known as GlaxoWellcome Turkey) was awarded MRPII 'Class A' certification in 1999 by business education consultants Oliver Wight Europe.

GSK Turkey launched a programme (known as EKIP) in January 1998 to improve company-wide communications and sustain a robust business planning process using MRPII 'best practice' principles.

Beginning in September 1998, the company improved and sustained a customer service level running at 97% and inventory turnover of around 5.0. The sales turnover in 1998 increased by 20% in real terms in spite of some supply shortfall from the corporate network in the first half. This was an even greater achievement in view of the adverse economic and political conditions of Turkey at the time. GSK Turkey was recognised as a major business in the pharmaceutical giant GSK Group and the business plan for 1999 was aiming at a turnover of US $110 million.

(continued)

(continued)

As part of the MRP II Class A programme, GSK Turkey installed an S&OP process, which was underpinned by a set of business planning meetings at various levels. In spite of the GW and SB merger and the corporate Lean Sigma initiative, the S&OP process has since been continued by the company every month, on an ongoing basis.

The vigour of the S&OP process, which is championed by the managing director, has helped the company to sustain and improve both the business benefits and its communication culture. This was particularly useful when they were challenged by a number of initiatives in hand, including:

- Transfer of office
- Rationalisation of factory and warehouse
- Corporate Lean Sigma programme
- Merger of GlaxoWellcome and Smith Kline Beecham

4.4.3. Self-Assessment and Certification

In order to maintain a wave of interest in the quality programme and also to market the competitive advantage that quality undoubtedly affords, many companies channelled their efforts in two respects. They directed their energies in the pursuit of an approved accreditation such as ISO 9000, or to a prize such as the Malcolm Baldridge Award (in the USA) or derivatives of the Baldridge Award (in other countries). The process of certification and awards has had a chequered history. After a peak during the early 1990s, the Baldridge Awards gradually lost their impact in the USA and companies such as GE or Johnson and Johnson started developing their own customised quality assessment process. Encouraged by customer demand for the ISO stamp of approval, there was a rush for ISO 9000 certification in the 1990s. However, many firms became disillusioned by the auditors' focus on ensuring compliance with

Table 4.3 Self-assessment options

Option	Pros	Cons
Standard Accreditation	• Proven process • Known to customers and suppliers • Trained auditors and consultants available • External networking	• Too generic to fit business • Invasion of auditors and consultants • More expensive • Not improvement driven
Customised Self-Assessment	• Process ownership • Customised to business needs • Improvement orientated • Common company culture • In-house knowledge based • Enables self-assessment	• Lack of external benchmark • Time to develop and pilot

mainly current procedures without necessarily improving standards. A number of consultancy companies attempted to introduce their own awards to progress an improvement programme (e.g. Class 'A' by Oliver Wight).

It is essential to incorporate a self-assessment process in a FIT Σ programme in order to sustain a performance and improvement culture. Put simply, there are two choices: either select an external certification or develop your own checklist based on proven processes. Table 4.3 highlights the relative pros and cons of these two options.

There are several examples where a company achieved an external award based on a set of criteria but without improving business performance. There are also cases where, after a burst of initial publicity, the performance level and pursuit for excellence were not maintained. If the process is not underpinned by self-assessment then the award will gradually lose its shine, just like lack of maintenance of an expensive new car. We therefore recommend that a FIT Σ programme should adopt a self-assessment process developed from proven procedures. Two such courses of action are described below: 'EFQM' and 'total solutions'.

EFQM (European Foundation of Quality Management)

The EFQM accolade is derived from America's Malcolm Baldridge National Quality Award. There are similar tributes available in other countries, such as the Canadian Excellence Awards and the Australian Quality Award.

The EFQM Award was established in 1991. It is supported by the European Union and countries within the EU have their own support unit (e.g. British Quality Foundation in the UK). As shown in Figure 4.11, the ERQM model provides a set of checklist questionnaires under nine categories, each providing a maximum number of points. They are:

1	Leadership	100 points
2	People Management	90 points
3	Policy and Strategy	80 points
4	Resources	90 points
5	Processes	140 points
6	People Satisfaction	90 points
7	Customer Satisfaction	200 points
8	Impact on Society	60 points
9	Business Results	150 points
	TOTAL:	1,000 points

The first five categories (Leadership to Process) can be seen as 'enablers' while the remaining four categories are 'performance' related.

Total Solutions

This holistic approach of self-analysis covering all aspects of the business has been described in detail in *Total Manufacturing Solutions* (Basu and Wright, 1997). As shown in Figure 4.12, 'total solutions' enables self-assessment against 20 defined areas ('foundation stones') to identify areas of improvement for achieving the full potential of the business.

The business is built from the foundation stones up, and consists of the 'six pillars' of total solutions. There are 200 questions in

EFQM Model

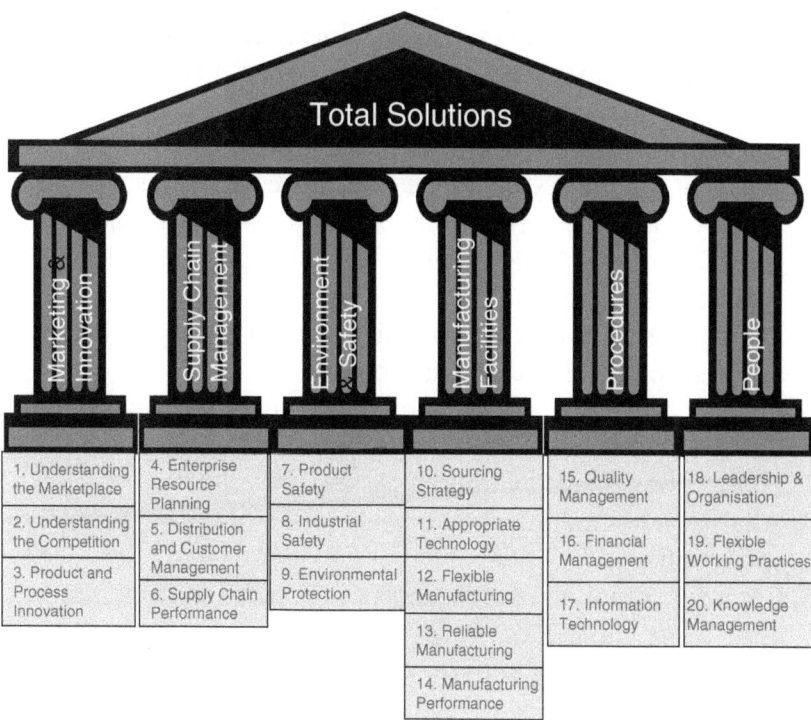

Figure 4.11 EFQM model

Figure 4.12 Total solutions: a holistic approach

the checklist, with ten questions for each foundation stone. These pillars are comprised as follows:

- Marketing and Innovation
- Supply Chain Management
- Environment and Safety
- Facilities
- Procedures
- People

Although the checklist is aimed at manufacturing operations, it can be adapted easily to service operations. A 'spider diagram' can be constructed from scores of each foundation stone to highlight the current performance profile and gaps (see Figure 4.13).

The recommended methodology of the self-assessment in a FIT Σ programme consists of the following features.

1. Establish the policy of external certification or customised self-assessment in line with the company culture and business characteristics.
2. Develop or confirm the checklist of assessment.
3. Train Internal Assessors in the common company assessment process (one Assessor for every 500 employees as a rough guide). These Assessors should also carry out normal line or functional duties.
4. Train Experts (Black Belts) and department managers in the self-assessment checklist and process.
5. Carry out quarterly self-assessment by department managers.
6. Ensure six-month (at the initial stage) and annual (at the later phase) assessments by Internal Assessors.
7. Analyse gaps and implement measures to minimise these shortcomings.
8. Consider corporate awards, depending on the performance attained, by the CEO.
9. Review the checklist with the change of business every two years.
10. Consider external accreditation if it adds value to the business.

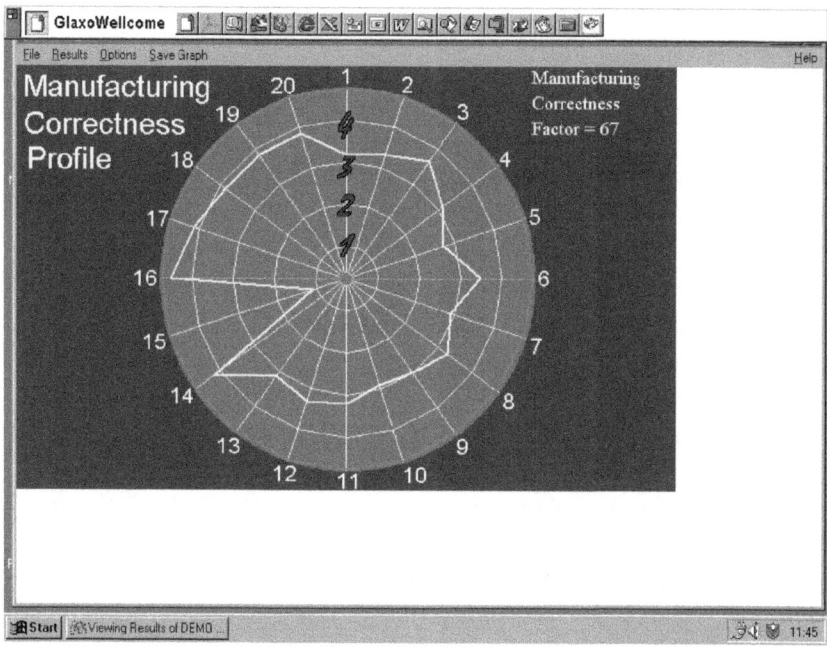

Figure 4.13 Manufacturing correctness profile
SOURCE: Basu and Wright (1997).

The above methodology is applicable to all types of business, both manufacturing and service, and all sizes of operations whether large, medium or small. A larger organisation is likely to possess its own resources to develop and maintain the process. A smaller organisation may require the assistance of external consultants to develop the procedure.

Case Example 4.7   Janssen-Cilag Applies 'Signature of Quality' for Continuous Self-Improvement

Janssen-Cilag is the pharmaceutical arm of the Johnson and Johnson Group with their European Head Office based in High Wycombe, Buckinghamshire. The origins of the company lie

(continued)

(continued)

as far back as the 1940s, with three firms initially in existence: Ortho Pharmaceutical in the UK, Cilag Chemie in Switzerland and Janssen Pharmaceutica in Belgium. The merger was completed in 1995 and Janssen-Cilag is now among the top 10 pharmaceutical companies in the world. The company markets prescription medicines for a range of therapeutic areas of gastroenterology, fungal infections, women's health, mental health and neurology.

The commitment of the company to the values and standards laid out in 'Our Credo' drives management to strive continually for excellence in a number of overlapping areas. Based upon the principles of the Baldridge Award, the quality management team of Janssen-Cilag developed a self-assessment process known as 'Signature of Quality (SoQ)'. The process is supported by a checklist on a carefully constructed questionnaire in five interdependent areas:

- Customer Focus
- Innovation
- Personnel and Organisational Leadership
- Exploitation of Enabling Technology
- Environment and Safety

SoQ is managed as a global process from the US office and each site is encouraged to prepare and submit a comprehensive quality report meeting the requirements. The assessment is carried out by specially trained quality auditors and a site may receive a SoQ Award based upon the results of the assessment.

SoQ has been reported to be successful in Janssen-Cilag as a tool for performing a regular 'health check' and as a foundation for improvement from internal benchmarking.

4.4.4.   Knowledge Management

Almost 400 years ago, Francis Bacon stated that 'Knowledge is power'. Peter Drucker (1995) wrote, 'Knowledge has become the key economic resource and the dominant, if not the only, source of comparative advantage' (mentioned in Ruggles, 1998).

Webster's dictionary defines knowledge as 'familiarity or understanding gained through experience or study'. In the context of a FIT Σ initiative, an essential sustainable driver of performance management is the sharing of knowledge and best practice. Although not explicit in his 14 points philosophy, Deming (1986) advocated the principle 'to find the best practices and train the worker in that best way'.

The key tenets of knowledge management in FIT Σ methodology are:

1. Systematically capture knowledge from proven 'good practices'.
2. Select examples of 'best practices' based upon added value to the business.
3. Do not differentiate between the sources, regardless of the level of technology or economic power.
4. Inculcate knowledge sharing between all units.

The essential ingredient for benefiting from knowledge management is the establishment of a 'learning organisation' culture. The key element here is the faith of the participants in the process. Unless members at all levels of a company involved in sharing knowledge believe that their business can benefit from it, then the exercise has little value. If a company thinks that they already know the best way or that the 'best practice' is actually not appropriate to their circumstances, then sustainable improvement just will not happen. The development of a 'learning organisation culture' does not, of course, happen overnight – it takes time and it requires the appropriate infrastructure to be in place. The experience suggests that time and money spent in knowledge management is also invested in the most valuable resource of competitive advantage – people. The support structure for such a knowledge sharing process should include:

- A champion to act as a focal point to coordinate the process
- A regular best practice forum to learn from each other and to allow networking
- Internal and external benchmarking to assess targets and gaps
- Continuous communication through websites, newsletters, videos and 'visual factors'

Case Example 4.8   GE Capital Shares Best Practice of 42 Branches

General Electric Inc. with its global business of over 120 billion per annum has been voted by Fortune as 'the most respected company'. GE is also known as the 'Cathedral of Six Sigma' and the high profile of the programme under the leadership of Jack Welch has been well publicised. GE licensed Six Sigma technology in 1994 from the Six Sigma Academy and rolled out the programme worldwide, achieving $2 billion savings in 1999.

GE Capital is the financial services arm of GE and accounts for approximately 40% of the group turnover. The success of Six Sigma in GE Capital has been a testament to the progress in service operations. One good early success story of GE Capital relates simply to the sharing of good practice.

GE Capital was fielding about 300,000 calls a year from mortgage customers who had to use voice mail or call back 24% of the time because the employees were busy or unavailable. A Six Sigma team found that in actual fact, one of their 42 branches had a near-perfect percentage of answered calls.

'The team analysed its systems, process flows, equipment, physical layout, and staffing, and then cloned it to the other 41 branches. Customers who once found us inaccessible nearly one quarter of the time now had a 99.9 per cent chance of getting a GE person on the first try' (Jack Welch, 2001).

4.5. Summary

FIT SIGMA is a natural extension of the third wave of the quality movement, offering a historically proven process to improve and sustain the performance of all businesses, both manufacturing and services, whether large or small. Green Six Sigma is an adaptation of FIT SIGMA specifically for climate change initiatives with DMAICS (Define, Measure, Analyse, Improve, Control and Sustain) in place of DMAIC (Define, Measure, Analyse, Improve and Control). Green Six Sigma includes additional tools in SUSTAIN to ensure the sustainability of the environment.

Green Six Sigma is not a statistic. It is both a management philosophy and an improvement process. The underlying belief is that of a total business-focused approach underpinned by continuous reviews and a knowledge-based culture to sustain a high level of performance. In order to implement the Green Six Sigma philosophy, a systematic approach is recommended. The process is not a set of new or unknown tools; in fact, these tools and cultures have been proven to yield excellent results in earlier waves.

The differentiation of Green Six Sigma is the process of combining and retaining success factors. Its strength is that the process is not a rigid programme in search of problems, but an adaptable solution for a specific climate change initiative or business.

Small wonder then that Green Six Sigma can be seen to offer new and exciting possibilities in the field of operational excellence and climate change initiatives. There is no magic formula in a new name or brand; what counts are the underlying total business philosophy process and culture of Green Six Sigma.

A unique selling proposition (USP) of Green Six Sigma is that it will form a bridge between the two camps of Lean and Six Sigma and the topic of climate change towards sustainability. It will thus act as a catalyst for the implementation of climate change initiatives.

Green Tips

- FIT SIGMA is a derivative of Lean Six Sigma aimed at all types of organisation with three fundamentals: fitness for purpose, sigma for improvement and integration and fitness for sustainability.
- Green Six Sigma is the adaptation of Lean Six Sigma and FIT SIGMA for climate change initiatives.

Chapter 5
Green Six Sigma Tools

'I have six honest working men
(They taught me all I know)
Their names are What and Why and When
And How and Where and Who.'

– Rudyard Kipling

5.1.   Introduction

The selection and application of appropriate tools is a critical success factor of a Green Six Sigma programmer. There are many tools and techniques available in the Six Sigma world (Basu, 2009), some of which are more advanced, such as Design of Experiments (DOE), Quality Function Deployment (QFD), Failure Mode and Effect Analysis (FMEA) and Statistical Process Control (SPC). In this chapter, we do not introduce any 'new' Green Six Sigma tools under the five steps of the DMAIC cycle and those discussed do constitute the more frequently and appropriately used Six Sigma and Lean tools. However, the new feature of Green Six Sigma is the introduction of the Sustain cycle to extend DMAIC to DMAICS. Thomas Edison once said, 'your idea has to be original only in its adaptation to the problem you are currently working on'. The adaptation of the existing DMAIC tools represents 'appropriate Green Six Sigma tools'.

These tools described here are the tools used more predominantly under the five steps of the DMAIC cycle and the new tools for sustainability.

5.2. Tools for Define

Tools for Define as described in this section are:

- Value Stream Mapping
- SIPOC Diagram
- Flow Diagram
- CTQ Tree
- Project Charter

D1: Value Stream Mapping

Definition

Value Stream Mapping (VSM) is a visual illustration of all activities required to bring a product through the main flow, from raw material to the stage of reaching the customer.

Mapping out the activities in a production process with cycle times, down times, in-process inventory and information flow paths helps us to visualise the current state of the process and guides us to the future improved state.

Application

VSM is an essential tool of Lean Manufacturing in identifying non-value-added activities at a high level of the total process.

According to Womack and Jones (1998), the initial objective of creating a Value Stream Map is to identify every action required to make a specific product. Thus, the first step is to group these activities into three categories:

- Those that actually create value for the customer
- Those that do not create value but are currently necessary (type one muda)
- Those that create no value as perceived by the customer (type two muda)

Once the third set has been eliminated, attention is focused on the remaining non-value-creating activities. This is achieved through making the value flow at the pull of the customer.

VSM is closely linked with the analytical tool of Process Mapping. Having established improvement opportunities at a high level by VSM, a detailed analysis of the specific areas of the process is effective with Process Mapping.

Basic Steps

1. The first step of VSM is to select the product or process for improvement.
2. Each component of production from the source to the point of delivery is then identified.
3. The entire supply chain of the product or process (e.g. through order entry, purchasing, manufacturing, packaging and shipping) is mapped sequentially.
4. The quantitative data of each activity (e.g. storage time, delay, distance travelled, process time and process rate) are then recorded.
5. Each component (i.e. activity) of production or process is evaluated to determine the extent to which it adds value to product quality and production efficiency.

(continued)

(continued)

6. These activities are then categorised as:
- Value added,
- Necessary non-value added,
- Unnecessary non-value added.

7. Areas of further analysis and improvement are then identified clearly.

Worked-Out Example

The following example is adapted from Womack and Jones (1998), pp. 38–43.

Consider a case containing eight cans of cola at a Tesco store.

Figure 5.1 shows a Value Stream Map of cola, from the mining of bauxite (the source of the aluminium in the cans) to the user's home.

The quantitative data related to the activities in the value stream are summarized in Table 5.1.

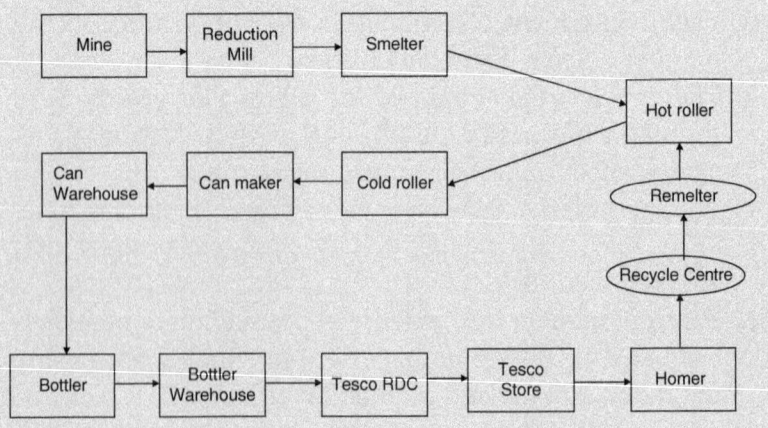

Figure 5.1 Value stream for cola cans

Table 5.1   Quantitative data of cola cans

	Incoming Storage	Process Time	Finished Storage	Process Rate	Cumulative Days
Mine	0	20 min	2 weeks	1000 t/hr	319
Reduction Mill	2 weeks	30 min	2 weeks	-	305
Smelter	3 months	2 hr	2 weeks	-	277
Hot Rolling Mill	2 weeks	1 min	4 weeks	10 ft/min	173
Cold Rolling Mill	2 weeks	< 1 min	4 weeks	2,100 ft/min	131
Can Maker	2 weeks	1 min	4 weeks	2,000/ min	89
Bottler	4 days	1 min	5 weeks	1500 min	47
Tesco RDC	0	0	3 days	-	8
Tesco Store	0	0	2 days	-	5
Home Storage	3 days	5 min	-	-	3
Totals	5 months	3 hr	6 months	-	319

It is evident from the details in Table 5.1 that value-added activities take only 3 hours compared to the total time (319 days) from the mine to the recycling bin. This proportion is surprisingly small when one considers the overall duration of the process.

Training Requirements

The basic principles of VSM are not new, but making sense of these ideas and applying them to practical problems clearly requires some tuition. There is no shortage of training consultants offering workshops and courses in the tools of Lean Manufacturing including VSM.

We recommend that the team members should undergo an education workshop of at least half a day's duration for VSM. This training programme should be combined with other relevant tools like Process Mapping.

D2: SIPOC Diagram

Definition

SIPOC is a high-level map of a process to view how a company goes about satisfying a particular customer requirement in the overall supply chain. SIPOC stands for:

Supplier: The person or company that provides the input to the process (e.g. raw materials, labour, machinery, information, etc.). The supplier may be both external and internal to the company.

Input: The materials, labour, machinery, information, etc. required for the process.

Process: The internal steps necessary to transform the input to output.

Process: The product (both goods and services) being delivered to the customer.

Customer: The receiver of the product. The customer could be the next step of the process or a person or organisation.

Application

A SIPOC diagram is usually applied during the data collection of a project or at the 'Define' stage of DMAIC in a Six Sigma programme. However, its impact is utilised throughout the project life cycle.

SIPOC not only shows the inter-relationships of the elements in a supply chain, but also any critical to quality (CTQ) indicators, such as 'delivered in 7 days'.

Basic Steps

1. Select the process for the SIPOC diagram and identify critical to quality (CTQ) parameters.
2. Determine the input requirements.
3. Identify the suppliers for each of the input elements.
4. Define the output and validate CTQ parameters.
5. Identify the customers.
6. Draw the SIPOC process diagram.
7. Retain the diagram for the rest of the improvement project.

Worked-Out Example

Figure 5.2 shows a SIPOC diagram for a company that leases equipment (adapted from George, 2002, p. 185).

Suppliers	Inputs	Process	Outputs	Customers
List the suppliers (internal or external) of any inputs to the process	List the transformed resource inputs to the process (materials, information, etc.)	Describe the process and/or list the key process steps	List the outputs of this process (goods and/or services)	Identify the customers (internal or external) of these process outputs
Sales department	Order specification	Customer order received	Lease agreement	Equipment lessor
Credit agency	Credit report	Customer credit review		
Engineering department	Equipment specification	Preparation of lease documents		
Transforming Resources		Signing off lease documents		
List the transforming resource inputs (staff, facilities, equipment, etc.) that are needed for the process				
IT system Finance department Staff		Dispatch of lease documents		

Figure 5.2   SIPOC process diagram

(continued)

(continued)

Training Requirements

The preparation and teaching of SIPOC should be amal-gamated with those for the CTQ tree and the IPO diagram since they complement one another. The combined training is expected to be carried out for both Black Belts and Green Belts in half a day.

D3: Flow Diagram

Definition

A Flow Diagram (also called a flow chart) is a visual representation of all major steps in a process. It helps a team to understand a process better by identifying the actual flow or sequence of events in a process that any product or service follows.

There are variations to a Flow Diagram depending on the details required in an application. We have included two other forms of illustration in this family. These are the Flow Process Chart and Process Mapping.

The type of Flow Diagram described in this section is a top level mapping of the general process flow and uses four standard symbols:

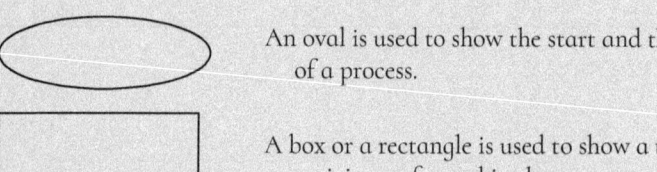

An oval is used to show the start and the end of a process.

A box or a rectangle is used to show a task or activity performed in the process.

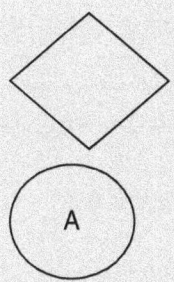

A diamond shows those points in the process where a decision is required.

A circle with either a letter or a number identifies a break and connects to another page or part of the diagram.

Application

A Flow Diagram can be applied to any type of process. It can be used for anything from the development of a product to the steps involved in making a sale or servicing a product.

It allows a team to come to a consensus regarding the steps of the process and to identify critical and problem areas for improvement.

In addition, it serves as an excellent training aid to understand the complete progression of the course of action.

Basic Steps

1. Select the process and determine the scope or boundaries of that process:
   (a) Clearly define where the process understudy starts and ends.
   (b) Agree the level of detail to be shown on the Flow Diagram.
2. Brainstorm a list of major activities and determine the steps in the process.
3. Arrange the steps in the order they are carried out. Unless you are developing a new process, sequence what actually is and not what should be.

(continued)

(continued)

4. Draw the Flow Diagram using the appropriate symbols.

5. There are a number of good practices when charting a process including:

   (a) Use Post-it™ notes so that you can move them around in a large process.

   (b) For a large-scale process, start by charting only the major steps or activities.

   (c) Come back to develop further details for major steps if necessary.

   (d) Consider Process Mapping to apply to a larger process.

Worked-Out Example

Figure 5.3 shows an example of a Flow Diagram to illustrate a purchase order process.

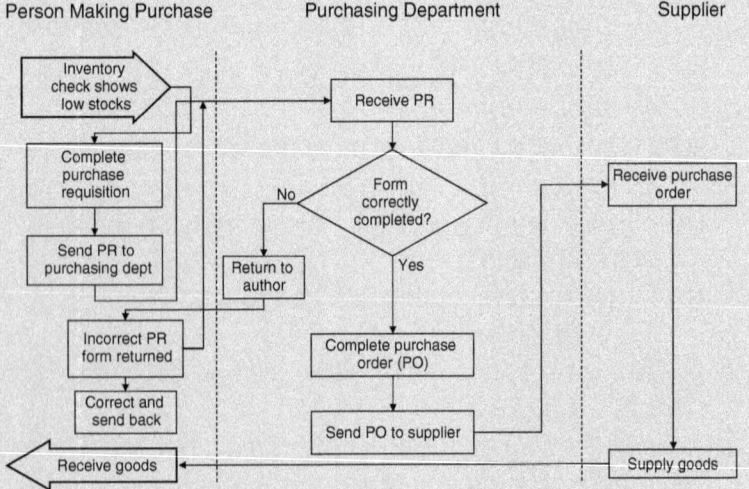

Figure 5.3   A Flow Diagram

Training Requirements

The basic principles of a Flow Diagram are very simple and can be acquired in a self-teaching process by the user. However, good experience is required to develop a Flow Diagram of a more complex process. This sort of knowledge can only be gained by working as a team involved with improvement projects.

D4: Critical to Quality (CTQ) Tree

Definition

'Critical to quality' (CTQ) is a term widely used within the field of Six Sigma activities to describe the key output characteristics of a process. An example may be an element of a design or an attribute of a service that is critical in the eyes of the customer.

A CTQ tree helps the team to derive the more specific behavioural requirements of the customer's general needs.

Application

A CTQ tree is a useful tool during the data collection stage (Define) of an improvement project. Once the project team has established who their customers are, the working party

(continued)

(continued)

should then move towards determining the customer needs and requirements. The 'needs' of a customer form the output of a process. 'Requirements' are the characteristics necessary to determine whether the customer is happy with the output delivered. These constitute what is 'critical to quality' and thus a CTQ tree helps to identify these CTQs in a systematic way.

Basic Steps

1. Identify the customer.
2. Pinpoint the customer's general needs in Level 1.
3. Distinguish the first set of requirements for that need in Level 2.
4. Drill down to Level 3 if necessary to ascertain the specific behavioural requirements of the customer.
5. Validate the requirements with the customer. The process of validation could be one-to-one interviews, surveys or focus groups depending on the CTQ.

Worked-Out Example

(Adapted from Eckes, 2001, p.55)

Figure 5.4 shows a worked-out example of a CTQ tree for room service in a hotel.

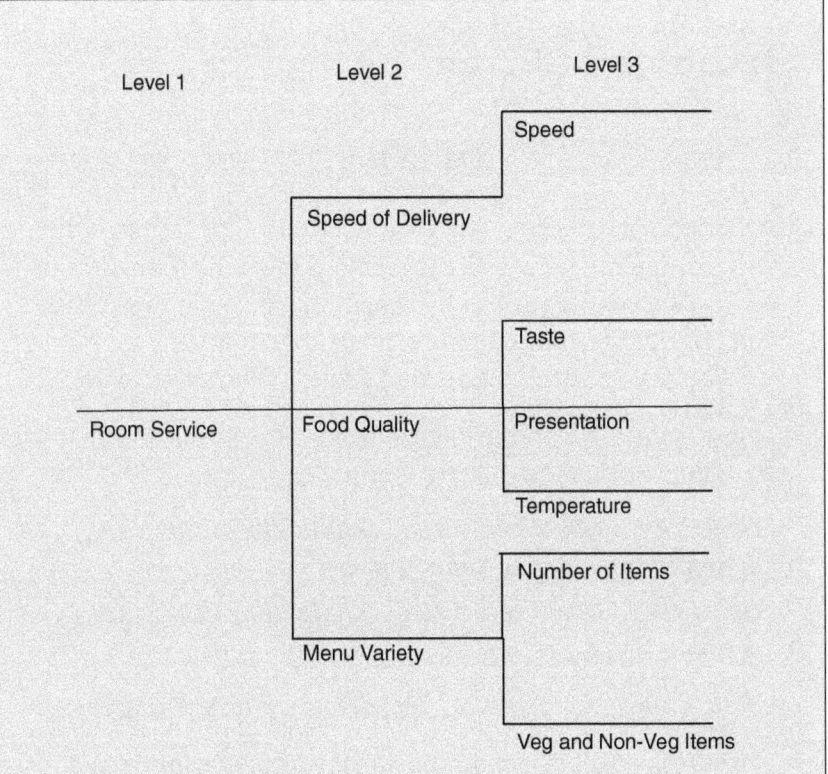

Figure 5.4 A CTQ tree

Training Requirements

A CTQ tree is a simple tool in principle and a one-hour training session (including an exercise) should be sufficient for a team member to get involved in developing a practical CTQ tree. This is appropriate for both Black Belts and Green Belts.

Final Thoughts

A CTQ tree is a simple but powerful tool for capturing the details of customer requirements and we recommend its use at the very early stage of a Six Sigma project.

D5: Project Charter

Definition

A Project Charter is a working document for defining the terms of reference of each Six Sigma project. The charter can make a successful project by specifying necessary resources and boundaries that will in turn ensure success.

The necessary elements of a Project Charter include:

Project Title: It is important to use a descriptive title that will allow others to quickly identify the project.

Project Type: Whether it is for quality improvement, increasing revenue or reducing cost.

Project Description: A clear explanation of the problem, the opportunity and the goal.

Project Purpose: Why you are carrying out this project.

Project Scope: Project dimensions, what is included and not included.

Project Objectives: Target performance improvement in measurable terms.

Project Team: Sponsor, Team Leader, and Team Members. It is important to identify Black Belts and Green Belts within the team.

Customers and CTQs: Both internal and external customers and CTQs specific to each customer.

Cost Benefits: A draft business case of savings expected and the cost required to complete the project.

Timing: Anticipated project start date and end date. Target completion dates of each phase (e.g. DMAIC) of the project are also useful.

Application

A Project Charter is the formalised starting point in the Six Sigma methodology. It takes place in the Define stage of DMAIC.

We recommend that larger (e.g. over $1 million savings) projects of a Six Sigma programme, which is usually led by a Black Belt, should have a Project Charter. In fact, a Project Charter can also be useful in a multi-discipline, medium-sized project.

A Project Charter should be used as a working document that is updated as the project evolves. The version control of the charter is therefore very important.

Basic Steps

1. Select the project by taking into account the following criteria:
   (a) Not capital intensive
   (b) Achievable in six months
   (c) High probability of success
   (d) Good fit with Six Sigma techniques
   (e) Clearly linked to real business need
   (f) Historical and current data accessible
2. Identify the customers and their specific critical to quality (CTQ) requirements by a SIPOC diagram.
3. Estimate an order of magnitude figures for the costs and savings for the project. (These estimates would be updated when more accurate data becomes available as the project advances.)
4. Obtain top management support and sponsorship.
5. Select the project team with clear leadership and ownership for delivery.

(continued)

(continued)

6. Develop the Project Charter following a defined template (see Figure 5.5).

7. Obtain the approval of the sponsor.

8. Review and update the charter with the necessary version control as the task progresses.

Worked-Out Example

Figure 5.5 shows an example of a Project Charter for a 'Safety Performance' scheme used by DuPont Teijin Films Ltd, UK.

Project:	Safety Performance Predictor Model
Date:	3/28/00
Project Type:	Quality
	X
	Revenue
	Cost Reduction
Problem Statement:	Plant needs early warning signals so programs can be put in place to prevent injuries/incidents
Goal Statement:	Predict injuries/incidents prior to occurring
	Performance Level: 1.47 DPMO
	Time Frame: 6 months
Project Scope and Approach:	Study safety data to determine what factors influence injuries and incidents. Use the most significant factors and develop a predictor model to serve as early warning signals for a potential deterioration in our safety performance.
Team Members:	Terry
	Leadership
	John
	Debbie
	Leader: Vickie
	Sponsor: Terry
	Mentor: Tim

Figure 5.5 Six Sigma Project Charter

Project:	Safety Performance Predictor Model				
Customers:	Leadership Terry Network Leaders				
CTQs:	Early warning signals of downward shifts in safety climate Combined data source for all site safety data To be able to identify problem areas before injuries occur				
Defect Definition:	Injuries and Incidents				
Opportunities per unit:	Exposure Hours				
Approx. DPMO:	1.47 Z st: 6.19				
Goal DPMO:	1.25 Z st goal: 6.19				
Stake:	Confidence Upper Lower Interval:				
Capital:					
Timing:	Define	Measure	Analyse	Improve	Control
Target Completion:	04/30/00	06/30/00	07/31/00	08/31/00	09/30/00
Data Issues:	Safety Climate Indicator measurements system needs to be validated				

Figure 5.5 (*Continued*).

Training Requirements

The training of a Project Charter is included in the education programmes for both Black Belt and Green Belt attainment. The basic principles of a Project Charter are relatively simple and can be explained to team members in less than an hour. The development of a chapter with appropriate data may need a couple of days.

5.3.   Tools for Measure

The Tools for Measure as described in this section are:

- Run Chart
- Histogram
- Cause and Effect Diagram
- Pareto Chart
- Control Charts

M1: Run Charts

Definition

A Run Chart is a graphical tool to allow a team to study observed data for trends over a specified period of time. It is basically a simple line graph of x and y axes.

Application

A Run Chart has a wide range of applications to detect trends, variation or cycles. It allows a team to compare performances of a process before and after the implementation of the solution. The application areas include sales analysis, forecasting, performance reporting and seasonality breakdown.

Basic Steps

1. Select the parameter and time period for measurement.
2. Collect data (generally 10–20 data points) to identify meaningful trends:
    (a) x axis for time or sequence cycle (horizontal),
    (b) y axis for the variable parameter that you are measuring (vertical).

3. Plot the data in a line graph along the *x* and *y* axes.
4. Interpret the chart. If there are no obvious trends then calculate the average value of the data points and draw a horizontal line at this mean value.

Worked-Out Example

Table 5.2 shows the operational efficiency (%) of a packaging machine.

The Run Chart for this data is shown in Figure 5.6.

Table 5.2 Operational efficiency

x	Jan	Feb	Mar	Apr	May	Jun	Jul	Aug	Sept	Oct	Nov	Dec
y	55	60	45	40	65	60	65	30	60	65	60	55

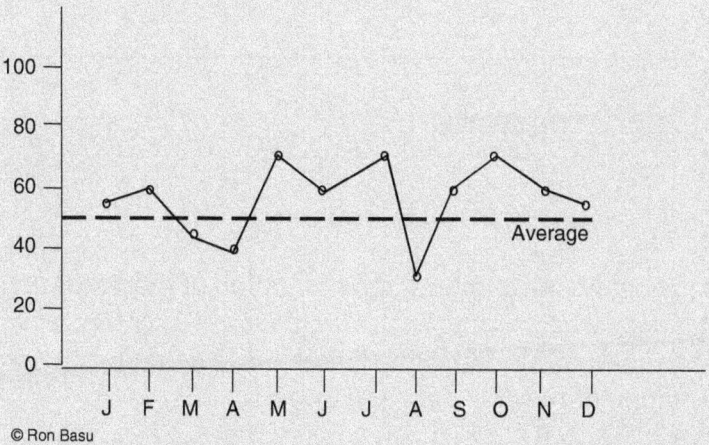

© Ron Basu

Figure 5.6 Example of a Run Chart

(continued)

(continued)

Training Requirement

The understanding and application of a Run Chart is so simple that it is not essential to conduct a classroom training specifically for it. The team members should be able to use a Run Chart after a preliminary briefing, in a practical application. The training process involving a Run Chart is usually included in an education programme for continuous improvement tools. Due to the fact that it could be seen as encompassing simplicity to a fault, a danger in using a Run Chart is the inclination to interpret every variation as being noteworthy. For any statistically significant result, Control Charts or Regression Analysis should be more appropriate. We recommend the use of a Run Chart for detecting a visual trend only and identifying areas of further analysis.

M2: Histograms

Definition

A histogram is a graphical representation of recorded values in a data set according to the frequency of occurrence. It is a bar chart of numerical variables giving a graphical representation of how the data is distributed.

Applications

The histogram is used extensively in both statistical analysis and data presentation. A histogram displays the distribution of data and thus reveals the amount of variation within a process. There are a number of theoretical models for various shapes of distribution of which the most common one is the normal or Gaussian distribution.

There are several advantages of applying histograms in continuous improvement projects including:

- It displays large amounts of data that are difficult to interpret in tabular form.
- It illustrates quickly the underlying distribution data revealing the central tendency and variability of a data set.

Basic Steps

1. Collect at least 50 to 125 data points for establishing a representative pattern.
2. Subtract the smallest individual value from the largest in the data set.
3. Divide this range by 5, 7, 9 or 11 depending on the number of data points. As a rough guide, take the square root of the total number of data points and round it to the nearest integer. For example, for 50 data points, divide the range by 7 and for 125 data points you should divide by 11.
4. The resultant value determines the interval of the sample. It should be rounded up for convenience.
5. Calculate the number of data points in each group or class.
6. Plot the histogram with the intervals in the x axis and the frequency of occurrence on the y axis.
7. Clearly label the histogram.
8. Interpret the histogram related to centring, variation and shape (distribution).

(continued)

(continued)

Worked-Out Example

The following example is taken from Schmidt et al. (1999), pp. 135–137.

Table 5.3 shows the data points of miles per gallon data of a car pool.

Since our smallest data point is 8 and the largest is 45, the interval should be $(45 - 8)/7 = 5.3$. We round it up to make it 6. In Table 5.4 we place individual data in each class as shown.

Table 5.3   Data points of a car pool

18	16	30	29	28	21	17	41	8	17
32	26	16	24	27	17	17	33	19	18
31	27	23	38	33	14	13	26	11	28
21	19	25	22	17	12	21	21	25	26
23	20	22	19	21	14	45	15	24	34

Table 5.4   Individual data in each class

Class No.	Class Range	Values	Frequency of Occurrence
1	6–12	8,11	2
2	12–18	16,16,17,17,14,12,14,17,17, 13,15,17	12
3	18–24	18,21,23,19,20,23,22,22,19,21, 21,21,21,19,18	15
4	24–30	26,27,25,29,24,28,27,26,25,24, 28,26	12
5	30–36	32,31,30,33,33,34	6
6	36–42	38,41	2
7	42–48	45	1

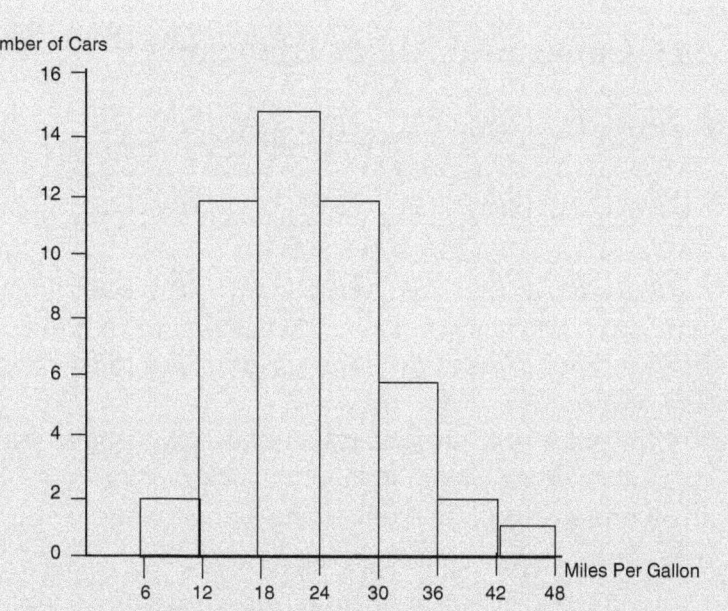

Figure 5.7 Example of a histogram

Next, we construct the histogram as shown in Figure 5.7. We see that the most values are between 12 and 30 mpg. with 18–24 mpg. representing the median. The data are also skewed to the right by some high mileage figures.

Training Needs

Although a histogram can lead to complex statistical analysis, its basic principles are relatively simple. Most members of the project team are likely to have some familiarity with and knowledge of histograms. However, a one-hour session of classroom training should be valuable to establish the methodology, especially related to the range, class and intervals.

M3: Cause and Effect Diagrams

Definition

The Cause and Effect Diagram is a graphical representation of potential causes for a given effect.

Since it was first used by Ishikawa, this type of illustration is also known as an Ishikawa diagram. In addition, it is often referred to as a 'fishbone' diagram due to its skeletal appearance.

The purpose of the illustration is to assist in brainstorming and enabling a team to identify and graphically display, in increasing detail, the root causes of a problem.

Application

The Cause and Effect Diagram is arguably the most commonly used of all quality improvement tools. The 'effect' is a specific problem and is considered to constitute the head of the diagram. The potential causes and sub-causes of the problem form the bone structure of the skeletal fish.

They are typically used both during the measurement and analysis phase of the project. Their wide application area covers Six Sigma teams, TQM teams or Continuous Improvement teams as part of brainstorming exercises to identify the root causes of a problem and offer solutions. It focuses the group on causes, rather than symptoms.

There are a number of variants in the application of a Cause and Effect Diagram. The two most common types are the 6M Diagram and CEDAC. Let us examine each of these terms a little more closely.

In a 6M Diagram, the main bone structure or branches typically consist of the self-explanatory '6Ms':

- Machine
- Manpower
- Material
- Method
- Measurement
- Mother Nature (Environment)

A CEDAC Diagram (Cause and Effect Diagram Assisted by Cards) works slightly differently. A blank, highly visible fishbone chart is displayed in a meeting room. Every member of the team must post both potential causes and solutions on a card (or Post-it™ notes) considering each of the categories.

A CEDAC also consists of two major formats:

- Dispersion Analysis Type
- Process Classification Type

Firstly, the Dispersion Analysis Type is used usually after 6M or CEDAC diagrams have been completed. The major causes identified are then treated as separate branches and their sub-causes are identified.

However, the Process Classification Type uses the major steps of the process in place of the major cause categories. This form is usually used when the problem encountered cannot be isolated to a single department. Each stage of the process is then analysed by using a 6M or CEDAC approach.

(continued)

(continued)

A typical sequence of Cause and Effect Diagrams for a complex problem could be:

Process Classification Type

↓

6M or CEDAC

↓

Dispersion Analysis Type

Basic Steps

1. Select the most appropriate cause and effect format. If the problem can be isolated to a single section or department choose either a 6M (small team) or a CEDAC (large team) approach.
2. Define with clarity and write the key effect of the problem in a box to the right-hand side of the diagram.
3. Draw a horizontal line from the left-hand side of the box. Draw main branches (fish bones) of the diagram after agreeing the major categories (e.g. 6M) of causes.
4. Brainstorm for each category the potential sub-causes affecting the category.
5. List the sub-causes of each category in a flipchart. In a CEDAC approach these would be a collection of Post-it™ notes for each section.
6. Rank the sub-causes in order of importance by a group consensus (or multi-voting) and select up to six top sub-causes for each category.
7. Construct the diagram by posting the top sub-causes in each category. These are the 'root causes'.
8. Decide upon further Dispersion Analysis or gather additional data needed to confirm the root causes.
9. Develop solutions and improvement plans.

Worked-Out Examples

The following example is taken from Basu and Wright (2003), pp. 29–30.

Consider the situation where customers of a large international travel agency sometimes find that when they arrive at their destination, the hotel has no knowledge of their booking.

In this case, to get started you might begin with 'Hotel Not Booked' as the effect and the 6Ms (Machine, Manpower, Method, Material, Measurement and Mother Nature) as the causes. When the sub-causes are further investigated the diagram may look like that shown in Figure 5.8.

The diagram points out that many sub-causes including training, e-mail systems and customer feedback appear to be worthwhile areas to follow up.

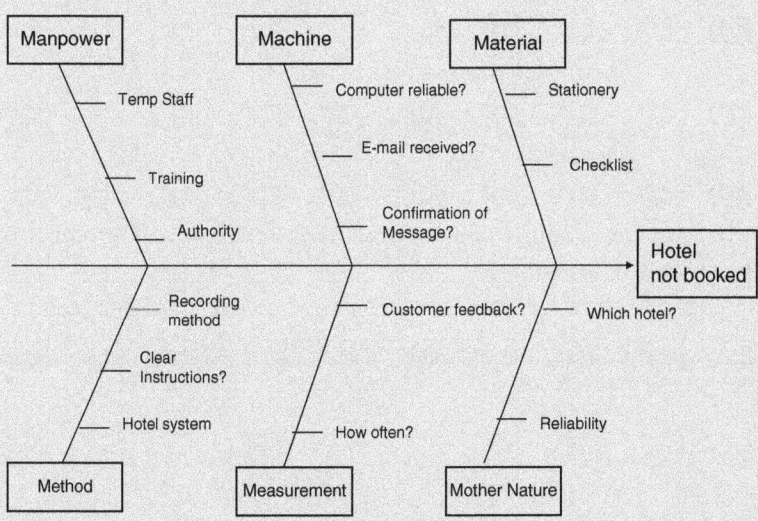

Figure 5.8 Cause and effect diagram

(continued)

(continued)

Training Requirements

As Cause and Effect Diagrams are essential to a quality improvement programme, it is important that members of the team receive at least one hour of hands-on training. An effective method of instruction is by participating in a brainstorming exercise where a Cause and Effect diagram is developed. It is more important to identify the root causes than to assign the cause to a specific category. For instance, in the example given in Figure 5.8, 'clear instructions' could also be grouped under Manpower while 'checklist' could be assigned to the category of Measurement.

M4: Pareto Charts

Definition

A Pareto Chart is a special form of bar chart that rank orders the bars from highest to lowest in order to prioritise problems of any nature.

It is known as 'Pareto' after a nineteenth century Italian economist Wilfredo Pareto, who observed that 80% of the effects are caused by 20% of the causes: 'the 80/20 rule'.

Applications

Pareto Charts are applied to analyse the priorities of problems of all types, e.g. sales, production, stock, defects, sickness, accident occurrences, etc. Improvement efforts are directed to priority areas that will have the greatest impact.

There are usually two variants in the application of Pareto Charts. The first type is the standard chart where bar charts are presented in descending order. The second category is also known as the 'ABC Analysis' where:

- Cumulative % values of causes are plotted along the x axis.
- Cumulative % values of effects are plotted along the y axis.
- 80% of the effects with corresponding % of causes are grouped as 'A' category.
- 80–96% of the effects and corresponding causes are 'B' items.
- The remaining values are 'C' category.

Basic Steps

The following steps apply for the preparation of a Pareto Chart:

1. Identify the general problem (e.g. IC Board Defects) and its causes (e.g. Soldering, Etching, Moulding, Cracking and other).
2. Select a standard unit of measurement (e.g. Frequency of Defects or Money Loss) for a chosen time period.
3. Collect data for each of the causes in terms of the chosen unit of measurement.

(continued)

(continued)

4. Plot the Pareto Chart with causes along the x axis and the unit of measurement along the y axis. The causes are charted in descending order of values from left to right.
5. Analyse the graph and decide on the priority for improvement.

The following steps apply for the preparation of an ABC Analysis:

1. Decide on the causes (e.g. number of customers) and effect (e.g. sales) of the problem areas that you want to prioritise.
2. Select a standard unit of measuring the effect (e.g. $ for sales values).
3. Collect data for each cause (e.g. customer) and the corresponding effect (e.g. sales in $).
4. Rank the cause according to the value of the effects (e.g. customers in descending order of $ sales).
5. Calculate the cumulative % values of the causes and effects.
6. Plot the cumulative % values of the causes (e.g. number of customers) along the x axis and the cumulative % values of effects (e.g. sales in $) along the y axis.
7. Identify A, B and C categories (e.g. A for 80% of sales, B for 80–96% of sales and C for the remainder).
8. Analyse the graph and decide on the priority for improvement.

Worked-Out Examples

The following example of a Pareto Chart is taken from Schmidt et al. (1999) p. 144.

Table 5.5 Major defects identified during manufacture of ICBs

Causes	Frequency	% Frequency
Soldering	60	40
Etching	40	27
Moulding	30	20
Cracking	15	10
Other	5	3
Total	150	100

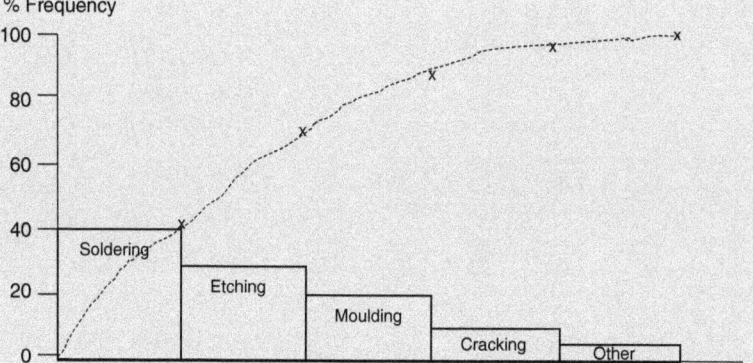

Figure 5.9 Pareto Chart

The major defects identified during the manufacture of Integrated Circuit Boards (ICBs) for a given period are given in Table 5.5.

We plot the causes along the x axis and frequencies along the y axis, as shown in Figure 5.9.

An example of ABC Analysis for a set of inventory items is shown in Figure 5.10.

(continued)

(continued)

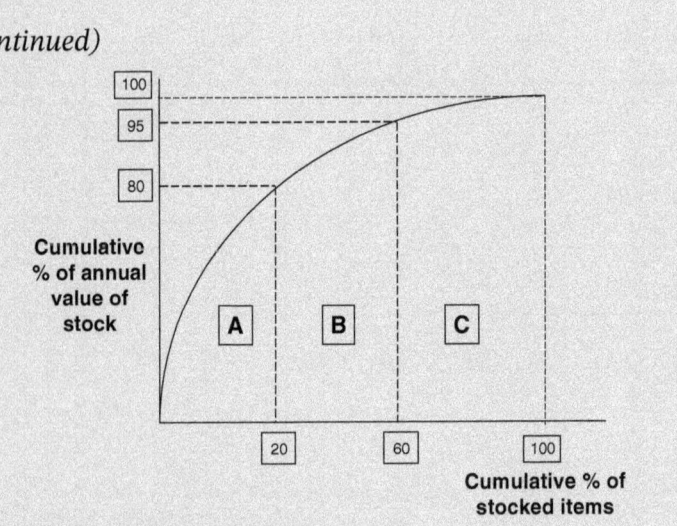

Figure 5.10 ABC Analysis

Training Needs

The basic principles of a Pareto Chart and ABC Analysis are easy to follow. The training for this tool of prioritising is usually included in the classroom education sessions related to the tools for measurement. A member of a team can be adept in the application of Pareto Charts after, say, one hour's practice on a few practical problems.

M5: Control Charts

Definition

A Control Chart consists of a graph with time on the horizontal axis and an individual measurement (such as mean or range) on the vertical axis.

A Control Chart is a basic graphical tool of Statistical Process Control (see Chapter 9) for determining whether a process is stable and also for distinguishing usual (or common) variability from unusual (special assignable) causes. Three control limits are drawn: the Central Line (CL), the Lower Control Limit (LCL) and the Upper Control Limit (UCL). The points above the UCL or below the LCL indicate a special cause. If no signals occur then the process is assumed to be under control, i.e. only common causes of variation are present.

Application

Control Charts can be used for examining a historical set of data and also for contemporary information. The current control based on current data underpins a feedback control loop in the process.

There are many good reasons why Control Charts have been applied successfully in both quality control and improvement initiatives since Walter Shewhart first introduced the concept at Bell Laboratories in the early 1930s.

Firstly, Control Charts establish what is to be controlled and force their resolution. Secondly, they focus attention on the process rather than on the product. For example, a poor product can result from an operator error, but a poor production process is not capable of meeting standards on a consistent basis. The third factor is that they comprise a set of prescribed techniques that can be applied by people with appropriate training in a specified manner.

(continued)

(continued)

For many probability distributions, most of the probability is within three standard deviations of the mean. So μ and σ are respectively the stable process mean and standard deviation; then

$$CL = \mu$$
$$UCL = \mu + 3\sigma$$
$$LCL = \mu - 3\sigma$$

When the mean (μ_s) and standard deviation (σ_s) values are calculated from a sample of n, then

$$\mu_s = \mu$$
$$\sigma_s = \sigma / \sqrt{n}$$

There are two types of Control Charts. A variable chart is used to measure individual measurable characteristics, whereas an attributes chart is used for go/no-go types of inspection.

The x-bar chart (also called the mean chart), the s-chart (also called the standard deviation chart) and the R-chart (also called the range chart) are used to monitor continuous measurement or variable data.

The stable Control Charts are used to determine process capability, that is whether a process is capable of meeting established customer requirements or specifications.

Basic Steps

1. Choose the quality characteristic to be charted. A Pareto analysis is useful to identify a characteristic that is currently experiencing a high number of non-conformities.
2. Establish the type of Control Chart to ascertain whether it is a variable chart or an attribute chart.

3. Choose the sub-group or sample size. For variable charts, samples of 4 or 5 are sufficient, whereas for attribute charts samples of 50 to 100 are often used.
4. Decide on a system of collecting data. The automatic recording of information by a calibrated instrument is preferable to manually recorded data.
5. Calculate the mean and standard deviation and then determine the control limits.
6. Plot the data and control limits on a Control Chart and interpret results.

Worked-Out Example

The following example illustrates the construction of variable Control Charts based on the data of packing cartons on a morning shift. The information in Table 5.6 is taken from Ledolter and Burnill (1999).

Table 5.6   Construction of variable Control Charts

Reading No.	Measurements				Average	Std Dev.	Range
1	25.1	25.5	25.0	25.1	25.175	0.222	0.50
2	24.8	25.2	25.1	24.9	25.000	0.183	0.40
3	25.1	25.2	25.2	25.2	25.175	0.050	0.10
4	25.1	25.4	24.8	25.0	25.075	0.250	0.60
5	25.2	24.7	24.9	25.3	25.025	0.275	0.60
6	25.2	25.2	25.0	25.1	25.125	0.096	0.20
7	25.2	25.2	25.2	25.3	25.225	0.050	0.10
8	25.2	25.1	25.3	25.0	25.150	0.129	0.30
9	24.9	25.1	25.2	24.8	25.000	0.183	0.40
10	25.1	25.1	25.3	25.4	25.225	0.150	0.30
Average					25.118	0.159	0.35

(continued)

(continued)

Hence

$$CL = \mu_s = 25.118$$
$$\sigma_s = \sigma / \sqrt{n} = 0.159 / \sqrt{10} = 0.159 / 3.163 = 0.05$$
$$UCL = \mu_s + 3\mu_s = 25.118 + 3 \times 0.05 - 25.27$$
$$LCL = \mu_s - 3\sigma_s = 25.118 - 3 \times 0.05 = 24.97$$

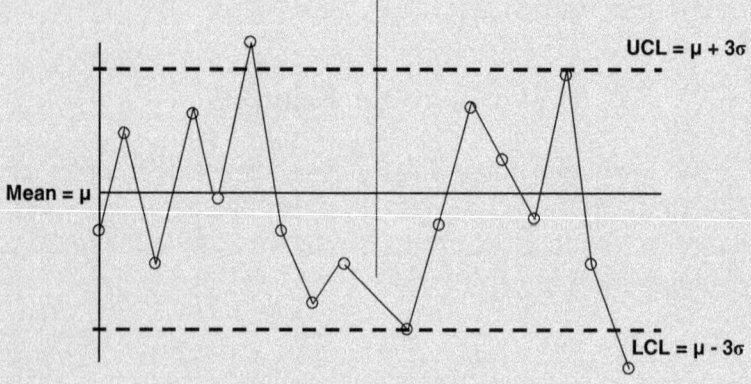

Figure 5.11 Control Chart

The control limits and the data are plotted as shown in Figure 5.11.

Similar charts are drawn for the Standard Deviation and the Range of the data. The control limits are constructed in such a manner that we expect approximately 99.7% of all data to fall between them. In Figure 5.11 all data are within the control limits, indicating that the process is stable.

Training Requirement

The construction and interpretation of Control Charts require a good understanding of Statistical Process Control.

The concepts of variable data vs attribute data, common causes vs special causes and control limits are essential to the effective application of Control Charts. Hence a few hours of classroom training is recommended before the members start the application of this tool. Care should be taken not to confuse a Control Chart with a Run Chart.

5.4. Tools for Analysis

Tools for Analysis as described in this section are:

Regression Analysis

Force Field Analysis

SWOT Analysis

PESTLE Analysis

Five Whys

Interrelationship Diagram

A1: Regression Analysis

Definition

Regression Analysis is a tool to establish the 'best fit' linear relationship between two variables.

The knowledge provided by the scatter diagram is enhanced with the use of regression.

(continued)

(continued)

Application

The topic of Regression Analysis is usually studied at school in algebra lessons where different techniques of 'curve fitting' are considered. Two common approaches are:

- Method of intercept and slope
- Method of least squares

In a practical business environment, the team members normally resort to drawing an approximate straight line by employing their visual judgement. Sometimes they use the 'method of intercept and slope'. Both of these practices are the estimated 'best fit' relationship between two variables. The reliability of such estimates depends on the degree of correlation that exists between the variables.

Regression Analysis is used not only to establish the equation of a line but also to provide the basis for the prediction of a variable for a given value of a process parameter. The scatter diagram, on the other hand, does not predict cause and effect relationships. Given a significant co-relation between the two variables, Regression Analysis is a very useful tool, enabling one to extend and predict the relationship between these variables.

Basic Steps

We have considered the 'method of intercept and slope' for developing the basic steps as follows (courtesy: M.J. Moroney, 1973, p. 284):

1. Consider the equation of $y = mx + c$, where m is the slope, c is the intercept and x and y are the two variables.
2. In the equation of $y = mx + c$, substitute each of the pairs of values for x and y and then add the resulting equations.

3. Form a second similar set of equations, by multiplying through each of the equations of Step 2 by its coefficient of m. Add this set of equations.
4. Steps 2 and 3 will each have produced an equation in m and c. Solve these simultaneous equations for m and c.
5. Plot the straight-line graph for $y = mx + c$ for the calculated values of m and c.

Worked-Out Example

The following example is taken from M.J. Moroney (1973), pp. 278–285.

Consider an investigation is made into the relationship between two quantities y and x and the following values were observed:

y	5	8	9	10
x	1	2	3	4

The values are plotted as shown in Figure 5.12. Now we follow the basic steps to calculate m and c in the equation $y = mx + c$.

Substituting the observed values of x and y, the resulting equations are:

$$
\begin{aligned}
5 &= m + c \\
8 &= 2m + c \\
9 &= 3m + c \qquad (1)\\
10 &= 4m + c \\
32 &= 10m + 4c
\end{aligned}
$$

(continued)

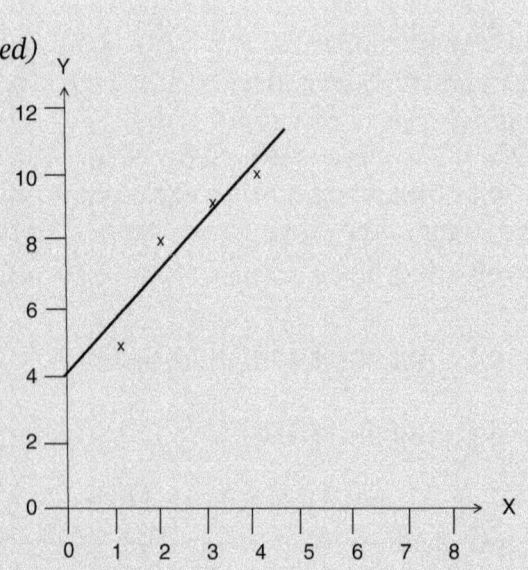

Figure 5.12 Regression Analysis

Multiplying each of the equations by its co-efficient of m, the resulting equations are:

$$5 = m + c$$
$$16 = 4m + 2c$$
$$27 = 9m + 3c$$
$$40 = 16m + 4c$$
$$88 = 30m + 10c \qquad (2)$$

We then solve simultaneously equations (1) and (2) for *m* and *c*.

We find that

$$m = 1.6$$
$$c = 4$$

Hence $y = 1.6x + 4$.

We calculate two pairs of values for x and y to draw a straight line, as shown in Figure 4.12:

y	4	8.8
x	0	3

Training Requirements

From the above, it will not surprise you to learn that the training of Regression Analysis is just like brushing up on school algebra! A few classroom exercises for approximately one hour should be adequate for team members to prepare themselves for the practical application of Regression Analysis.

A2: Force Field Analysis Diagram

Definition

The Force Field Analysis Diagram, or simply Force Field Diagram, is a model built on the concept by Kurt Lewin (1951). According to this theory, change is characterised as a state of equilibrium between driving forces (e.g. new technology) and opposing or restraining influences (e.g. fear of failure).

In order for any change to occur, the driving forces must exceed the restraining forces, thus shifting the equilibrium.

(continued)

(continued)

Application

The Force Field Diagram is a useful tool at the early stage of change management leading to improvement. It is often used:

- to investigate the balance of power involved in an issue or obstacle at any level (personnel, project, organisation, network),
- to identify important players or stakeholders – both allies and opponents,
- to identify possible causes and solutions to the problem.

Basic Steps

According to Lewin (1951), three key steps are involved in the concept of change management by the Force Field Diagram:

- Firstly, an organisation has to unfreeze the driving and restraining forces that hold it in a state of apparent equilibrium.
- Secondly, an imbalance is introduced to the forces, either by increasing the drivers or reducing the restrainers, or both, to enable the change to take place.
- Thirdly, once the change is complete and stable, the forces are brought back to equilibrium and refrozen.

A Force Field Diagram is constructed by a team and the following basic steps are suggested:

1. Agree on the current problem or issue under investigation and obtain the desired situation.
2. List all forces driving changes towards the desired situation.
3. List all forces resisting changes towards the desired situation.
4. Review all forces and validate their importance.

5. Allocate a score to each of the forces using a numeric scale (e.g. 5 = most important and 1 = least important.
6. Chart the influences by listing the driving forces on the left and restraining forces to the right.
7. Decide how to minimise or eliminate the restraining forces and increase the driving force.
8. Agree on an action plan.

Worked-Out Example

The issue identified is how to increase the usage of purchase orders in a pharmaceutical company. The driving and restraining forces were identified by the team and also rated in a scale of 1 to 5 (1 = low, 5 = high). This was then represented in a Force Field Diagram, as shown in Figure 5.13.

The driving forces show a total score of 13 against an overall score of 11 demonstrated by the restraining forces.

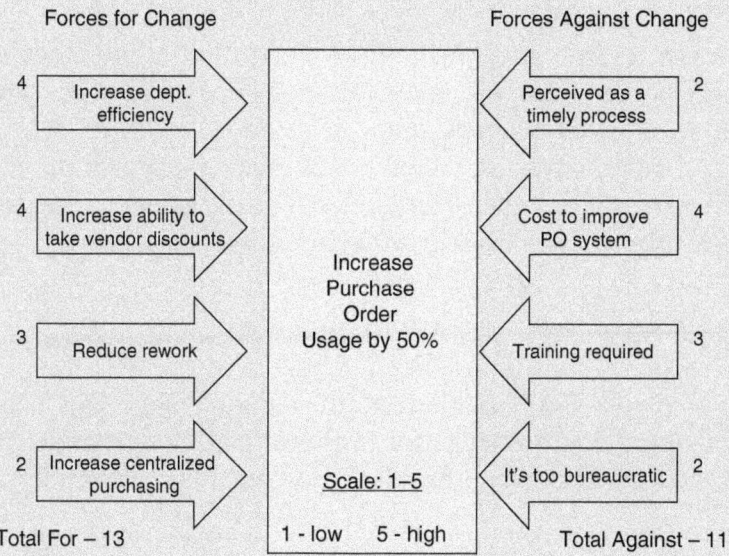

Figure 5.13   Force Field Diagram

(continued)

(continued)

Training Requirements

The knowledge and application of a Force Field Diagram are best derived by 'on the job' training during a brainstorming exercise on an actual problem. The facilitator should have experience in change management in applying a number of Force Field Diagrams to direct the team and gain a consensus of identifying forces and allocating scores.

A3: SWOT Analysis

Definition

A SWOT (Strengths, Weaknesses, Opportunities and Threats) is a tool for analysing an organisation's competitive position in relation to the opposition.

In the context of a quality improvement programme, a SWOT Analysis refers to a summary of the gaps and positive features of a process following the analytical stage.

Application

Based on a SWOT framework, the team members can focus on alternative strategies for improvement. For example, an S/O (Strengths/Opportunities) approach may be considered to consolidate the strengths and open further leverage from the process. Similarly, an S/T (Strengths/Threats) policy could be borne in mind in order to maximise the strength of the process and minimise risks.

Thus, a SWOT Analysis can help the team to identify a wide range of alternative tactics for the next stage.

Basic Steps

1. Create two categories (internal factors and external factors) and then further sub-divide into positive aspects (Strengths and Opportunities) and negative aspects (Weaknesses and Threats).
2. Ensure that the internal factors may be viewed as a strength or weakness of a process depending on their impact on the outcome or the process output.
3. Similarly assess the external factors bearing in mind that threats to one process could be viewed as an opportunity for another procedure.
4. Summarise the key features and findings derived from previous analyses in each of the SWOT categories.
5. Develop the improvement strategy for the next stage as pointers from the SWOT Analysis.

Worked-Out Example

The following example is taken from Kotabe and Helsen (2000), p. 277.

(continued)

(continued)

Table 5.7 shows the framework of a SWOT Analysis.

Table 5.7 Framework of a SWOT Analysis

	Internal Factors	Strengths	Weaknesses
External Factors		Brand name, human resources, technology, advertising	Price, lack of financial resources, long product development cycle
Opportunities	Growth market, de-regulation, stable exchange rate, investment grant	S/O Strategy Maximise Strengths and maximise Opportunities	W/O Strategy Minimise Weaknesses and maximise Opportunities
Threats	New entrants, change in consumer preference, local requirements	S/T Strengths Maximise Strengths and minimise Threats	W/T Strategy Minimise Weaknesses and Minimise Threats

Training Requirements

The training of the SWOT Analysis should be conducted in stages. The first part is in a classroom where the basic principles can be explained based on a known marketing product. The second aspect of the tuition is delivered to the team member when the results following the analysis of process are summarised.

A4: Pestle Analysis

Definition

The PESTLE (Political, Economic, Social, Technical, Legal and Environmental) Analysis is an analytical tool for assessing the impact of external contexts on a project or a major operation and also the impact of a project on its external circumstances. There are several possible contexts including:

- Political
- Economic
- Social
- Technical and
- Environmental

This is remembered easily by the acronym 'PESTLE' or 'Le Pest' in French. It is thus also known as the PEST Analysis.

Application

Very few significant changes, whether they are caused by a major operation or a project, are unaffected by the external surrounds.

Political: A project is affected by the policies of international, national or local government. It is also influenced by company policies and those of stakeholders, managers, employees and trade unions.

Economic: The project is affected by national and international economic issues, inflation, interest rates and exchange rates.

(continued)

(continued)

Social: The change is influenced by social issues, the local culture, the lives of employees, communications and language.

Technological: The success of implementation is affected by the technology of the industry and the technical capability of the parent company.

Legal: The project is affected by the legal aspects of planning, registration and working practices.

Environmental: The impact of the change on environmental emission, noise, health and safety is assessed.

Basic Steps

A PESTLE Analysis is carried out in four stages:

1. Develop a good understanding of the deliverables of the operation and the project. At this stage, the relevant policy and guidelines of both the local company and the parent organisation are reviewed.
2. List the relevant factors affecting the various aspects of the project related to PESTLE. It is important that the appropriate expertise of the organisation is drawn into the team for this analysis.
3. Validate the factors in Step 2 with the stakeholders and functional leaders of the company.
4. Review progress and decide on the next steps by asking two questions:
   How did we do?
   Where do we go next?
5. For more information on the PESTLE Analysis, see Turner and Simister (2000), pp. 165–215.

Worked-Out Example

Consider the policy renewal management process of an insurance company based in Finland. The company implemented an online renewal process within Finland and wanted to expand the process in the European Union (EU).

A PESTLE Analysis was carried out as shown in Table 5.8.

Table 5.8 PESTLE Analysis

Contexts	Key Factors	Impact on Company (0–10)
POLITICAL	• Within the EU, countries are moving towards a more common political structure	6
ECONOMIC	• Slowing economy of Finland; GDP forecast to grow by 3.9% in 2003 • Dynamic changes in client business environment in Finland and Europe	8
SOCIAL	• Difference in buying habits in Finland vs EU	7
TECHNOLOGICAL	• Accelerating pace of change in ICT in Finland • Online opportunity in EU with little extra cost • New cyber-related risk in client business	9
LEGAL	• New constraints or requirements initiated by regulatory bodies, e.g. Insurance Supervisory Authority in the EU	9
ENVIRONMENTAL	• No significant impact	1

(continued)

(continued)

The PESTLE Analysis shows that the expansion of an online service, in general, has a direct influence upon and opens up opportunities in the EU.

Training Requirements

The principles of PESTLE Analysis are best learned by the process of the group working together during the project life cycle. The programme of Black Belt training normally includes a session on PESTLE Analysis and team leaders should receive a broad understanding of this tool. The analysis is of a strategic nature, and thus it may not involve all members of the project team.

A5: The Five Whys

Definition

The Five Whys is a systematic technique of asking five questions successively. The aim is to probe the causes of a problem and thus hopefully get to the heart of the issue.

Application

The Five Whys is a technique that is widely used to analyse problems in both manufacturing and service operations. It is a variation on the classic Work Study approach of 'critical examination' involving six questions: Why, What, Where, When, Who and How?

The objective is to eliminate the root cause rather than merely 'patch up' the effects.

Basic Steps

1. Select the problem for analysis.
2. Ask five 'close' questions, one after another, starting with why.
3. Do not defend the answer or point the finger of blame at others.
4. Determine the root cause of the problem.

Worked-Out Example

The following example is taken from Stamatis (1999), p. 183.

Consider a problem: 'Deliveries are not completed by 4 pm'.

Question 1: Why does it happen?

Answer: The routing of trucks is not optimised.

Question 2: Why is it not optimised?

Answer: Goods are loaded based on their size rather than the location of the delivery.

Question 3: Why are they loaded by size?

Answer: The computer defines the dispatch based upon the principle of 'large items first'.

Question 4: Why are large items given preference?

Answer: Large items are delivered first.

Question 5: But why?!

Answer: Current prioritisation policy puts large items first on the delivery schedule.

(continued)

(continued)

Training Requirements

As can be seen from the above question and answer model, the principle of this analytical tool is very straightforward. Thus the application of the Five Whys does not require any rigorous classroom training. The members of a problem solving team can easily understand and apply this simple tool after just one such group exercise.

Final Thoughts

The Five Whys is an uncomplicated but very effective tool that can be used to identify the root causes of a problem. We recommend that, taking advantage of the fact that it is such a quick an unfussy approach, it can be utilised on a far wider basis than at present.

A6: Interrelationship Diagram

Definition

An Interrelationship Diagram (ID) is an analytical tool to identify, systematically analyse and classify the cause and effect relationships among all critical issues of a process. The key drivers or outcomes are identified, leading to an effective solution.

Application

An Interrelationship Diagram is often applied to enable the further examination of causes and effects after these are recorded in a Fishbone Diagram. ID encourages team members to think in multiple directions rather than merely in a linear sense.

This simple tool enables the team to set priorities to root causes even when credible data does not exist.

Basic Steps

1. Assemble the team and agree on the issue or problem for investigation.
2. Lay out all of the ideas or issues that have been brought from other tools (such as a Cause and Effect Diagram) or brainstormed.
3. Look for the cause and effect relationships between all issues and assign the 'relationship strength' as:

   3 – Significant

   2 – Medium

   1 – Weak

4. Draw the final Interrelationship Diagram in a matrix format and insert the 'relationship strength' given by members.
5. Total the relationship strength in each row to identify the strongest effect of an issue on the greatest number of issues.

Worked-Out Example

The following example is taken from Bassard and Ritter (1994), p. 81.

(continued)

(continued)

Consider five key issues to improve customer service:

- Logistics Support
- Customer Satisfaction
- Education and Training
- Personal Incentives
- Leadership

The Interrelationship Diagram is plotted in a matrix (see Figure 5.14) with appropriate 'relationship strengths'.

	Logistics Support	Customer Satisfaction	Training	Personal Incentives	Leadership	**Total**
Logistics Support		◯	▭	△	▭	8
Customer Satisfaction	◯		▭	◯	▭	10
Training	▭	▭		▭	◯	9
Personal Incentives	△	◯	▭		◯	9
Leadership	▭	▭	◯	◯		10

Relationship Strength
◯ Significant 3
▭ Medium 2
△ Weak 1

Figure 5.14 Interrelationship Diagram

From the above analysis in the 'Total' column, it is evident that Customer Satisfaction and Leadership are the two most critical issues.

Training Requirements

The team can be adept in the application of ID after less than one hour's training in a classroom or a practical environment. The principles are simple, but it is important that a consensus is reached in attributing the relationship strength numbers.

5.5. Tools for Improvement

Tools for Improvement as described in this section are:

- Single Minute Exchange of Dies (SMED)
- Five S
- Mistake Proofing
- Brainstorming
- Overall Equipment Effectiveness (OEE)

I1: SMED

SMED or Single Minute Exchange of Dies is the name of the approach used for reducing output and quality losses due to changeovers and setups.

'Single Minute' means that necessary setup time is counted on a single digit.

(continued)

(continued)

Application

This method has been developed in Japan by Shigeo Shingo (1985) and has proven its effectiveness in many manufacturing operations by reducing the changeover times of packaging machines from hours to minutes.

The primary application area of SMED is the reduction of setup times in production lines. This process enables operators to analyse and find out themselves why the changeovers take so long and how this time can be reduced. In many cases, changeover and setup times can be condensed to less than ten minutes, so that the duration of the changeover can be expressed with one single digit. It is therefore called 'Single Minute Exchange of Dies'.

SMED is considered as an essential tool in Lean Manufacturing and it is instrumental in the reduction of non-value-added activities in process times. Changeover deficit is one of the six big losses that have been defined within the Total Productive Maintenance (TPM). It is important to note that SMED is directly linked with the analytical process of OEE (Overall Equipment Effectiveness).

With due respect to the success of the SMED method, it is fair to point out that the basic principles are fundamentally the application of classical industrial engineering or work study.

Basic Steps

1. Study and measure the operations of the production line to discriminate:
   - Internal Setup (IS), the operation that must be done, which machine is stopped.
   - External Setup (ES), the operation that possibly can be done while the machine is still running.

2. Suppress non-value-added operations and convert IS operating into ES. The data from OEE and the preparations of prerequisites (e.g. tools, changeover parts, preassemblies, preheating, mobile storage, etc.) are reviewed to achieve results. Some internal setups are converted to external setups.
3. The next stage is to simplify the design of the machine, especially fillings and tightening mechanisms. Some examples of the design simplification are U-shaped washers, quarter-turn screws and cam and lever tights.
4. Balance the work content of the line and ensure teamwork. For example, in one automatic insertion machine, one operator sets up on the machine front while the other operator feeds components on the other side.
5. Minimise trials and controls. Use of Mistake Proofing or Poka-Yoke enables the standard way to be carried out each time.

Worked-Out Example

The following example is taken from Basu and Wright (1997), p. 97.

Consider the setup time reduction of a packing machine.

The internal and external setup times have been measured. As shown in Figure 5.15, the total setup duration is reduced by overlapping external setup times on the internal setup phase.

Training Requirements

The training of SMED is likely to be more effective on team members with a good understanding of work study

(continued)

(continued)

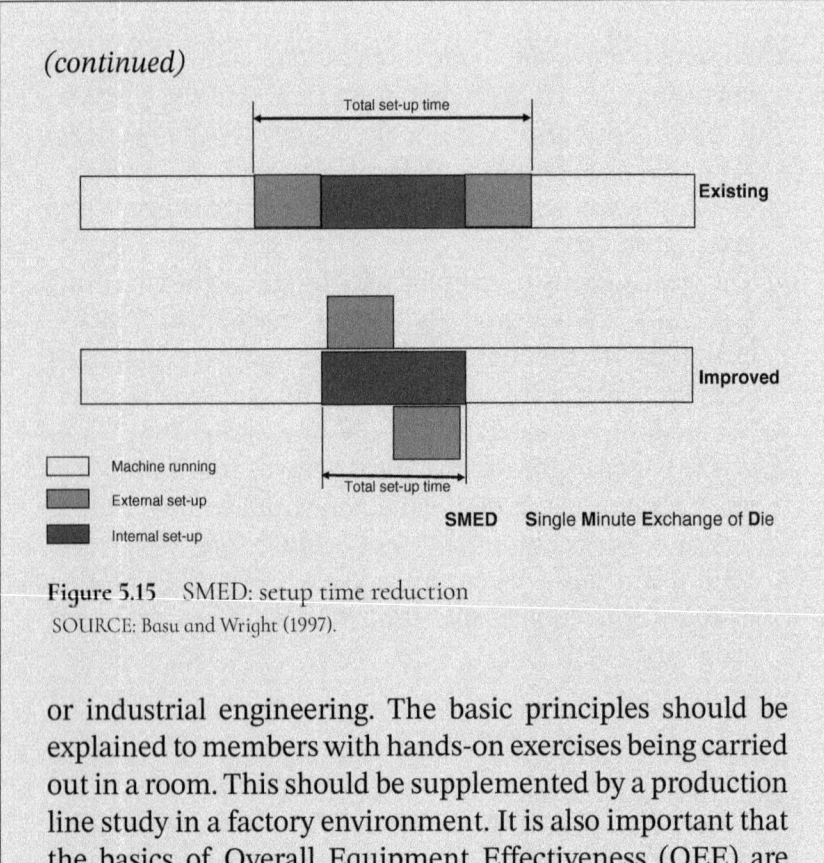

Figure 5.15 SMED: setup time reduction
SOURCE: Basu and Wright (1997).

or industrial engineering. The basic principles should be explained to members with hands-on exercises being carried out in a room. This should be supplemented by a production line study in a factory environment. It is also important that the basics of Overall Equipment Effectiveness (OEE) are covered during a SMED training session.

I2: Five S

Definition

Five S is a tool for improving the housekeeping of an operation, developed in Japan, where the five Ss represent five Japanese words all beginning with 's':

- Seiri (Organisation): Separate what is essential from what is not.
- Seiton (Neatness): Sort and arrange the required items in an orderly manner and in a clearly marked space.
- Seiso (Cleaning): Keep the work station and the surrounding area clean and tidy.
- Seiketson (Standardisation): Clean the equipment according to laid down standards.
- Shitsuke (Discipline): Follow the established procedure.

In order to retain the name 'Five S', a number of English language versions have evolved. These include:

- Seiri: Sort
- Seitor: Set in order/Stabilise
- Seiso: Shine
- Seiketsu: Standardise
- Shitsuki: Sustain

Application

The Five S method is a structured sequential programme to improve workplace organisation and standardisation. Five S improves the safety, efficiency and orderliness of the process and establishes a sense of ownership within the team.

Five S is used in organisations engaged in Lean Sigma, Just in Time (JIT), Total Productive Maintenance (TPM) and Total Quality Management (TQM). This principle is widely applicable not just for the shop floor, but for the office too. As an additional bonus there are benefits to be found in environmental and safety factors due to the resulting reduction in disorder and confusion. Quality is improved by better organisation, and productivity is increased due to the

(continued)

(continued)

decline in the amount of time spent in searching for the right tool or material at the workstation.

Consider the basic principle of a parent tidying a small child's room that is overflowing with clutter and where parts of some playthings are lost. By sorting through the various types of toys, grouping together pieces of missing jigsaw, Lego™ and so forth to reduce muddle, eventually no toy or game will be missing a vital part of the set. The end product should be a neater, warmer, brighter and more civilised play environment. The parent hopes that this will encourage the child to utilise all toys and equipment more productively because all relevant pieces are together, space is enhanced and mess is reduced. Till the next time!

It is useful to note that the quality gurus of Japan like numbered lists, e.g. the Seven Mudas, the Five Whys, and the Five Ss. However, the exact number of Ss is less important than observing the simple doctrine of achieving the elimination of wastes.

As the Five S programme focuses on attaining visual order and visual control, it is thus a key component of Visual Factory Management.

Basic Steps

1. Sort: The initial step in the Five S programme is to eliminate excess materials and equipment lying around in the workplace. These non-essential items are clearly identified by 'red-tagging'.
2. Set in order: The second step is to organise, arrange and identify useful items in a work area to ensure their effective retrieval. The storage area, cabinets and shelves are all labelled properly. The objective of this step is, as the old mantra says, 'a place for everything and everything in its place'.

3. Shine: This third action point is sometimes known as 'sweep' or 'scrub'. It includes down-to-basics activities such as painting equipment after cleaning, painting walls and floors in bright colours and carrying out a regular housekeeping programme.
4. Standardise: The fourth point encourages workers to simplify and standardise the process to ensure that the first three steps continue to be effective. Some of the related activities include establishing cleaning procedures, colour coding containers, assigning responsibilities and using posters.
5. Sustain: The fifth step is to make Five S a way of life. Spreading the message and enhancing the practice naturally involves people and cultural issues. The key activities leading to the success of Five S include:
   • Recognise and reward the effort of members.
     ◦ Top management awareness and support.
     ◦ Publicise the benefits.
6. The final step is to continue training and maintaining the standards of Five S.

Worked-Out Examples

As Five S is primarily a visual process, a good example of promoting its message would be to display pictures of a workplace with photographs showing both 'before' and 'after' depictions of the implementation of Five S.

The following example is taken from Skinner (2001) to illustrate the benefits of a Five S programme.

Northtrop Grumman Inc. in the USA first deployed Five S on a part delivery process. The work area assembled a variety of components into a single product.

(continued)

(continued)

Before Five S, the area was not well organised and the process was inefficient. With Five S implementations, the area saw a huge 93% reduction in the space employees travel to complete tasks as well as a 42% reduction in the overall floor space.

The system has become a one-piece flow operation between assembly and mechanics, enabling everyone involved to know what the station has and what it needs.

Training Requirements

Five S is a conceptually simple process, but it requires both initial and follow-up training to inculcate the methodology to all employees. The classroom training sessions should be followed by, as far as practicable, a visit to a site where visual changes due to Five S could be observed. A second-best option is to show the members photography or videos illustrating the 'before and after' status of the workplace involved in a Five S programme.

I3: Mistake Proofing

Definition

Mistake Proofing is an improvement tool to prevent errors being converted into defects. It comprises two main activities: preventing the occurrence of a defect and detecting the defect itself.

Mistake Proofing is also known as Poka-Yoke. The concept was developed by Shigeo Shingo and the term 'poka-yoke' comes from the Japanese words 'poka' (inadvertent mistake) and 'yoke' (prevent).

Application

Mistake Proofing is applied in fundamental areas. Although Poka-Yoke was devised as a component of Shingo's 'Zero Quality Control' for Toyota production lines, it is very easy to understand and grounded in basic common sense.

The process of Mistake Proofing is simply paying careful attention to every activity in the process and then placing appropriate checks at each step of the process. Mistake Proofing emphasises the detection and correction of mistakes at the design stage before they have a chance to become defects. This is then followed by checking. It is achieved by 100% inspection while the work is in progress by the operator and not by the quality inspectors. This inspection is an integral part of the work process.

There is an abundance of examples of simple devices related to Mistake Proofing in our everyday surroundings including limit switches, colour coding of cables, error detection alarms, a level crossing gate and many more.

Basic Steps

1. Perform Shingo's 'source inspection' at the design stage. In other words, identify possible errors that might occur in spite of preventive actions. For example, there may be some limit switches that provide some degree of regulatory control to stop the machine automatically.
2. Ensure 100% inspection by the operator to detect that an error is either taking place or is imminent.

(continued)

(continued)

3. Provide immediate feedback for corrective action. There are three basic actions in order of preference:
- Control: an action that self-corrects the error, e.g. spell checker,
- Shutdown: a device that shuts down the process when an error occurs, e.g. a limit switch,
- Warning: alerts the operator that some error is imminent, e.g. alarm.

Worked-Out Example

Consider the situation leading to the development of a level crossing. This is a place where cars and trains are crossing paths and the chances of accidents are very high.

The possible errors that might occur would relate to car drivers, who might be preoccupied or distracted while driving (source inspection).

Both the level crossing operator and the car driver should ensure safety features while the work is in progress (judgement inspection).

In order to prevent drivers from making mistakes when a train is approaching, traffic lights were installed to alert the driver to stop (warning).

The lights might not be completely effective, so a gate was installed when a train was coming (shutdown or regulatory function).

The operation of the gate was controlled automatically as the train was approaching (control).

With the above Mistake Proofing devices in place, an accident can only occur if either the control and regulatory measures are malfunctioning or the driver willfully drives around the gate.

Training Requirements

There is no 'rocket science' involved in Mistake Proofing and it may be perceived in a dismissive fashion: 'that's only common sense'. However, it is critical that there should be some basic training in the principles and applications of Mistake Proofing. Furthermore, employees need to be empowered to make improvements in the process by using Mistake Proofing. A half day workshop should be sufficient to meet these training requirements.

I4: Brainstorming

Definition

Brainstorming is an improvement tool for a team to generate, creatively and efficiently, a high volume of ideas on any topic by encouraging free thinking.

There are a few variations on the brainstorming process, of which two methods are more frequently used. First is the structured approach (known as the 'round robin') where each member is asked to put forward an idea. The other technique is unstructured and is known as 'free-wheeling', in which ideas are produced and expressed by anyone at any time.

(continued)

(continued)

Application

Brainstorming is employed when the solution to a problem cannot be found by quantitative or logical tools. It works best by stimulating the synergy of a group. One member's thoughts trigger the idea of another participant, and so on. It is often used as a first step to open up ideas and explore options, which are then followed up by appropriate quality management tools and techniques.

It has the advantage of getting every member involved, avoiding a possible scenario where just a few people dominate the whole group.

There are some simple ground rules or codes of conduct to observe:

- Agree to a time limit with the group.
- Accept all ideas as given and do not interpret or abbreviate.
- Do not evaluate ideas during the brainstorming process.
- Encourage quantity rather than quality of ideas.
- Discourage the role of an expert.
- Keep ideas expressed in just a few words.
- Emphasize causes and symptoms as opposed to solutions.
- Write clearly and ensure the ideas are visible to everyone.
- Have fun!

Basic Steps

1. Clearly state the focused problem selected for the brainstorming session.
2. Form a group and choose a facilitator, agree on a time limit and remind members of the ground rules.

3. Decide whether a structured approach or a free-wheeling basis will be used. For a larger group, a structured process will allow everyone to get a turn and subsequently this could be switched to the free-wheeling method.
4. Write clearly on a flipchart or a board any ideas as they are suggested. The facilitator will motivate and encourage participants by prompting them, 'What else?'
5. Review the clarity of the written list of ideas, allow them to settle and discard any duplication.
6. Apply filters to reduce the list. Typical filters could include cost, quality, time and risk.
7. Ensure that everyone concurs with the shortlist of ideas.

Worked-Out Example

Consider the following focused statement for brainstorming.
What are the key selection criteria of a family holiday?
The five members of a family generated 26 ideas or issues. These were then filtered by a budgeted cost of £4,000 for the whole family and the following key criteria were derived.

- Two weeks in August
- Seaside resort
- Indoor and outdoor recreational facilities
- Not near a nightclub
- Rich local culture
- Opportunities for sightseeing

Training Requirements

The application of brainstorming does not require any formal training in a classroom. A facilitator with some previous experience in the process can conduct a successful brainstorming session after briefing the team with the ground rules.

I5: Overall Equipment Effectiveness (OEE)

Definition

The Overall Equipment Effectiveness (OEE) is an index of measuring the delivered performance of a plant or equipment based on good output.

The method of monitoring OEE is devised in such a way that it would highlight the losses and deficiencies incurred during the operation of the plant and identify the opportunities for improvement.

There are many ways to calculate OEE (see Shirose,1992, and Hartman,1991). In this section we describe the methodology of OEE that was developed and applied by the author in both Unilever[1] and GlaxoWellcome.[2]

Overall Equipment Effectiveness (OEE) is defined by the following formula:

$$OEE(\%) = \frac{\text{Actual Good Output}}{\text{Specified Output}} \times 100$$

where Specified Output = Specified Speed × Operation Time.

Application

The application of OEE has been extensive, especially when driven by the TPM (Total Productive Maintenance) programmes, to critical plant and equipment. It can be applied to a single equipment, a packing line, a production plant or processes. In order to appreciate the usefulness of OEE it is

---

[1] In Unilever Plc, the methodology was known as PAMCO (Plant and Machine Control).
[2] In GlaxoWellcome it was called CAPRO (Capacity Analysis of Production).

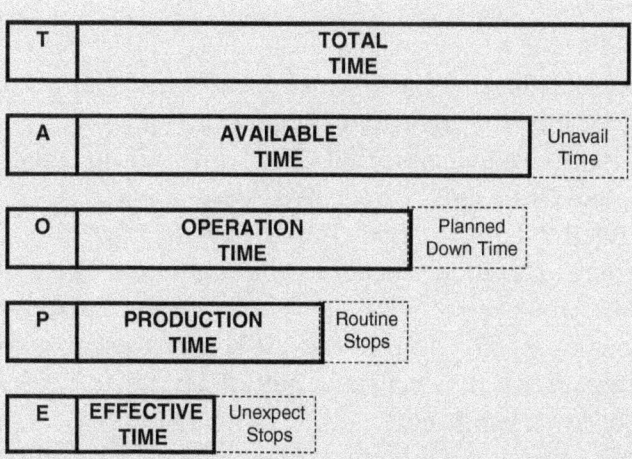

Figure 5.16 Equipment time analysis

important to understand equipment time analysis as shown in Figure 5.16 and described below.

Total Time defines the maximum time within a reporting period, such as 52 weeks a year, 24 hours a day, 8,760 hours in a year.

Available Time is the time during which the machine or equipment could be operated within the limits of national or local statutes, regulation or convention.

Operation Time is the period during which the machine or equipment is planned to run for production purposes. The operational time is normally the shift hours.

Production Time is the maximum phase during which the machine or equipment could be expected to be operated productively after adjusting the operation time for routine stoppages such as changeover and meal breaks.

Effective Time is the duration needed to produce a 'good output delivered' if the machine or equipment is working at

(continued)

(continued)

its Specified Speed for a defined period. It includes no allowances for interruptions or any other time losses.

It is important to note that Effective Time is not recorded; it is calculated from the Specified Speed as

Effective Time = Good Output/Specified Speed

where Specified Speed is the optimum speed of a machine or equipment for a particular product without any allowances for loss of efficiency. It is expressed as quantity per unit such as tons per hour, bottles per minute, cases per hour or litres per minute.

In addition to OEE, two other indices are commonly used, as shown below:

$$\text{Production Efficiency}(\%) = \frac{\text{Effective Time}(E)}{\text{Production Time}(P)} \times 100$$

$$\text{Operational Utilisation}(\%) = \frac{\text{Operation Time}(O)}{\text{Total Time}(T)} \times 100$$

A properly designed and administered OEE scheme offers a broad range of benefits and a comprehensive manufacturing performance system. Some of its key benefits are:

- It provides information for shortening lead time and changeover time and a foundation for SMED.
- It provides essential and reliable data for capacity planning and scheduling.
- It identifies the 'six big losses' of TPM (Total Productive Maintenance) leading to a sustainable improvement in plant reliability.
- It provides information for improving asset utilisation and thus reduced capital and depreciation costs in the longer term.

Basic Steps

1. Select the machines, equipment or a production line where the OEE scheme could be applied. The selection criteria will depend on the criticality of the equipment in the context of the business. It is useful to start with a single production line as a trial or pilot.
2. Establish the specified speed of the production line governed by the control or bottleneck operation. As shown in the following example (Figure 5.17) of a soap packaging line, the specified speed is 150 tablets per minute, i.e. this constitutes the speed of the wrapper (which is the slowest piece of equipment).

1. Set up a data recording system so that the output data and various stoppages and losses can be recorded.
2. Compile the data every day and validate the results. At this stage, detailed calculations are not necessary.
3. Monitor the results, comprising OEE and key indices, major losses as a percentage of the Operation Time and the trends of indices. The reporting is normally on a weekly basis for the department and on a monthly basis for senior management.
4. Use the results for continuous improvement, planning and strategic changes.

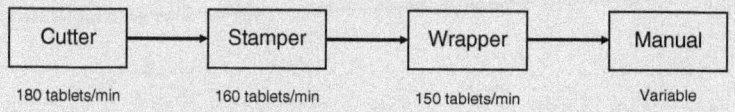

Figure 5.17   Soap production line

(continued)

Worked-Out Example

Consider the production data of a toilet soap packing line (see Table 5.9) where the control station governing the Specified Speed is an ACMA 711 wrapping machine.

Given that each case contains 144 tablets,

$$\text{Good Output} = 4232 \times 144 = 609,408 \text{ tablets}$$

$$\text{Effective Time} = \frac{\text{Good Output}}{\text{Specified Speed}} = \frac{609,408}{150 \times 60} = 67.71 \text{ hours}$$

$$\text{Production Time} = \text{Operation Time} - \text{Routine Stoppages}$$

$$= 128 - 11.5 = 116.5 \text{ hours}$$

$$\text{Total Time} = 7 \times 24 = 168 \text{ hours}$$

$$\text{OEE} = \text{Effective Time} / \text{Operation Time} = \frac{67.71}{128} = 0.53 = 53\%$$

$$\text{Production Efficiency} = \frac{\text{Effective Time}}{\text{Production Time}} = \frac{67.71}{116.5} = 58\%$$

$$\text{Operation Utilisation} = \frac{\text{Operation Time}}{\text{Total Time}} = \frac{128}{168} = 76\%$$

Table 5.9 Data of a toilet soap packing line

Week Number:	31
Operation Time:	128 hours
Specified Speed:	150 tablets per minute
Good Output:	4232 cases
Routine Stoppages:	11 hours 30 minutes
Unexpected Stoppages:	27 hours 15 minutes

It is important to note that the Effective Time was calculated and not derived from the recorded stoppages. There will be an amount of unrecorded time (also known as Time Adjustment) as, in the example, given by:

$$\text{Unrecorded Time} = \left(\text{Production Time} - \text{Unexpected Stoppages}\right)$$
$$- \text{Effective Time}$$
$$= \left(116.5 - 27.25\right) - 67.71$$
$$= 21.54 \, \text{hours}$$

Training Requirements

The success of an OEE scheme depends heavily on the rigour of continuous training. It is important that each operator, supervisor and manager of a production department receives a half day training programme covering the definitions, purpose and application of the OEE scheme. The training is continuous because of the turnover of staff. Senior management should also benefit from a one-hour awareness session.

5.6. Tools for CONTROL

Tools for Control as described in this section are:

- Gantt Chart
- Activity Network Diagram
- Radar Chart
- PDCA Cycle

C1: Gantt Chart

Definition

A Gantt Chart is a simple tool that represents time as a bar or a line on a chart. The start and finish periods for activities are displayed by the length of the bar and often the actual progress of the task is also indicated.

A Gantt Chart is also known as a bar chart.

Application

The most common form of scheduling is the application of Gantt Charts. The merits of Gantt Charts are that they are simple to use and they provide a clear visual representation of both the scheduled and actual progress of activities. The current time is also indicated on the graph.

In addition, Gantt Charts are used to review alternative schedules by using movable pieces of paper or plastic channels. The graphs can be drawn easily by standard software tools such as Powerpoint or Excel. However, a Gantt Chart is not an optimising tool and therefore does not determine the 'critical path' of a project.

Basic Steps

1. Identify the key activities or the tasks related to the project and describe each action using selective key words.
2. Prepare a scheduling board and, depending on the duration of the project, draw vertical lines to divide the board in monthly, weekly or daily intervals.
3. Arrange the activities in a sequence of estimated start dates and post them on the extreme left-hand column of the board.

4. Estimate the start and finish dates of each activity and draw horizontal bars or lines along the time scale to reflect the start and duration of each of the activities.
5. On completion of each activity, show the actual start and duration of the activity by using a bar of a different colour.
6. Include a 'Time Now' marker on the chart; review and maintain the chart until the end of the project.

Worked-Out Example

Figure 5.18 shows an example of a Gantt Chart showing the planned and completed activities of a Green Six Sigma programme.

Training Requirements

The application of Gantt Charts does not require extensive training. Team members are usually experienced in the use of Gantt Charts. A briefing session in front of the scheduling board should be adequate.

Activity	Week 1	Week 2	Week 3	Week 4	Week 5	Week 6	Week 7	Week 8	Week 9
A	2	2							
B			2	2					
C			6	6					
D					3	3			
E					1	1	1	1	
F									2
Total	2	2	8	8	4	4	1	1	2

Figure 5.18 A Gantt Chart
SOURCE: Basu and Wright (2003).

C2: Activity Network Diagram

Definition

An Activity Network Diagram is a control tool to determine and monitor the most efficient path, known as the critical path, and a realistic schedule for the completion of a project. The diagram is represented graphically showing a brief description of all tasks, their sequence, their expected completion time and the jobs that can be carried out simultaneously.

An Activity Network Diagram with some variations is also referred to as PERT (Project Evaluation and Review Technique), CPM (Critical Path Method), a Precedence Diagram and, finally, as Network Analysis.

Application

The Activity Network Diagram was extensively used in most projects during the 1960s and 1970s. As larger undertakings became increasingly complex and comprising numerous tasks, its popularity by manual methods started to diminish. However, with the advent of software systems such as Primavera and MS Project, its application at the higher level of the project has increased significantly. It offers a number of benefits:

- The team members can visualise the criticality of major tasks in the overall success of the project.
- It highlights the problems of 'bottlenecks' and unrealistic timetables.
- It provides facilities to review and adjust both the resources and schedules for specific tasks.

Basic Steps

There are normally two methods applied for the construction of an Activity Network Diagram: the 'activity on arrow' method and the 'activity on node' approach. It is the former that has been used most widely and the steps for the application of the arrow technique can be outlined as follows:

1. Assemble the project team with the ownership and knowledge of key tasks.
2. List the key tasks with a brief description for each one.
3. Identify the first task that must be carried out, the tasks that can be done in parallel and the sequential relationship between tasks.
4. Draw arrows for each task, which are labelled between numbered nodes, and estimate a realistic time for the completion of each of these tasks.
5. Avoid feedback loops in the diagram. Unlike Gantt Charts, the length of the arrows does not have any significance.
6. Determine the longest cumulative path as the critical path of the project.
7. Review the Activity Network Diagram and adjust resources and schedules if appropriate.

For more detailed information on the Activity Network Diagram, see Wild (2002), pp. 403–450.

Worked-Out Examples

Consider a project of writing and submitting the draft manuscript of a technical book such as this one to a publisher. Table 5.10 lists all the activities that constitute such

(continued)

(continued)

Table 5.10 List of project activities for production of a technical book

Resource	Activity	Description	Predecessor	Duration (Weeks)
Author	A	Prepare proposal	-	2
Publisher	B	Approve proposal	A	4
Author	C	Preliminary research	A	2
Author	D	Detailed research	C	10
Author	E	Write Chapters 1–3	B	3
Author	F	Write Chapters 4–6	E	3
Author	G	Write remaining chapters	F	4
Admin	H	Type Chapters 1–3	E	2
Admin	I	Type Chapters 4–6	F, H	2
Admin	J	Type remaining	G, I	3
Author	K	Compile full draft	D, J	2
Author	L	Obtain copyright clearance	B	12
Author	M	Submit manuscript	K, L	1

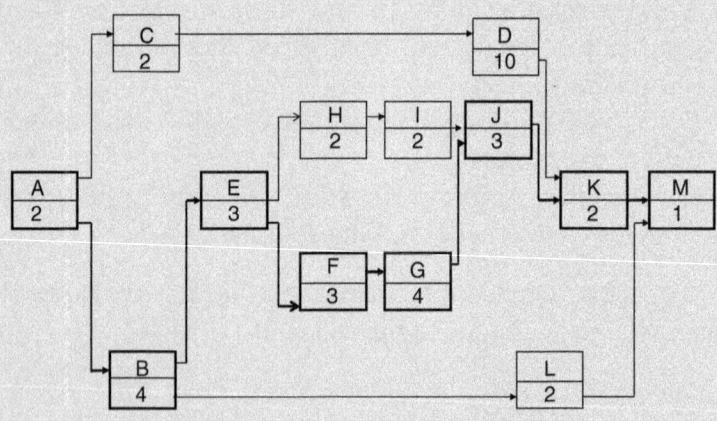

Critical path: ABEFGJKM 22 weeks

Figure 5.19 Activity Network Diagram

an endeavour, including their dependent relationship and estimated duration.

The Activity Network Diagram is shown in Figure 5.19.

The critical path is A, B, E, F, G, J, K and M with a total project duration of 22 weeks.

Training Requirements

The basic principles of an Activity Network Diagram are not difficult to follow and can be covered in a half-day workshop with practical exercises.

A detailed analysis of an Activity Network Diagram can be complex when the variable estimates of duration, 'float' or 'slack', resource levelling and the probability of occurrence are considered. We suggest that the advanced applications should be treated for academic research.

C3: Radar Chart

Definition

A Radar Chart is a polar graph to show using just one graphic the size of the gaps in the performance levels of key performance indicators.

A Radar Chart is also known as a Polar Graph and, because of its appearance, as a spider diagram.

Application

A Radar Chart is a useful visual tool to display the important metrics of performance at the Control stage of a quality improvement programme. The other benefits of this chart include:

(continued)

(continued)

- It highlights the strengths and weaknesses of the total process, programme or organisation.
- It can define full performance in each category.
- It can act as a focal point to capture and review the different perceptions of all stakeholders of the organisation related to relevant performance metrics.
- Given a range of rating (say on a scale of 1 to 5), it can drive a total or average score of all entities.

However, a limitation of a Radar Chart is that it tends to provide just a snapshot of the performance levels at any given time.

Basic Steps

1. Select and define the performance categories. The chart can handle 10–20 categories.
2. Some performance metrics are likely to be easily quantifiable and expressed as a percentage. Other metrics may be qualitative and not represented by numbers.
3. Normalise all performance metrics in a scale of 1 to 5 with appropriate guidelines according to the following grades:

   1 – Poor

   2 – Fair

   3 – Good

   4 – Very Good

   5 – Excellent

4. Construct the chart by drawing a wheel with as many spokes as the performance categories and marking each spoke with '0' at the centre and '5' on the rim.

5. Connect the ratings for each performance category and highlight the gaps.
6. Use the results for consolidating strengths and improving weaknesses.

Worked-Out Example

The example of a Radar Chart (Figure 5.20) is adapted from Slack et al. (2012), p. 42.

Consider five aspects of operations performance, which as a whole will affect the customer service when a product is delivered to the customer. These aspects are:

Quality: doing things right

Speed: doing this fast

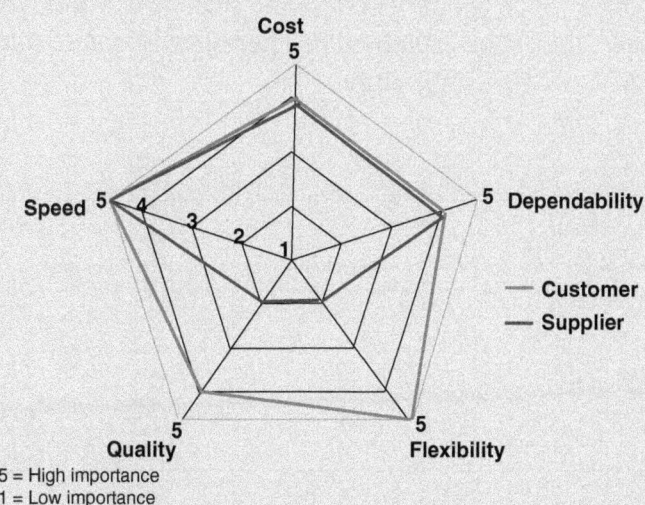

5 = High importance
1 = Low importance

Figure 5.20   Radar Chart

(continued)

(continued)

Dependability: doing things on time

Flexibility: ability to change

Cost: doing things cheaply

Table 5.11 shows the actual performance of the supplier and the expectation of the customer for the above five aspects of customer service in a scale 1 to 5, where 5 is high performance and 1 is low performance.

Training Requirements

The application of a Radar Chart does not require any significant classroom-based training. However, it does necessitate a good understanding of how to rate all performance categories. This awareness, and the selection criteria of the metrics, should be explained in a period of about an hour as part of a training programme.

Table 5.11 Actual performance of the supplier and the expectation of the customer

Five Aspects	Supplier	Customer
Quality	2	4
Speed	5	5
Dependability	4	4
Flexibility	2	5
Cost	4	4

C4: The PDCA Cycle

Definition

In a central process, the actual results of an action are compared with a target or a set point. The difference between the two is then monitored and corrective measures are adopted if the disparity becomes large. The repeated and uninterrupted nature of continuous improvement follows this usual definition of Control and is represented by the PDCA (Plan-Do-Check-Act) Cycle.

This is also referred to as the Deming Wheel, named after W.E. Deming (1986). Another variation of PDCA is PDSA (Plan, Do, Study, Act).

Application

The application of the PDCA Cycle has been found to be more effective than adopting the 'right first time' approach of concentrating on developing flawless plans (Juran, 1999, p. 41.3). The PDCA Cycle means continuously looking for better methods of improvement.

The PDCA Cycle is effective in both doing a job and managing a programme. The extent to which the PDCA Cycle is applied to the task level depends on the self control of the operators. Education and training enhance the self-control capacity of workers. At the programme level, the PDCA Cycle acts as a process of repeatedly questioning the detailed working of the operations and thereby helps to sustain the improved results.

The PDCA Cycle enables two types of corrective action – temporary and permanent. The temporary action is aimed

(continued)

(continued)

at results by practically tackling and fixing the problem. The permanent corrective action, on the other hand, consists of investigating and eliminating the root causes and thus targets the sustainability of the improved process.

Basic Steps

1. **P (Plan) Stage:** The cycle starts with the Plan stage, comprising the formulation of a plan of action based on the analysis of the collected data.
2. **D (Do) Stage:** The next step is the Do or implementation period. This may involve a mini-PDCA cycle until the issues of implementation are resolved.
3. **C (Check) Stage:** The next step is the Check phase where the results after implementation are compared with targets to assess if the expected performance improvement has been achieved.
4. **A (Act) Stage:** At the final Act juncture, if the change has been successful then the outcome is consolidated or standardised.
5. If the change has not been successful, however, the lessons are recorded and the cycle starts again. Even if the change is successful, the results are sustained by going through the PDCA Cycle over and over again.

Worked-Out Example

The following example is taken from Juran (1999), pp. 32.8–32.10.

In this illustration, a healthcare organisation in the USA was adhering to the traditional reliance on extensive internal and external inspection to maintain quality standards. This resulted in a medical record system whose size, complexity and format were wasteful and cumbersome.

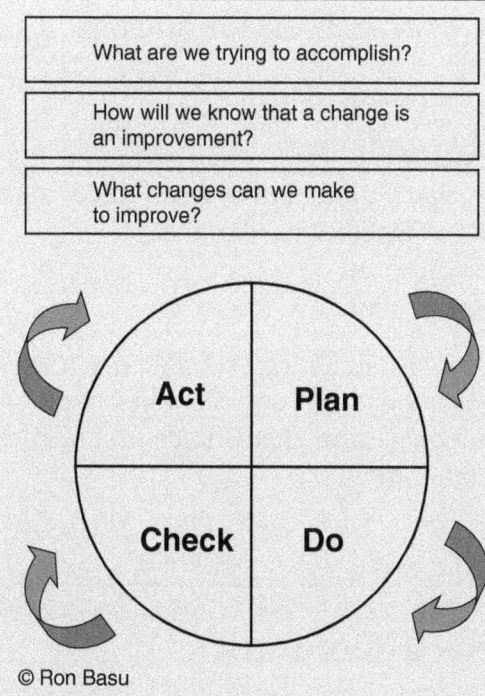

What are we trying to accomplish?

How will we know that a change is an improvement?

What changes can we make to improve?

© Ron Basu

Figure 5.21   PDCA Cycle

The aspects of the PDCA Cycle (see Figure 5.21) were applied to their internal quality assurance procedures and the medical record procedures were simplified.

Training Requirements

The importance of training for the PDCA Cycle, especially for first time workers, has been well recognised at the early stage of the quality movement and thus the concept of the Quality Circle was born. During the late 1950s, about 100,000 transcripts of radio broadcast text for quality circles were sold in Japan. The teaching of the PDCA Cycle, although simple in principle, should be inculcated in everyone within the organisation on a continuous basis. This tool then becomes most effective when it becomes a way of life in the organisation.

5.7. Tools for Sustain

Tools for Sustain as described in this section are:

- Balanced Scorecard
- EFQM (European Foundation of Quality Management)
- S&OP (Sales and Operations Planning)
- Material Flow Account
- Carbon Footprint Tool

Three tools for sustainability (viz. Balanced Scorecard, EFQM and S&OP) have already been described in Chapter 4. These three tools are presented again in this Chapter 5 under Sustain in the same format as other tools.

S1: Balanced Scorecard

Definition

The term Balanced Scorecard (BSC) refers to a performance management metric covering all aspects of the business (e.g. R&D, financial, marketing, operations and human resources). As shown in Figure 4.7 (see Chapter 4), it covers both leading indicators (e.g. Financial and Learning and Growth) and lagging indicators (e.g. Customer and Internal Business Processes).

Application

This strategic management tool was introduced (Kaplan and Norton, 1996) to translate strategy into action and has been applied extensively to a variety of improvement initiatives including:

- Total Quality Management
- Just in Time (JIT) production system
- Lean production/lean enterprise
- Management of major projects
- Activity-based cost management
- Supply chain management

Basic Steps

Balanced Scorecard is a company-wide performance management process covering four key perspectives (viz. Financial, Customer, Internal Business Processes and Learning and Growth) where the interests and involvement of all business units are required. The following steps are recommended by Kaplan and Norton to design and implement a Balanced Scorecard.

1. Select a core organisation unit to develop key performance indicators (KPIs) in all perspectives.
2. Conduct first round of interviews to agree the KPIs and their definitions.
3. Conduct the first executive workshop to review KPIs and ensure top management support.
4. Conduct a pilot exercise to try out the KPIs and seek agreement of a respective business unit.
5. Conduct the second executive workshop to agree an implementation plan.
6. Implement the agreed Balanced Scorecard.
7. Continuously review and improve the performance management system based on the Balanced Scorecard.

(continued)

(continued)

Worked-Out Example

As part of their Lean Six Sigma programme GlaxoSmithKline (GSK) introduced a Balanced Scorecard after following the above seven steps. It included 12 KPIs at the top level supported by 23 key performance measures. A standard template was used for each KPI, showing its definition, formula for calculation and a numerical example, as shown below as a sample for the KPI, cost of poor quality.

Title: COST OF POOR QUALITY (COPQ)

FORMULA: COPQ = Sum of cost of recalls + cost of rejects + cost of rework + cost of material failures + cost of adverse regulatory events + cost of waste

GLOBAL TARGET: 75% reduction from 2004 baseline

DEFINITION: The cost of poor quality is calculated by determining what was required to repair the defect and what was impacted by the defective product in the market.

PURPOSE: To identify major areas of poor quality in the business and develop a prioritized list of improvement projects.

EXAMPLE:

Recalls	£4,340
Rejects	£35,500
Rework	£4,400
Material failure	£13,000
Non-compliance	£25,000
Waste	£7,800
TOTAL	£90,040

Training Requirements

The importance of understanding the calculation and significance of each top level KPI and the buying in of the Balance Scorecard has been emphasized by Kaplan and Norton (2004). It is recommended that in addition to the executive workshops for senior managers, each department should also conduct training workshops for employees.

S2: EFQM (European Foundation of Quality Management)

Definition

The EFQM Excellence Model (British Quality Foundations, or BQF, 1999) is a framework for assessing business excellence. It serves to provide a stimulus to companies and individuals to develop quality improvement initiatives and to demonstrate sustainable superior performance in all aspects of the business.

Application

The EFQM excellence model is intended to assist European managers to better understand best practices and how to support them in quality management programmes. The

(continued)

(continued)

EFQM currently has nineteen national partner organisations in Europe, and the British Quality Foundation is such an organisation in the UK. Over 20,000 companies, including 60% of the top 25 companies in Europe, are members of the EFQM.

The model has been used for several purposes, of which the four main ones are given below:

1. Self-assessment: The holistic and structural framework of the model helps to identify the strengths and areas for improvement in any organisation and then to develop focused improvements.
2. Benchmarking: Undertaking the assessment of defined criteria against the model, the performance of an organisation is compared with that of others.
3. Excellence Awards: A company with a robust quality programme can apply for a European Quality Award to demonstrate excellence in all nine criteria of the model. Although only one EQA is made each year for company, public sector and SME (small and medium enterprise), several EQAs are awarded to companies who demonstrate superiority according to the EFQM excellence model.
4. Strategy formulation: The criteria and sub-criteria of the model have been used by many companies to formulate their business strategy.

Basic Steps

1. As shown in Figure 4.11 (see Chapter 4), the model is structured around nine criteria and thirty-two sub-criteria

with a fixed allocation of points or percentages. The criteria are grouped into two broad areas:

Enablers: how we do things – the first five criteria.

Results: What we measure, target and achieve – the second four criteria.

2. For each of the nine criteria there are questions for assessment in 32 sub-criteria.

3. The scoring of each sub-criterion is guided by the RADAR logic which consists of four elements:
   - Results
   - Approach
   - Deployment
   - Assessment and Review

4. The words on the RADAR scoring matrix reflect the grade of excellence for each attribute and what the Assessor will be looking for in an organisation.

Worked-Out Example

The model has been extensively applied in manufacturing, services and project management. It is an important tool of self-assessment to ensure the culture of sustainability in a Green Six Sigma programme.

Following an internal self-assessment, the percentage scores of each criteria were adjusted by the weighting factor for each criteria to calculate the overall score, as shown in Table 5.12.

(continued)

(continued)

Table 5.12   An example of EFQM self-assessment scores

Criteria	Score for the criteria (%)	Weighting factor	Net score (%)
Leadership	82	0.1	8.2
People	88	0.09	7.9
Policy and Strategy	80	0.08	6.4
Partnership and Resources	78	0.09	7.0
Processes	96	0.14	13.4
People Results	86	0.09	7.7
Customer Results	84	0.2	16.6
Society Results	70	0.06	4.2
Key Performance Indicators	88	0.15	13.2
		OVERALL	84.6

Training Requirements

EFQM licensed two- or three-day training courses are designed to enable individuals to help their organisations plan, manage and support an internal improvement process. These courses also prepare individuals to complete an internal assessment of their organisation.

S3: S&OP (Sales and Operations Planning)

Definition

Sales and Operations Planning (S&OP) is a senior management review process of establishing the operational plan and other key activities of the business to best satisfy the current levels of sales forecasts according to the delivery capacity of the business. S&OP is also known as the senior management review.

Application

Every organisation usually has some form of regular planning meeting in which the financial and business plans are reviewed and often some marketing and operational targets are discussed by a group of managers. These monthly meetings tend to deal with short-term problems and opportunities and usually decisions are made by the subjective judgments of an influential senior manager. In many companies, what passes for S&OP is often little more than a monthly review of the performance of the master production schedule. This approach of short-term planning fails to achieve the very real business benefits that an effective S&OP process can deliver. S&OP should be treated as a longer-term planning and a short-term execution process through a set of progressive meetings with specific departments.

It is an important tool of regular review to ensure the culture of sustainability in a Green Six Sigma programme. The agenda for the S&OP meeting with the general manager or chief executive officer should include a progress report of Green Six Sigma projects.

Basic Steps

The key steps of S&OP have been illustrated in Figure 4.9 (see Chapter 4). These steps are summarized below:

1. It starts with the sales and marketing departments comparing actual demand to the sales plan, assessing the marketplace potential and projecting future demand.

(continued)

(continued)

2. The updated demand plan is then communicated to the manufacturing, engineering and finance departments, which offer to support it.
3. Any difficulties in supporting the sales plan are worked out with a formal meeting chaired by the general manager or chief executive officer.

Worked-Out Example

As part of the MRP II Class A programme, GSK Turkey installed a Sales & Operations Planning (S&OP) process that is underpinned by a set of business planning meetings at various levels. The company went through major changes following the 'Class A' award, including the global merger with another multinational pharmaceutical company and the corporate Lean Six Sigma programme. In spite of these seismic changes, the S&OP process has been continued by the company every month.

The rigour of the S&OP process, which is championed by the managing director, has helped the company to sustain and improve the business benefits and communication culture, especially when they were challenged by a number of local initiatives in hand, including:

- Transfer of head office
- Rationalization of factory and warehouse
- New products introduction
- Sustaining Lean Six Sigma performance indicators

Training Requirements

The training syllabus of Black Belts and Green Belts should include Sales & Operations Planning meetings. In addition, special training workshops are required for senior managers and key stakeholders of the planning processes. The participants at each stage of S&OP also learn by taking part in meetings.

S4: Material Flow Analysis

Definition

Materials Flow Analysis is a quantitative process for determining the flow of materials through the total enterprise or an ecosystem. When the study of material flows is applied to an economic sector or a nation or a region it is also called material flow accounts.

Application

Material Flow Analysis (MFA) has many application areas of which three areas are most prominent. These are:

- On a national or regional scale. In this type of application material exchanges between an economic sector and the nation or region are analysed. This process is also known as material flow accounts or material flow accounting.
- On a corporate level. This process involves the supply chains of a number of companies in the corporate group. The goal of MFA within a company is to calculate the balance of the input and output of materials so that materials are more efficiently used.

(continued)

(continued)

- In the life cycle of a product. In this application MFA is used to compile the life cycle inventory to optimise the balance and waste reduction.

In each application of MFA the central focus is the principles of the circular economy by recycling and waste reduction.

Basic Steps

1. Select the domain of MFA as to whether the analysis is for a nation, region, corporation or a product life cycle.
2. Make precise use of the term 'material' as to whether it is a transforming material or a finished product.
3. Establish the unit of analysis, e.g. bottles of whisky or kilograms of transforming materials.
4. Measure the input and output of materials in each stage of the process or supply chain.
5. Present the quantitative data in a material flow diagram.
6. Analyse the material balance and losses in each stage.
7. Apply the principles of the circular economy to optimise the usage of materials.

Worked-Out Example

The MFA diagram in Figure 5.22 paints a picture of the scale and nature of Scotland's whisky production by calculating all the raw materials used to make whisky, local consumption and exports. The units are proportionate for the material balance but not the total balance.

The example demonstrates how resources from Scotland are combined with a flow of imported materials to

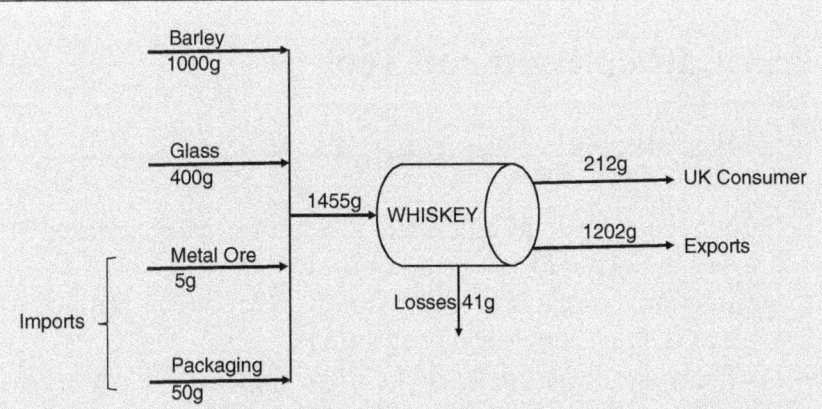

Figure 5.22 Material Flow Analysis diagram

make a bottle of whisky. The materials used to produce the whisky have been measured against UK consumption and as exported material. The process also identified 2.8% wastes for further reduction.

This also enables users to explore Scotland's material flow accounts and compare Scotland's material consumption with additional indicators such as population, GDP and carbon footprint data. Moving towards a circular economy is one of the solutions that will maximise value from the goods we already have in circulation while relieving pressure on finite natural materials.

Training Requirements

It is important to understand how to construct a Material Flow Analysis diagram and recognize its subtle differences with material flow accounts. Workshops on MFA also assist in team building, which is critical to collect and verify materials data from multiple sources. The training programmes for Black Belts and Green Belts should also include Material Flow Analysis.

S5: Carbon Footprint Tool

Definition

Carbon footprint is the amount of greenhouse gases released into the atmosphere as a result of the activities of a particular individual, organization, service, product or community expressed as carbon dioxide equivalent.

There are three categories of scopes of carbon footprint as follows:

- Scope 1 covers the greenhouse gas emissions that are made directly, e.g. running a car.
- Scope 2 covers the emissions it makes indirectly, e.g. energy bought for heating.
- Scope 3 covers the emissions by suppliers to make the products along the supply chain.

Application

The application of carbon footprint was first promoted by BP plc in an attempt to move public attention away from the activities of fossil fuel companies and onto individual responsibility. It has become a very useful tool for many applications including:

- For an organisation to determine the degree of carbon offsetting by planting trees
- To determine the impact on climate change for a new strategy, especially sourcing strategy
- To determine the carbon footprint per capita for a country
- To develop and validate climate change initiatives by governments, local governments and organisations

- To assess the impact of individual travel and lifestyles on climate change
- As a regulatory for larger companies to comply with SECR (Streamlined Energy and Carbon Reporting)

For calculating personal carbon footprints, several free online carbon footprint calculators exist. A high-level guide is shown in Appendix 1.

Basic Steps

1. Select the area for measuring the carbon footprint (e.g. whether a project, department or enterprise).
2. Define the boundary of calculation (e.g. which locations should be included in the inventory).
3. Develop likely greenhouse gas inventory (e.g. only CO_2 or also other greenhouse gases)
4. Determine consumption values for each component of emissions (e.g. quantify the energy consumption).
5. Calculate your carbon footprint (e.g. by using a software or standard-compliant emission factors).
6. Develop a climate strategy and reduction targets (e.g. introduce KPIs for climate change).
7. Report your carbon footprint (e.g. prepare a report with a profile of your carbon footprint, strategy and risk analysis).

Worked-Out Example

A large service company in the UK has been publishing their Carbon Footprint Report since 2008. The report is comprehensive, containing a summary and also detailed

(continued)

(continued)

Table 5.13　CO_2 emissions: performance summary

	Year 2019	Change from 2018
Net Emissions	20,252 tonnes CO_2 e	+9.7%
Employees	3,290	+12.9%
Intensity per Employee	6.16 tonnes CO_2 e	− 2.9%

Table 5.14　CO_2 emissions: car travel

	Mileage	Emission (tonnes CO_2 e)	Percentage of Total Emissions
Commuting	12,177	2,735	13.5%
Company Car	474	70	0.3%
Rental Car	408	92	0.5%

Table 5.15　CO_2 emissions: wastes

Type of Wastes	Treatment	Volume (tonnes)	Tonnes CO_2 e
Organic	Compost	247	1.5
Paper	Recycled	246	5.2
Glass	Recycled	19	0.4
Plastic	Recycled	15	0.3
Mixed	Incinerated	165	3.5

emissions of different areas of activities. The following tables (Tables 5.13, 5.14 and 5.15) show the performance summary and details of two areas.

Training Requirements

It is important to explain the purpose and method of calculating carbon footprints to all employees in an organisation to enhance the awareness and urgency of climate change initiatives. The team with the responsibility of preparing and calculating greenhouse gases inventory will gain competence with experience.

Carbon footprint is a vital tool of the Sustain stage of Green Six Sigma.

5.8. Summary

The success of a quality programme is underpinned by the selection and application of appropriate tools and Green Six Sigma is no exception to that. The recommendation is to start with simple tools first, as described in this chapter (Basu, 2004). Arguably in this section, only the Control Chart would require a good understanding of Statistical Process Control. Other tools can be applied without the 'fear' of advanced statistics associated with Six Sigma. It is recognised that more advanced tools and techniques (e.g. DOE, FMEA, QFD, SPC, DFFS, Monte Carlo Simulation and TRIZ) are required to solve more complex problems to near perfection. A separate book, *Implementing Six Sigma and Lean* (Basu, 2009), is recommended for helping the reader to tackle this area.

Green Tips

- For the majority of Green Six Sigma projects for climate change, simpler tools described in this chapter should be adequate.
- For larger projects, including R&D projects for climate, more advanced tools (e.g. DOE, SPC, TRIZ, etc.) may be required.
- There are additional tools for Green Six Sigma under the project cycle Sustain. These include Material Flow Analysis and carbon footprint.

Chapter 6
The Digital Revolution and Climate Change

'Whether you like it or not we are now in a digitally interconnected world.'

– Barak Obama

6.1. Introduction

Nicholas Negroponte (1995) predicted over three decades ago: 'Like a force of nature the digital age cannot be denied or stopped. It has four very powerful qualities that will result in ultimate triumph: decentralizing, globalizing, harmonizing and empowering.' The digital revolution is definitely here to stay, and we can safely say that each generation will become more digitally competent than the preceding one. It is reinventing business models, reshaping economic sectors as well as changing societal infrastructures. Big Data and Artificial Intelligence along with several other technological developments are now fundamentally altering the ways in which economies work and how we live our lives. Perhaps surprisingly, this movement to digital technologies is also envisaged to play a significant role in the planet's ecosystem along with climate change.

The focus of information and communication technology within organisations has shifted dramatically over the last forty years, moving from improving the efficiency of business processes within companies to enhancing the effectiveness of the value chain reaching suppliers, customers and consumers. During the 1960s and 1970s, businesses focused on the use of mainframes to process large quantities of data. In the 1980s and early 1990s organisations concentrated instead on using personal desktop computers to improve individual efficiencies.

The last decade, with the revolution of the widespread use of the Internet, has seen the use of technologies to create electronic communication networks within and between organisations and individuals. The implementation of Enterprise Resource Planning (ERP), websites, e-Commerce and e-mail systems during the past 15 years have allowed individuals within organisations to communicate together and share data. Information technology (IT) has now grown into information and communication technology (ICT). In this chapter we consider the following broad areas:

- Information technology and systems
- e-Business
- Big Data and Artificial Intelligence
- Digital tools for Green Six Sigma
- Digital applications in climate change

6.2.   Information Technology and Systems

Information technology (IT) is rapidly changing and becoming more powerful. It is a continuing source of competitive advantages for manufacturers and the supply chain if used correctly. By 2000 the personal computer (PC) on the desk of an average operations manager even then offered more computing power than the average £100 million a year manufacturing plant had provided 10 years earlier in 1990. The beauty of it was that this amazing IT revolution was available to everyone. However, it is how a company puts it to work that determines the extent of their competitiveness in the global market.

The rapid growth of information technology has created both problems and challenges. Many senior managers of companies lack any detailed understanding of the complexity of technology. They either follow the current fashion (e.g. 'no one was ever fired for choosing IBM') or they are discouraged by the cost of technology, or by a lack of evidence that savings can be made in a new field. When executives read about all the clever things that seemingly low-cost computer technology can do, understandably they feel frustrated when the systems experts caution them, 'But it will take three years to develop the software'.

Most senior managers also feel lost in a blizzard of buzz words and are conscious of well publicised failures. A notorious example can be found in the UK National Health Service's electronic care records project of 2002–2011. This scheme was discontinued after £2.3 billion had been spent, and was described by members of parliament as one of the worst and most expensive contracting fiascos ever encountered. Further examples of mismanagement of the potential of technology can be seen in the US Air Force Enterprise Resource Planning project 2005–2012, which was cancelled at a cost of $1.1 billion, and in Denmark's 2007–2012 da:Polsag plan concerning police case file management. This scheme was cancelled after an enormous DKK500 million expenditure. The list of similar and extremely costly failures is, unfortunately, endless.

Yet another issue is the implementation of systems for the benefit of the users. When a company looks for an IT solution to a problem without re-engineering the process, instead seeking to refine the existing database or concentrating upon training the end users, the application is doomed to fail. Real disasters can be very expensive. For example, the $60 million Master Trust accounting system for Bank of America had to be scrapped because it could not fulfil the simple brief of keeping accurate accounts.

Figure 6.1 shows a framework of IT strategy comprising three levels of hardware strategy, software strategy and implementation strategy.

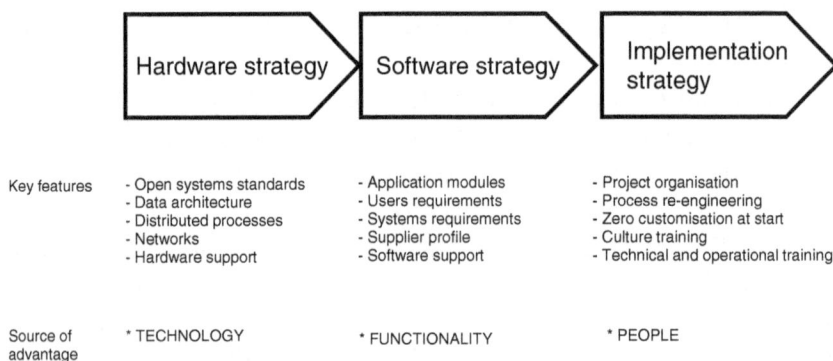

Figure 6.1   Information technology strategy

6.2.1.   IT Hardware Strategy

Hardware requires auditing with a refresh cycle of ideally three years but no more than five years. Chief information officers (CIOs) have the ongoing challenge of possessing sufficient IT capability to respond to new business needs and balancing the cost of capital spending with operating efficiency, while at the same time they must be mindful of risk. The rapid growth in data storage has placed pressure on CIOs and has tempted them to retain old storage hardware. However, keeping older and not always reliable unsupported hardware can be costly and risky. Using hardware until it breaks down or the supporting application is no longer available might save capital expenditure in the short term but could prove disastrous over a longer period. Across a supply chain there will be significant differences in the way organisations run their operations and in the applications that are used. New hardware is quicker, consumes less power, requires less maintenance, is more reliable and reduces labour (help desks, fixing and maintenance). A well-managed refresh audit will ensure the correct tradeoffs between capital expenditure and lowering maintenance and power costs, as well as identifying actual and expected needs.

The hardware strategy should also include the capability of local hardware support both by suppliers and the company's own staff. The support capability may influence the selection of hardware.

A sensible strategy is to go with the market leaders who are setting the de facto standards.

Enterprise Resource Planning (ERP) systems are supply chain IT systems that exchange information across all functions of an organisation or enterprise and can be extended across the supply chain to gain integration and the sharing of information. There are several modules of an ERP system that can be installed and are either standalone or function by interaction with other modules. Some of the key components are finance, purchasing, master production scheduling, materials management, sales and distribution, supplier management and human resources. ERP systems clearly hold major advantages over 'legacy systems' in terms of functionality, scope and flexibility of applications.

6.2.2.   IT Software Strategy

At the early stage of information technology, applications software was limited to financial and commercial areas. Now a company is faced with a bewildering array of software ranging from design/process engineering, to manufacturing, to supply chain, to administration. Versions of specific software and systems technology will continue to change. Therefore, it is vital that a manufacturing company formulates a software strategy by careful planning.

The first step is to identify the areas of application depending on the size of activities and priorities of the company. Figure 6.2 shows a framework of application software in five key areas, namely financial administration, supply chain management, factory administration, and 'client' work station. The traditional computing modules of accounts and payroll are in the realm of financial management. The biggest area of application lies in supply chain management, starting from sales forecasting and ranging to customer service and electronic data interchange (EDI). At the factory shop floor there are two application areas, namely factory administration – comprising management information systems – and factory automation – encompassing design, process engineering and automation of equipment.

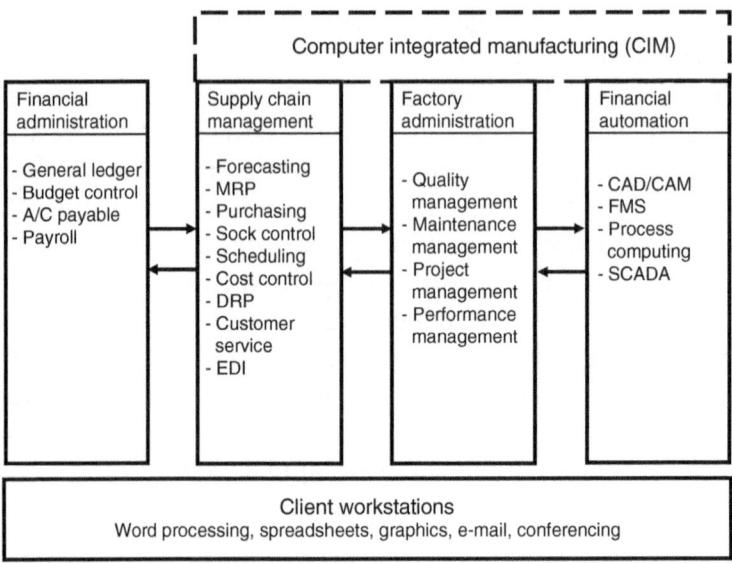

Figure 6.2   Application software modules

The software for client work stations is PC based. During the late 1980s many manufacturing companies searched for one turn-key package and invested in what is known as computer-integrated manufacturing (CIM), although with limited success. If a company follows an 'open systems' policy for a hardware and relational data-base then different proprietary software packages stand a better chance of being interfaced and database information can be shared in a client-server environment. Probably the most significant advantage lies in the enterprise-wise view of a business that ERP (Enterprise Resource Planning) systems allow.

The software policy should include standard packages for the company in specific areas of application. The selection of software should conform to the key criteria of user requirements, systems requirements, supplier profile and software support. The earlier examples of applications software were relatively inflexible and the approach was to 'systematise the customer' rather than 'customise the system'. Many disillusioned customers attempted to build their own software and burnt their fingers in the process. In the present

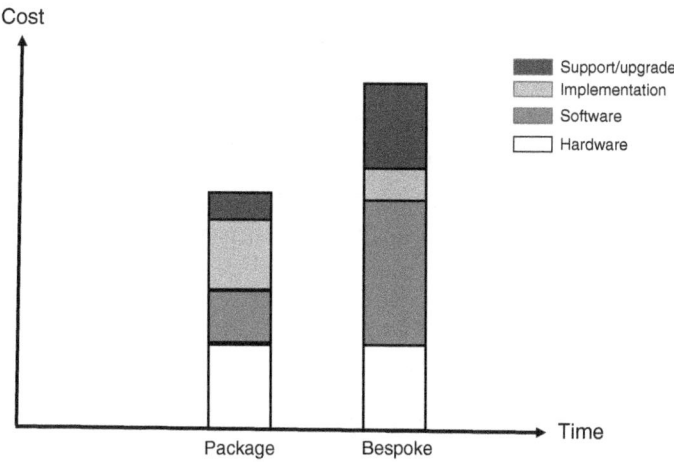

Figure 6.3   Software development strategy

climate, software tools have become flexible, the IT technology is advancing rapidly and competitive expert support is provided by specialist software houses, and thus it is prudent to buy appropriate software rather than to develop your own (see Figure 6.3). The software should conform to open systems requirements and the supplier should be both reputable and locally available for support. The company should also build up its own IT support staff, especially a 'user support' service.

There is a major conflict in developing a software strategy between a 'best of breed' approach and a 'single integrator' methodology. In a 'best of breed' methodology the optimum functionality solution of each individual function is chosen and companies attempt to integrate different types of systems. Although the business is likely to obtain the best solutions in each area, the problems of integration often offset the advantages of such top-quality solutions. ERP providers offer flexible modules that allow a single integrated framework of different functions of a supply chain stage. A single integrator approach also offers the advantage of technical support and a maintenance contract with a single source supplier.

6.2.3. Market Making Applications

There are broadly two types of market making applications. The first allows businesses to buy or sell by online auctions or bidding. Buyers place an open order to purchase an item and the sellers have the opportunity to bid. The second mechanism is the exchange or two-way auction platform containing a high-speed bid/ask bartering process.

6.2.4. Enterprise Resource Planning (ERP) Applications

Internet technology has certainly enhanced the collaborative business culture by enabling the transparency of online information and transactions. Company-centric enterprise application vendors, including SAP and Oracle (JD Edwards Enterprise One), have extended into supply chain supervision and customer relationship management.

6.2.5. Customer Relationships Management (CRM) Solutions

It is fair to state that most businesses regard the retention of customers as an important goal and therefore the criteria of CRM are not new or unfamiliar to most enterprises. However, the collaborative power of the Internet-based network has enhanced the need for customer intimacy and personalisation. A number of software solutions have been developed to provide some powerful holistic functionalities including:

- A customer database for knowing and understanding customer characteristics
- Managing the relationship with key business partners, (e.g. customers)
- Providing value-added services to retain customer loyalty
- Transparency and real-time acceptability of information for both customers and suppliers
- Optimising cross-selling opportunities

6.2.6.   Supply Chain Management (SCM) Solutions

There are now few companies that do not recognise that the Internet has had a profound effect on supply chain performance. Applications that fall into this category are essentially decision support software packages for optimising multiple levels of demand and supply in the global supply chain.

The CPFR (Collaborative Planning Forecasting and Replenishment) for key stakeholders of the total supply chain has emerged. In CPFR, data and process model standards are developed for collaboration between suppliers and an enterprise with prescribed methods for planning (agreement between the trading partners to conduct business in a certain way), forecasting (agreed-to methods, technology and timing for sales, promotions and order forecasting) and replenishment (order generation and order fulfilment). These solutions take into account the constraints of transportation, supply capacity and inventory requirements. The ultimate objective is order fulfilment within the set time and at a cost acceptable to customers.

The early leading vendors in the market, e.g. i2 (now part of IBM) and Manugistics (acquired by JDA Software in 2006), have been surpassed by SAP and Oracle's JD Edwards Enterprise One.

6.2.7.   Implementation Strategy

The success of an IT strategy depends on well-managed implementation as much as it does on the selection of the appropriate hardware and software.

Similar to a company-wide programme such as TQM, the implementation must have top management commitment. This should be reflected in setting up a project team comprising members from all users (marketing, logistics, manufacturing, accounts) and business systems. The project manager is usually chosen from the main user group. For example, if the application software is for supply chain management, then the project manager should ideally have a logistics background.

The project team should receive both technical training and operational coaching (functionality of the software). The project manager then prepares a clearly stated action plan with target dates and resources for key activities. This plan must include review points and steering by the members of the board.

It is essential that the existing procedures and processes are thoroughly and systematically reviewed. There are various tools for analysing the flow and requirements of these existing systems. Statistical Process Control (SPC) techniques are widely used. Nowadays some companies are applying computer-aided software engineering (CASE) tools to analyse the structure, database and flows of the existing processes and compare them with the proposed software for implementation. With the success of the Business Process Re-engineering (BPR) approach of Hammer and Champy (1993), some companies are utilising an IT application as a catalyst and applying the principles of BPR to re-engineer the total business processes of the company. The approach chosen should depend on the depth and breadth of the application systems, but there is no doubt that the existing procedures must be reviewed and refined when implementing a new method.

One important rule is that the user should not try to customise the system at the outset. Often, having acquired experience on the new system, the user may find that, in reality, the need for and nature of customisation could be very different. However, it is necessary that a 'prototype' is tested for any new system using the company's own data.

After the preparation and teaching of the project team, the training programmes should be extended to all potential users of the system. The training features should contain both cultural education to establish acceptance by everyone concerned and operational instruction to understand the functionality and operations of the new system. Training documents must be designed specifically for the users' needs. The next stage is the data input and 'dry run' of the new system in parallel with the existing procedure before the system goes live. There are numerous benefits to forming user groups for exchanging experience, with members drawn both from within and from outside the company.

6.3.   E-business

One might gain the impression from today's press that all business problems can be solved by e-business whilst, at the same time, the media do tend to blame all business failures and any economic downturn on e-business as well! Given the volume of news items on the subject, it may appear that defining 'e-business' is merely to state the obvious – or is it?

The distinctions between e-commerce, e-marketplace, and e-Business are poorly interpreted. For example, the most popular perception of e-business is that it is best exemplified by online shopping. However, it should be noted that in 2015 in the UK only 25% of retail sales were made online, rising to only 26.2% of sales in 2020, even taking into account the effect of Covid lockdowns (Coppola, 2021).

Let's take a moment to clarify some aspects. E-commerce is the transactional electronic exchange that takes place involving the buying and selling of goods and services.

The 'e-marketplace' is the online intermediary for electronic transactions between buyers, sellers and brokers. This is also referred to as the digital marketplace, portals, or hubs.

Early opportunities were observed in the enabling infrastructures and Internet-based networks (Internet, Intranet and Extranet), which replaced existing telephone, fax and EDI networks. The early success of e-procurement vendors (e.g. Commerce One, Ariba, Info Bank) was well received. However, the old suppliers suffered many problems including that of authorisation with no conformity of systems between business partners. It was rather like having different telephone systems for each of the people to whom you speak. This has been transformed by Trading Portals that interconnect the contents of different suppliers, thus making them usable by all buyers.

A report by Basu (2002) indicated that the complex web and infrastructure of e-business applications have been simplified, as shown in Figure 6.4 which illustrates the 'building blocks'.

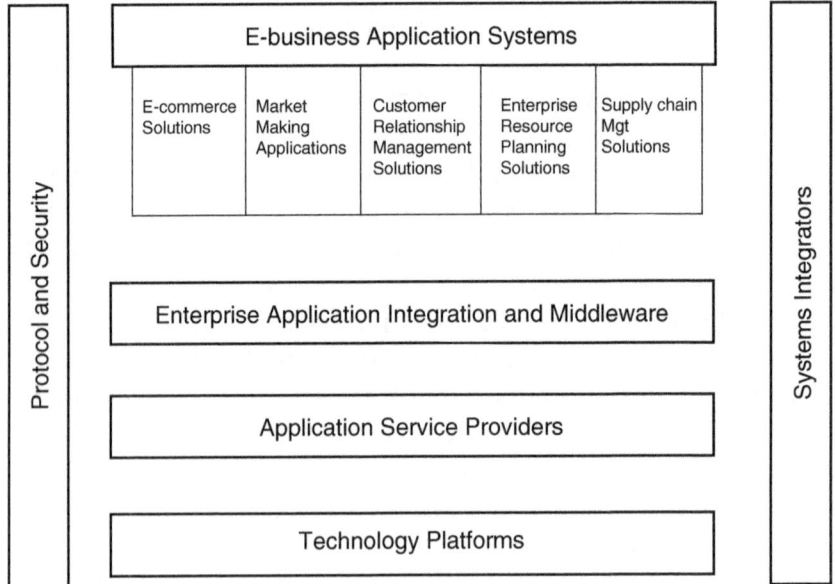

Figure 6.4 E-business building blocks

There are five key types of e-business application systems that enable businesses to trade and conduct electronic transactions or communications. These are:

- E-commerce solutions for both the 'sell side' and 'buy side' applications.
- Market making applications that enable multiple buyers and sellers to collaborate and trade.
- CRM solutions to facilitate improved business partnerships with customers.
- ERP solutions for site-based planning and execution of operations.
- SCM solutions for optimising the demand and supply in the total supply network including for the suppliers.

6.3.1. E-commerce Solutions

The buy-side applications of e-commerce, initially targeted at larger buyers, enable companies to levy across new or existing vendors. Solutions are increasingly aiming at integrating ERP systems with the organisation's own suppliers and customers. The new application developers are utilising the opportunities created by the lack of integration of ERP systems with other Internet systems and outside companies.

Initially, buy-side application vendors (including Commerce One and Ariba) were driven by pure-play solutions for the purchase of MRO (maintenance, repairs and operations) or indirect goods. The huge potential of e-procurement offered by 'pure companies' has been recognised and seized by established ERP vendors such as SAP and Oracle and software vendors like Netscape and Datastream.

The buy-side vendors, whether pure-play or not, are focussing on packaged buy-side application suites and looking to move into the direct procurement area. This requires a greater degree of understanding of business processes in specific industries and rigorous validation of the data processing.

The sell-side application vendors are looking to provide services content management and transaction processing. Hence, there are some sub-categories of software within this group. These include cataloguing, profiling, configurations and payment technologies. As a result, this sector is highly fragmented.

6.4.   Big Data and Artificial Intelligence

The term 'Big Data' refers to piles of data that are meaningless unless you have the power to analyse them. Everyone has a limited vertical view of data sitting in its own silo. The advantage of Big Data is that it lets you get a 360 degree view of information in both vertical and horizontal planes and right across your organisation. Data from discrete silos is brought together by a single data lake in web services (such as AWS or Amazon Web Services), now commonly known as cloud computing.

A typical flow of Big Data Analytics is shown Figure 6.5, where unprocessed information from multiple sources is extracted into a daily batch of raw evidence. This data is then cleansed and brought into a data lake using cloud computing. The data is then transformed and queried by a set of web services tools (e.g. Apache) and then personalised and visualised by using Tableau.

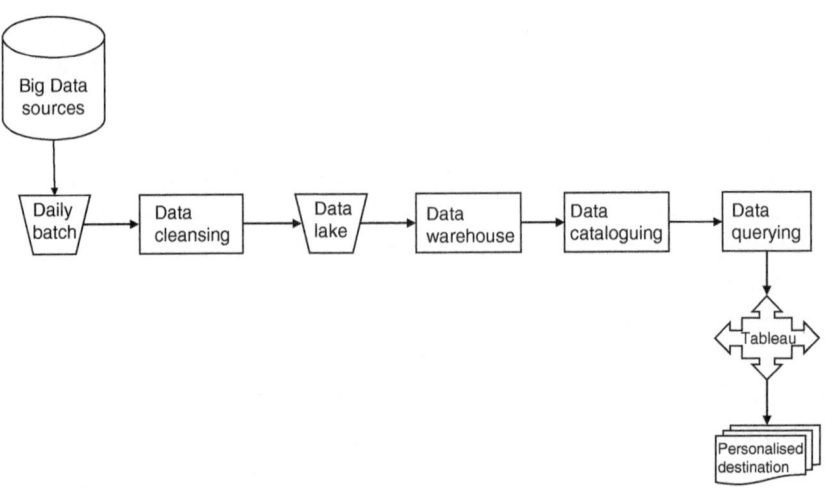

Figure 6.5   A typical flow of Big Data Analytics

One of the key benefits of cloud computing is the opportunity to replace up-front capital infrastructure expenses with low variable costs that scale with your business. Companies no longer need to plan for and procure servers and other IT infrastructure weeks or months in advance. As part of cloud computing, small and medium enterprises (SMEs) can afford to invest in licensed and expensive ERP systems (also called 'on demand software') on a so-called SaaS (Software as a Service) platform.

Artificial intelligence (AI) is the simulation of human intelligence processes by computer systems. AI research has been divided into sub-fields such as particular goals (e.g. 'robotics') and the use of specialised tools ('machine learning'). Specific applications of AI include expert systems, natural language processing (NLP), speech recognition and machine vision.

AI programming concentrates upon three cognitive skills: learning, reasoning and self-correction. Learning processes of AI programming focus on acquiring data and creating rules or algorithms to provide computing devices with step-by-step instructions for how to complete a specific task. Machine learning (ML), a fundamental concept of AI research, is the study of computer algorithms that improve automatically through experience. Reasoning processes of programming focus on choosing the right algorithm to reach a desired outcome. Finally, self-correction processes of programming are designed to continually fine-tune algorithms and ensure they provide the most accurate results possible.

AI is relevant to any intellectual task and advanced robotics. Modern AI applications are too numerous to list here; however, some high-profile examples include autonomous vehicles (such as drones and self-driving cars), medical diagnosis, creating art (e.g. poetry), proving mathematical theorems, playing games (such as chess), search engines (for instance, Google Search), online assistants (such as Siri), image recognition in photographs, spam filtering, the prediction of judicial decisions and the forecasting of demands, to name a few.

Since the introduction of iPhone by Apple Inc. in June 2007, the iPhone iOS has dominated the mobile market, but Google Android has now demonstrably overtaken iPhone in terms of market share. In addition to the social media revolution, mobile technology and its 'apps' have encroached upon and indeed come to dominate our daily lives. Mobile and wireless devices are also enabling organisations to conduct business more effectively. Mobile applications can be used to support e-commerce with customers and suppliers, and to conduct e-business within and across organisational boundaries. There are two broad choices involved in deploying a system to mobile users, such as creating custom native apps targeted at major mobile platforms or developing a web application optimised for mobile access.

The Internet of Things (IoT) describes the network of physical objects connecting and exchanging data with other devices and systems over the Internet. IoT technology is generally related to smart homes including security devices and home appliances that can be controlled by smart phones. The IoT can also be used in industries and healthcare systems. There are, however, some concerns regarding IoT, especially in the areas of security and privacy.

A significant disruption in digital technology has been created by 'blockchain technology', which is popularly used as a generic term that most people associate with cryptocurrency (e.g. bitcoin). However, arguably it is more useful as distributed ledger technology, also known as 'trustware', because it replaces interpersonal trust with technological verification. This new form of technological trust can reduce the capacity of operators to behave opportunistically, enhance input verification and ensure transparency and traceability during transaction time.

6.5.   Digital Tools for Green Six Sigma

Like pure-play Six Sigma, Green Six Sigma is also a data-driven process. Both the simpler tools (e.g. Histogram, Pareto Chart and Standard Deviation) and more complex instruments and techniques (e.g. ANOVA Report, Process Capability Analysis and Design of Experiment) require statistical analyses. There are many software systems available for such statistical evaluations, the most commonly used of which are Minitab and SPSS.

Minitab (Minitab.com) is a statistics package developed at Pennsylvania State University and distributed by Minitab LLC. This powerful statistical analysis package is a favourite with Six Sigma practitioners and offers three areas of functions – Discover, Predict and Achieve. Minitab can empower all parts of an organisation to predict better outcomes, design enhanced products and improve processes. It can access modern data analysis and explore data even further with advanced analytics and open source integration. Visualisations can help present the findings through scatterplots, bubble plots, histograms, parallel plots, time series plots and more.

The many areas of Minitab output include:

Graphics
- Scatterplots, boxplots, histograms, time series plots

Basic Statistics
- Descriptive statistics
- Correlation and covariance
- Normality test

- Linear regression
- Nonlinear regression
- Partial least squares
- Orthogonal regression
- Poisson regression
- Plots: residual, factorial, contour, surface, etc.

Analysis of Variance
- ANOVA
- MANOVA
- Test for equal variances
- Analysis of means

Quality Tools
- Run chart
- Pareto chart
- Cause and effect diagram
- Process capability
- Variability chart

Design of Experiments
- Definitive screening designs
- General factorial designs
- Response surface designs
- Taguchi designs
- User-specified designs
- Response prediction and optimisation

Another type of software package is SPSS (Pallant, 2010) which is used for interactive, or batched, statistical analysis. It has been produced by SPSS Inc. for some years and was acquired by IBM in 2009. The initial Version 1 appeared in 1968 and SPSS has now reached Version 26. The package has run on MS Windows since Version 16. Like Minitab, SPSS is a powerful data analysis package that can handle complex statistical processes. It is assumed that the user is versed in the fundamentals of statistics; in fact, instruction in statistics and the use of Minitab and SPSS constitute a vital part of Black Belt training.

SPSS tools and techniques for statistical data analyses include:

Descriptive Statistics
- Histogram and assessing normality
- Checking outliers
- Bar chart and line chart
- Scatter diagram
- Box plot

Statistical Techniques
- Regression analysis
- Correlation analysis
- Factor analysis
- T-tests
- ANOVA
- MANOVA
- Analysis of co-variance

6.6.   Digital Technology Applications in Climate Change

Various approaches and tools are currently being tried and advocated regarding how best to tackle climate change and sustainable development and the creation of ecological value. To this, digital sustainability activities can be added that focus on digital innovations to create scalable socioecological value. The technologies most commonly used in such digital sustainability tasks include distributed ledger technologies (blockchain), artificial intelligence and machine learning, Big Data Analytics, mobile technology and applications, sensors and other IOT devices, and additional tools like satellites and drones.

George et al. (2020) explore the opportunities and challenges of digital technology in climate change initiatives and define them as 'digital sustainability activities'. The authors give credit to entrepreneurial organisations who have adopted innovative approaches to ecological challenges and support them with examples including the following:

- Poseidon, a Malta-based foundation, is tokenising carbon credits by blockchain tokens from conservation programs in the Andean rainforest. It changes or tokenises those credits into 'carbon by the gram'.
- Ecosia is a search engine that uses 80% of its advert revenue to plant trees to fight global warming. Ecosia enables users to contribute to tree planting by simply installing Ecosia as their default search engine.
- Efforce is a blockchain-based energy-saving trading platform seeking to revolutionise the market for Energy Performance Contracting (EPC) to achieve infrastructure upgrades that reduce energy costs. An energy service company (ESCO) proposes improvements to an industrial facility, which are then funded by a finance partner.
- At the supply stage, Olam, an agribusiness multinational based in Singapore, is working to digitise the origination process for crops like cocoa across its global network. By equipping small-scale farmers with mobile phones armed with a digital sales platform, Olam cuts out price-setting middlemen and provides higher prices to farmers.

There are many proven software tools already available in the market to measure and monitor carbon footprint of business operations (e.g. *evizi*, *Emitwise*, *GaBi* and more). These digital tools are providing practical help in climate change initiatives.

6.7. Summary

When looking at information technology I have taken a more general approach. This section is equally applicable to all functions of the organisation involved in climate change initiatives. The key issue in any new IT system is knowing what you want, going with a system that has local support and initially making do with off-the-shelf software.

I have not discussed topics such as uninterrupted power supply, disaster recovery, the need to back up files and so on. All these issues are 'nuts and bolts' and should be second nature to your IT manager. This section was not written for the professional IT executive, but rather to give the average manager an understanding of the strategy of IT implementation. I have also addressed the opportunities and challenges emerging from e-business technologies, Big Data Analytics, Artificial Intelligence, mobile technology, IoT and blockchain technology.

During the last ten years we have experienced the growth of e-business applications and enabling infrastructures that have rapidly increased productivity by streamlining existing business processes. The time has come to take a fresh look at Internet technology, cloud computing and Artificial Intelligence. We need to see such digital technology as a powerful enabling tool that can be used in almost any business and become part of almost any strategy. The key question now is not whether to implement digital technology, but how to deploy it.

The proactive and ambitious international and national plans and support for meeting the challenge of the Paris Climate Agreement cannot be doubted, along with their laudable ambition to achieve net-zero carbon emissions by 2050. However, the challenge is to make it happen at the sources of emissions including power plants, factories, infrastructures, transport systems and buildings. Both sustainable digital activities and Green Six Sigma tools and techniques, underpinned by its holistic approach, can be vital factors in such implementation programmes.

Green Tips

- As part of the green supply chain large organisations are benefitting from comprehensive information systems such as ERP and CRM and Internet-based e-business.
- SMEs are taking advantage from the services of SaaS platform and cloud computing.
- Keep an eye on the dynamic contributions from disruptive technology such as AI, Big Data Analytics and blockchain.
- Complex statistical analysis using advanced Green Six Sigma techniques have the digital support of Minitab and SPSS.
- Use proven software to measure and monitor the carbon footprint.

Chapter 7

Green Six Sigma and Clean Energy

'I would like nuclear fusion to become a practical power source. It would provide an inexhaustible supply of energy without pollution or global warming.'

– *Stephen Hawking*

7.1.   Introduction

In preceding chapters I have addressed the existential challenges facing our planet caused by greenhouse gas emissions, as well as the extent of both global and national initiatives to mitigate these perils. I have also described some of the available tools and processes offered by Green Six Sigma and digital technology to accelerate the implementation of these initiatives. Although neither these strategies nor the wisdom of the carbon neutral target by 2050 are in doubt, it is important to note that in reality the reduction of greenhouse gas emissions can only be delivered by tackling its sources, such as power stations, factories, buildings, land usages and transport systems.

Table 7.1   Green Six Sigma by economic sector

Economic Sector	Percentage (%)	Chapters and Topics
Electricity and Other Energy	35	Chapter 7: Clean Energy
Agriculture and Land	24	Chapter 8: Green Supply Chain
Industry	21	
Transports	14	Chapter 9: Green Transport
Building	6	Chapter 10: Retrofitting Buildings

Table 1.3 in Chapter 1 indicated that the biggest source of greenhouse gas emissions is the energy sector, contributing 35% of total releases. This chapter will analyse the challenges and opportunities in this sector as well as the role of Green Six Sigma to accelerate and sustain the desired outcomes. Before I address the issues of clean energy, Table 7.1 illustrates how the share of greenhouse gas emissions by economic sector has been grouped to describe the impact of Green Six Sigma in each sector; this will be addressed in the later chapters of the book.

7.2.   Guiding Factors of Clean Energy

There are a number of aspects that arise if we scrutinise articles or plans regarding Clean Energy and the shaping of its future direction. The good news is that even though the energy sector constitutes only 35% of greenhouse gas emissions it represents much more than 35% of the potential solution. This is because energy generation and supply are at the start of the greenhouse gases value chain. Industry, transport and buildings, and even agriculture, are all driven by the supply of energy.

The first guiding factor is the basic demand for power to support the energy supply of a house, city or a country. Although this demand varies according to seasonality, degree of industrialisation and the time of the day, Table 7.2 is indicative of how much power we need to support us.

Table 7.2 How much power do we need?

Location	Power Supply
Average household	1 KW
Medium-sized city	1 GW
UK	35 GW
USA	1,000 GW
World	5,000 GW

SOURCE: Gates (2021).

Table 7.3 Fuel share of primary energy in 2019

Fuel Source	Share of Energy (%)	Percentage Change from 2028
Oil	33.1	- 0.2
Gas	24.2	+ 0.2
Coal	27	- 0.5
Hydro	6.4	0.0
Renewables	5.0	+0.5
Nuclear	4.3	+0.1

SOURCE: BP Statistical Review of World Energy (2020).

The global requirement for electricity and energy is growing, and this is bearing in mind that currently some 860 million people (including 600 million in Africa) do not have access to any electricity at all.

We are highly dependent on fossil fuels (84.3% for combined oil, gas and coal) for the generation of primary power, as shown in Table 7.3.

There are positive growths for renewables and nuclear sources of primary energy but these advances are not enough to meet the carbon target of 2050. Another worrying trend is that gas consumption is also increasing.

In the UK as well, most of the primary energy is produced by fossil fuels, mainly natural gas (45%) and coal (9%). However, shares of renewables (25%) and nuclear (21%) are also relatively high.

Table 7.4   Power density of energy sources

Energy Source	Watts per Square Metre
Fossil fuels	500 to 10,000
Nuclear	500 to 1,000
Hydro	5 to 50
Solar	5 to 20
Wind	1 to 2

SOURCE: Gates (2021).

The space required for primary power generation is also an important guiding factor. Power density is a useful metric, allowing us to understand the amount of power generated per square metre of land and water for different energy sources, as shown in Table 7.4.

In terms of the required space, power plants run by fossil fuels have a clear advantage over renewables. However, one benefit of wind turbines is that they could be installed on otherwise unusable land and water.

Then there is the small matter of the cost advantage of an installation. Detailed cost benefit analyses are beyond the scope of this book, but we can discuss some of the principles involved. Zero-carbon solutions are in general more expensive than fossil fuel power plants. When we consider the cost of the environmental damage caused by fossil fuels or the government imposed 'carbon tax' then renewable alternatives may seem more viable. Some protagonists of fossil fuels have suggested 'direct air capture' (DAC) as a feasible alternative. With DAC, emissions are blown over a device that absorbs carbon dioxide and the output is then stored for safekeeping. However, DAC is a very expensive and largely unproven technology.

A novel concept of the Green Premium is advocated by Bill Gates (2021). The Green Premium is the difference between the cost of a green solution and the alternative or existing option. There are many such Green Premiums – some for electricity from various fuels, others for cement, steel and so on. The size of the Premium depends upon, firstly, what you are replacing and, secondly, what you are substituting it with. In rare cases, a Green Premium can be negative – for example, it may be cheaper to replace your gas cooker with an electric one.

7.3. How Clean Energy Solutions Can Reduce Greenhouse Gas Emissions

The primary objective of Clean Energy solutions is to generate carbon-free electricity. We know that the key suppliers of Clean Energy are renewable sources, which are natural sources that are constantly replenished. These constitute

- Wind energy
- Solar energy
- Hydropower
- Geothermal energy
- Tidal energy
- Biomass
- Hydrogen

Nuclear energy is also a source of carbon-free electricity although the material (e.g. uranium) used in nuclear power plants is not a renewable source. Nuclear energy is considered to be an effective way of producing power without the harmful by-products emitted by fossil fuels.

If we combine the energy from renewable sources and nuclear energy we get Clean Energy without any greenhouse gas emissions. The biggest share of the 2,790 gigawatts of Clean Energy in 2019 came from hydropower (42%), as shown in Table 7.5.

The portion of hydroelectricity has been stable for several years. The share of wind and solar energy is growing while the segment of nuclear energy is in decline, especially after the 'Great East Japan Earthquake' in 2011. Thanks to wind and solar power, renewable energy experienced a record growth in 2019, accounting for 40% of

Table 7.5   Share of Clean Energy in 2019

Source	Share of Clean Energy (%)
Hydropower	42
Wind energy	20
Solar energy	17
Nuclear energy	16
Others (Bio, Geothermal, etc.)	5

SOURCE: BP Statistical Review of World Energy (2020).

the expansion in primary energy. This is undoubtedly a good sign for Clean Energy.

Hydropower that harnesses the strength of water is the oldest source of energy. In Ancient Greece flowing water was used to turn the wheels of flour mills. The most common type of hydroelectric plant is called an impounded facility. Here a large reservoir is created by building a dam and the flow of controlled water drives a turbine, thereby generating electricity. This natural energy source has the advantage of being more reliable than wind or solar power. Furthermore, electricity can be stored for potential use at a time of peak demand. In another type of plant, called a diversion plant, a series of canals are used to channel a flowing river towards the turbines. A third type of operation, called a pumped storage facility, is where the plant collects energy produced from renewable sources by pumping water uphill from a pool at a lower level to a reservoir situated at a higher point. When a greater demand for electricity occurs, water from the reservoir is released to turn the turbines.

Table 7.6 shows ranking in the hydropower capacity of the top five countries.

Wind is a plentiful source of Clean Energy. It captures the natural airstream in our environment and converts the wind motion into electricity by using wind turbines. The spinning blades of these wind turbines are connected to electromagnetic generators that create electricity. This electricity is then fed into the national grid. However, there are some locations better suited for wind power than others. In general, wind speeds are higher near the coast and

Table 7.6 Hydropower

Rank and Country	Hydropower (GW)
1. China	341
2. USA	102
3. Brazil	100
4. Canada	81
5. Russia	51

SOURCE: EY Global Renewables (2020).

Table 7.7 Wind power

Rank and Country	Wind Power (GW)
1. China	288
2. USA	122
3. Germany	63
4. India	29
5. Spain	27

SOURCE: EY Global Renewables (2020).

offshore as there are fewer obstructions. A group of large structures of wind turbines, called wind farms, are familiar sights both in the outskirts of towns and also at sea. There are also some domestic or 'off grid' wind energy generation systems available.

The main advantages of wind energy are that it is a clean renewable form of power and has low operational and maintenance costs. However, as the wind speed varies both throughout the day and on an annual basis, wind energy presents an intermittency issue for the power grid. Fortunately, reliable storage systems, including battery storage, compressed air storage and pump storage are now available. The price of wind energy is declining and the share of renewable energy by wind is increasing.

Table 7.7 shows ranking in the wind power capacity of the top five countries.

Like wind, sunlight is one of our most abundant and freely available resources. Solar energy is absorbed in specially designed and

Table 7.8   Solar power

Rank and Country	Solar Power (GW)
1. China	205
2. USA	76
3. Japan	63
4. Germany	49
5. India	38

SOURCE: EY Global Renewables (2020).

manufactured solar panels to generate electricity directly. Solar panels are made out of photovoltaic cells (or PV cells) that convert the Sun's energy into electricity. A single PV cell can produce typically around 0.58 volts. PV cells are sandwiched between layers of silicon. When hit by photons from sunlight each layer creates an electric field that creates the direct current (DC) needed to produce electricity. This current is then passed through an inverter to convert it into an alternating current (AC), which then can be connected to the National Grid or used by a building with solar panels. Solar energy is carbon free and renewable and thus has many benefits, including its diverse applications for generating both electricity and heat, as well as its low maintenance costs. However, there are also disadvantages, such as the initial high cost, weather dependency and storage expenses.

Table 7.8 shows ranking in the solar power capacity of the top five countries.

Nuclear power is controversial with environmental activists primarily for the risks of radioactive waste storage and disposal that it poses. However, it is the only carbon-free energy source that reliably delivers electricity throughout every season almost anywhere in the world. The process of obtaining energy by splitting the atom is known as nuclear fission. The released energy is capable of generating steam and can then be used to turn a turbine and thus produce electricity. The most commonly used fuel for fission is uranium. In theory, fission power offers the exciting prospect of an almost inexhaustible source of energy for future generations. Nuclear fuels (uranium and plutonium) can be used to create nuclear weapons

Table 7.9   Ranking in the nuclear power capacity of the top five countries

Rank and country	Nuclear power (GW)
1. USA	97
2. France	61
3. China	48
4. Japan	38
5. Russia	29

SOURCE: EY Global Renewables (2020).

as well as nuclear reactors. Hence, only nations that are part of the Nuclear Non-Proliferation Treaty (NPT) are allowed to import nuclear fuels. In spite of the possible risks of radioactive wastes and misuse of nuclear fuels, nuclear energy has been found to be the cheapest and most continuously available path towards the goal of achieving the net-zero carbon target.

China is often criticised as a leading emitter of greenhouse gases. However, the above data shows that in fact the country ranks first in global terms in renewable power generation (hydro, wind and solar) and is in third place for the generation of nuclear power.

Having discussed the opportunities and challenges of clean energy initiatives in our battle against climate change, it is useful to describe a few well-known clean energy plants as case studies for successful clean energy endeavours.

One of the most famous renewable projects is the Three Gorges Dam in China, the largest hydroelectric dam in the world. Almost 100 years after it was envisioned and following two decades of construction the dam became operational in 2012. Built across the Yangtze River in western China the construction is 185 metres high and stretches over a length of 2 km. The reported cost of the project was £17 billion, but the efficacy of its operations is clear. The water flows over 32 turbines capable of producing 700 MW of power. It is providing 1.7% of China's electricity, reducing carbon dioxide emissions by 10 million tonnes every year.

Walney Offshore Windfarm is located off the coast of Cumbria, England, and is the largest wind energy provider in the world. It was built at a cost of £1.6 billion and began generating power from the beginning of 2011. The farm, stretching over 145 square km, has a total of 189 wind turbines, each standing 190 metres high. It has a total capacity of 600 MW, which is enough to power 600,000 homes.

A further interesting example can be found in the Ivanpah Solar Electric Generating system, located in the Mojave Desert of Southern California, which is the largest solar energy facility in the world. The scheme was created jointly by Bechtel and BrightSource Energy with a total investment of £2.4 billion and began operations in 2013. About 300,000 large (10 ft × 7 ft) mirrors (called heliostats) are digitally controlled to reflect sunlight to 140 metre towers fitted with solar panels. The concentrated sunlight heats water stored at the top of the three towers to create steam for turbines. The three plants together can produce 392 MW of electricity, sufficient to power 140,000 homes.

The largest nuclear plant in the world is the Kashiwazaki-Kariwa plant in Japan. It is owned by the Tokyo Electric Power Company (TEPCO) and has a gross installed capacity of 8,200 MW. It has seven boiling water reactors (BWR) and all units became fully operational from 1997. However, activities at the plant stopped in May 2012 following the Fukushima nuclear disaster. New safety guidelines from the Japan Nuclear Regulatory Authority are being implemented and all reactors of the plant are expected to be operational again from 2022.

7.4. How Six Sigma Is Helping Clean Energy Initiatives

There are good applications of Six Sigma and Lean Six Sigma in the renewable energy sector, especially in wind energy. However, Six Sigma projects seem to be almost non-existent with no mention of them in the published papers related to hydropower nuclear power plants. There are some academic publications on Six Sigma applications in thermal power plants (Kharub et al., 2018). The following case examples illustrate how Six Sigma can help in the renewable energy sector to save money and achieve sustainable improvements.

Case Example 7.1   Six Sigma Ivanpah Solar Electric Generating System

As stated earlier, the Ivanpah Solar Electric Generating system in California is the largest solar energy facility in the world and was a joint venture of Bechtel and BrightSource. Bechtel is a global project management organisation that has used Six Sigma to deliver many major projects to customers. Ivanpah was considered an appropriate venture for applying Six Sigma because the scheme had a budget of £2.4 billion over several years and Ivanpah had a lot of repetitive operations. The project was operationally challenging, requiring the design, construction and installation of around 300,000 large mirrors or heliostats.

Bechtel's project team joined with engineering and construction experts from BrightSource to form a Six Sigma group and all colleagues went through the Black Belt and Green Belt training programme together. The team identified five areas for process improvements by using Six Sigma: material handling, heliostat assembly, field transportation, heliostat installation and tower erection. In each of these spheres, especially in heliostat assembly, the team found new or more efficient ways of achieving results. For example, by using Six Sigma tools group members managed to redesign a stable process that would enable craftsmen to assemble 500 heliostats per day. The Six Sigma philosophy of 'continuous improvement' also carried over to the daily work of craftsmen.

All the processes involved in the heliostats, including transportation, had to be developed from scratch. This kind of complexity was a good fit for the Six Sigma approach. Bechtel used Six Sigma tools and processes to address the design, procurement and construction challenges of heliostats. The result was the development of new procedures that helped to meet sustainable performance goals and execute the project successfully. Six Sigma methodology was also instrumental for ensuring teamwork amongst project group members while simultaneously building trust and credibility with stakeholders.

Case Example 7.2 Vestas India Saved $10 Million Through Lean Six Sigma Initiatives

Vestas Wind Systems A/S is the largest manufacturer and installer of wind turbines in the world and is headquartered in Aarhus, Denmark. (Other notable large manufacturers are GE Renewable Energy, USA, and Goldwind, China.) Vestas' subsidiary in India is based in Chennai. Vestas India saved US $10 million over three years through the implementation of Lean Six Sigma methodology in its wind turbine manufacturing and supply operations. The company engaged a local consulting firm, Millennium Global Business Solutions (MGBS), in 2006 for coaching 50% of its employees in Green Belt and Yellow Belt training. The majority of them were schooled in the basic level of the Yellow Belt tools. Quality Director Dhananjay Joshi claimed, 'This enhanced collective competency as opposed to that of just a few employees at the senior level, as in the Black Belt methodology' (The Economic Times, 2009).

According to Mr Joshi, employees trained as Yellow Belts implemented two to four projects per year based on Lean Six Sigma methodology. These projects were chosen from their own departments and their own domain of expertise. This enabled each Yellow Belt to take his or her own decisions based on available data, rather than being dependent on a team leader. The company spent Rs 50,000 (£500) per employee on training while the savings per employee constituted up to Rs 5 lakh (£5,000). Over three years (2006 to 2008) Vestas India saved an equivalent of US$ 10 million and achieved sustainable performance to boot.

Case Example 7.3   Business Integration at GE Wind Energy

General Electric (GE) is considered to be a real champion of the application of Six Sigma. As a leading manufacturer and supplier of wind turbines GE has implemented the Six Sigma methodology very successfully in the renewable energy sector. Goel and Chen (2008) describe the re-engineering process of GE's wind energy division to integrate business operations across its globally dispersed acquisitions. The practice involved defining metrics and evaluating alternative processes through those metrics by deploying Six Sigma methodology. The application of Six Sigma ensured the sustainable best practices for process integration across global operations.

Case Example 7.4   Improving the Quality of the Road for Wind Farms

An Indian organisation engaged in the installation of wind turbines utilised Six Sigma methodology for the development of sustainable wind farm roads. Gijo and Sarkar (2013) explain that the data-driven approach of Six Sigma identified the root causes and solutions for road damage. The implementation plan also ensured good teamwork and sustainable processes.

Case Example 7.5   Six Sigma in Renewable Hydrogen Energy

In spite of the growth in renewable energy, it is envisaged that fossil fuels will continue to be used in the energy sector for the near future. As an alternative energy source, hydrogen is also

(continued)

(continued)

regarded as a viable source of energy for renewable power systems. A research report by Apak et al. (2017) shows how Six Sigma methodology has been applied to hydrogen energy to boost energy efficiency. The authors also emphasize the importance of hydrogen energy in exploring potential future sources of sustainable, reliable and competitively priced energy. This study was an initiative to implement the Six Sigma methodology in a hydrogen power plant in Turkey, with the aim of encouraging governments to support the use of hydrogen as a source of renewable energy.

7.5. How Green Six Sigma Can Help Clean Energy Initiatives Further

There is strong evidence of the application of Six Sigma/Lean Six Sigma methodology in solar power and wind power initiatives. Six Sigma has also been applied in thermal power plants. However, there is little testimony regarding Six Sigma methodology in hydropower and nuclear power projects.

Green Six Sigma should be very effective in all new Clean Energy projects, whether they are for hydropower, solar power, wind energy or nuclear plants. The existing clean energy installations, especially hydropower and nuclear plants, should consider proactively the application of the Green Six Sigma approach. The case example of Vestas India clearly demonstrates that a modest investment to develop employees even up to the basic Yellow Belt level can deliver big savings and sustainable processes.

The distinctive additional contributions of Green Six Sigma include:

- A comprehensive performance management system supported by a periodic self-assessment to monitor and sustain performance levels. (See Chapter 4.)

- A regular senior management review (e.g. Sales and Operations Planning) to include Green Six Sigma projects. (See Chapter 4.)
- Application of carbon footprint tools and software. (See Chapters 5 and 6.)
- Application of Material Flow Account. (See Chapter 5.)

7.6. Summary

We know that the energy sector is the top contributor of greenhouse gas emissions and its mitigation will come from all Clean Energy initiatives including nuclear energy. There is evidence of good progress within the realm of wind energy initiatives, with the solar energy sector coming close behind. Although natural gas is the least of the carbon polluters amongst fossil fuels, the faster growth in natural gas consumption is not promising with regard to attaining the net-zero carbon target. The big advantage of nuclear energy sources is that they can deliver more electricity day and night without interruption. Therefore, greater national efforts should be focussed on developing the field of nuclear energy.

This chapter has dealt with four main sources of Clean Energy, but there are of course other energy supplies. One example would be geothermal, using deep underground hot rocks. High-pressure water can be pumped down into these rocks and the water with absorbed heat comes out from another hole; in turn this can spin a turbine to generate electricity. Another example is hydrogen, which serves as a key ingredient of fuel cell batteries. We can use the intermittent supply of electricity from solar or wind farms to create hydrogen and then put hydrogen in fuel cells to generate electricity on demand.

Green Six Sigma is not a silver bullet to solve all Clean Energy demands. However, it can play a significant role in accelerating the initiatives at power plants and renewable farms as well as being instrumental in sustaining improved processes and environmental targets.

Green Tips

- Emissions come from five economic sectors, including a third from energy supply, and we need solutions in all of them.
- For kilowatt think of a house and for Gigawatt think of a city.
- Unfortunately, 85% of the energy supply comes from fossil fuel and we have to depend on natural gas for several years to keep our lights on.
- There has been good progress with the renewable energy both by wind power and solar energy.
- Green Six Sigma can play a significant role in the decarbonisation of the energy sector.

Chapter 8
Green Six Sigma and Green Supply Chain

'When we walk away from global warming, when we don't advance and live up to our own rhetoric and standards we set a terrible message of duplicity and hypocrisy.'

– John Kerry

8.1. Introduction

A supply chain, in simple terms, is a network between the suppliers to source the materials, the producer to convert them into products and the distributors to distribute the products to customers. The network could be complex involving many activities, people, facilities, information, processes and systems. In a typical supply chain, raw materials are procured (some local and some imported) and items are produced at one or more factories, transported to warehouses for intermediate storage and then transported locally and internationally to retailers or customers. With supply chain management the flow of materials and flow of information across traditional functional boundaries is seen as a single process. These flows

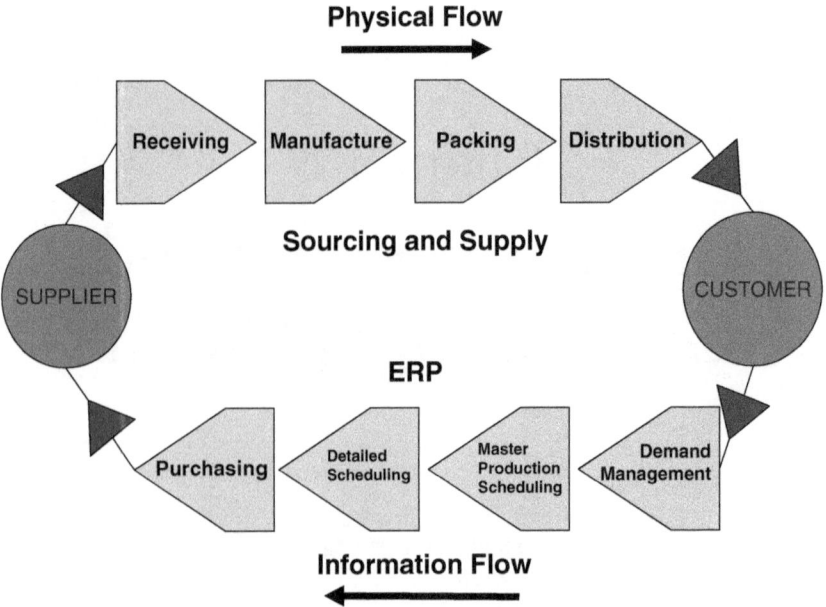

Figure 8.1   Supply chain management

are depicted in a simplified model in Figure 8.1. Thanks to ease of travel, the media and the 'world wide web' customers have never been more informed than they are today and they know what they want. This is especially true in service industries. As a result of the heightened expectations of customers, operations managers in service sectors also have been forced to using the principles of supply chain management.

If we look at a supply chain in another way, it is made of how we grow and procure things (land and agriculture), how we make things and provide services (industry) and how we get around (transport). As shown in Table 7.1, this chapter on green supply chain will include agriculture and land and industry. The green supply chain in total accounts for 45% of greenhouse gas emissions. This chapter will analyse the challenges and opportunities in green supply chain and also the role of Green Six Sigma to accelerate and sustain the outcomes.

Environmental regulations are also changing the way in which supply chains are designed and managed. The problem is that the sheer number of rules, other influences such as changing consumer sentiment, and the complexity of global trade make it difficult for companies to decide exactly how they should respond to these pressures. Firms must also address the ethical requirements of their corporate social responsibility (CSR).

On a global scale, industrial pollution is one of the main contributors to the so-called 'greenhouse' effect and global warming. It is important to note that environment and safety are not just social or political issues; they are vital ingredients contributing to the performance of an organisation. In manufacturing industries, there is much scope for environment and safety. The agriculture sector appears to present a picture of green pastor but a large proportion of methane gas is emerging from the cattle and sheep farming activities. Apart from humanitarian reasons it is a truism that accidents cost money. Likewise, many businesses and organisations are facing declining reserves of natural resources, increased waste disposal costs, keener interest in their human rights records and tighter legislation.

These rising environmental pressures and social expectations can be turned to commercial advantage if a strategic approach is taken to develop a Green Thinking policy as described in the next section. Green Thinking is exactly on the same page as climate change initiatives. The strategic approach of Green Thinking entails complex longer-term considerations involving not just industry but environment protection by regulations as an important international issue. Therefore, it is inevitable that no organisation can in the long term hope to avoid legislation and regulations designed to support the spirit of Green Thinking. In fact, well-designed Green Thinking strategies can lead to sustainable business advantages.

Such a policy should be supported by a process to implement its objectives. Here Green Six Sigma can play its part and contribute its own specific role in this global challenge and opportunity. In the domain of quality and holistic processes, the specific methodology of Green Six Sigma (which, as we know, is evolved from Six

Sigma methodology) could be such a process to support a Green
Thinking Strategy. The aim of this chapter is to review some of the
critical issues and initiatives of Green Thinking under the following headings:

- Green Thinking and Climate Change Initiatives
- Why Green Six Sigma Is Relevant to Green Supply Chain
- Green Initiatives by Manufacturers and Suppliers
- Green Initiatives by Retailers
- Green Initiatives by Consumers
- Green Initiatives by Farmers
- Green Initiatives by Government and Non-profit Organisations
- How Green Six Sigma Can Help Green Supply Chain

8.2.   Green Thinking and Climate Change Initiative

The concept of Green Thinking is not new. Pearce (1992) analysed
the relationship with Nature and the environmental strategies
identified with the Green Movement. Elkington (1994) coined
the phrase 'triple bottom line' as a new concept of accounting
practice. The triple bottom line or TBL (and also known as 'people, planet, profit') captures an expanded spectrum of values and
criteria for measuring organisational success: economic, environmental and social. TBL is not without its critics and it is now more
aligned with corporate social responsibility (CSR). Sustainability or sustainable development was first defined by the Brundt-
land Commission of the United Nations (1987) as 'the needs of
the present without compromising the ability of future generations to meet their own needs'. As discussed in Chapter 2, this
then led to the United Nations initiative of the UNFCCC environmental treaty addressing climate change signed by 158 states at
Rio de Janeiro in 1992 and then other international and climate
change initiatives.

With the above background the author has developed the 3Es
model (Efficiency, Environment and Ethics) as the three dimensions of Green Thinking. As shown in Figure 8.2, each aspect

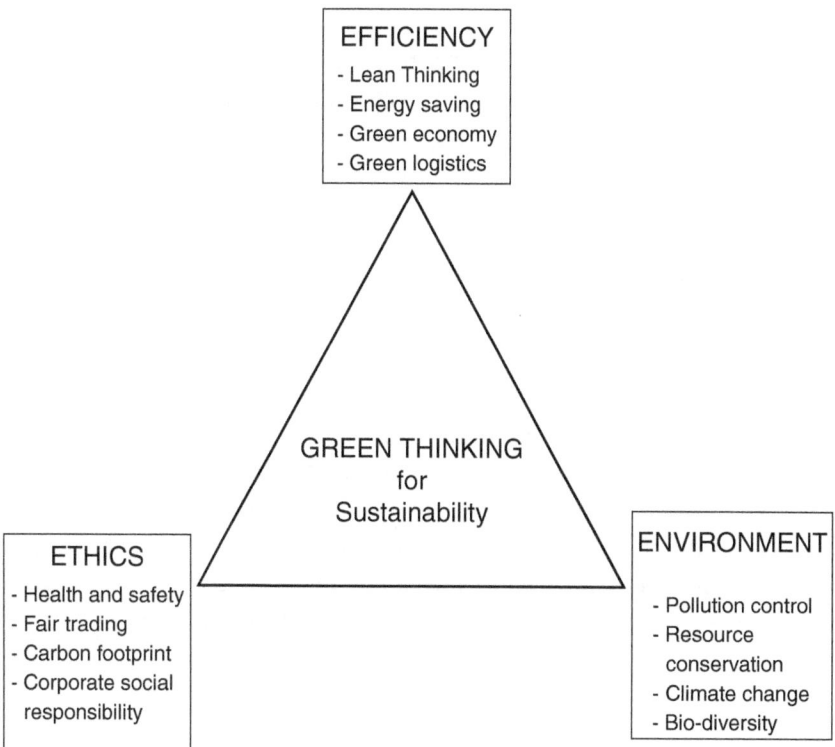

Figure 8.2 Green Thinking concept

includes specific attributes, e.g. Efficiency relates to Lean Think-ing, Energy Saving, the Green Economy and Green Logistics. Bet-ter training, greater awareness and improved communication on green issues characterise the Green Economy of an organisation. Green logistics refer to buyer companies requiring a certain level of environmental responsibility in the core business practices of their suppliers and vendors. Ethics include issues and processes related to health and safety, fair trading, carbon footprint and CSR. The most important dimension is Environment containing pollution control, resources (including energy), conservation, cli-mate change and biodiversity. Climate Change relates to the fac-tors (such as CO_2 emission) causing the longer-term alterations in weather statistics. Major energy companies like BP (www.BP/sustainability) are focusing on new energy technology and low carbon energy products in alternative sources, such as wind, solar, biofuels and carbon capture and storage (CCS). The variety of life on Earth or its biological diversity is commonly referred to as 'biodiversity', where each species, no matter how small, has an important role to play.

The primary focus of Green Thinking is on the Environment and its sustainability while Efficiency and Ethics contribute to the quality and sustainability of Environment. Therefore, the three dimensions and their attributes are interrelated. For example, energy saving and green logistics in Efficiency are closely linked to Environment. Likewise, the pillars of fair trading and carbon footprint within Ethics are intimately related to Environment.

The concept of Green Thinking is clearly incontrovertibly linked to climate change initiatives. Therefore Green Initiatives, based on the concept of Green Thinking, also mean climate change initiatives.

8.3. Why Green Six Sigma is Relevant to Green Supply Chain

As discussed in Chapter 4, the significant bottom line results and extensive training deployment of Six Sigma and Lean Six Sigma must be sustained with additional features for securing the long-term competitive advantage of a company. If Lean Six Sigma provides agility and efficiency, then measures must be in place to develop a sustainable fitness. The process to do just that is FIT SIGMA (Basu, 2011). In addition, the control of variation from the mean in the Six Sigma process (σ) is transformed to company-wide integration via FIT SIGMA methodology (Σ). FIT SIGMA is therefore synonymous with 'FIT Σ'. Furthermore, the philosophy of FIT Σ should ensure that it is indeed fit for all organisations – whether large or small, manufacturing or service. Green Six Sigma is the recast of FIT SIGMA adapted specifically for Green Thinking or climate change initiatives with additional processes to ensure the sustainability of the environment.

Four additional features are embedded in the FIT SIGMA philosophy to create the sustainability of processes and performance levels. These are:

- A formal senior management review process at regular intervals, similar to the Sales and Operational Planning procedure
- Periodic self-assessment with a structured checklist that is formalised by a certification or prize, similar to the EFQM award but with more emphasis on self-assessment
- A continuous learning and knowledge management scheme
- The extension of the programme across the whole business to ensure Green Thinking with the shifting of the theme from the variation control (σ) of Six Sigma to the integration of a seamless organisation (Σ)

The additional features of Green Six Sigma to ensure the sustainability of the environment are:

- A formal extension of DMAIC (Define, Measure, Analyse, Improve and Control) methodology to DMAICS (Define, Measure, Analyse, Improve, Control and Sustain)
- Inclusion of the above features of FIT SIGMA to create the sustainability of the processes and performance levels
- Additional processes to ensure the sustainability of the environment with additional processes and tools including Material Flow Account and Carbon Footprint Tool

Green Thinking can leverage the contents of Green Six Sigma to achieve the specific environmental and business goals of supply chain stakeholders. For example, the Value Stream Mapping of Lean Six Sigma (to pinpoint waste) can be adapted to create Green Value Stream Mapping (to identify carbon footprints). Likewise, 'Voice of Environment' can represent the growing prevalence of environmental drivers not captured in 'Voice of Customer'.

8.4. Green Initiatives by Manufacturers and Suppliers

It is reasonable to state that manufacturing industries are major players regarding greenhouse gas emissions accounting for 21% of the total. Industries in the green supply chain must address health and safety in addition to the environment. However, when the issues relate to health and safety, whether for products or workplaces, they apply seriously to both manufacturing and service organisations. Lack of safety in the product or in the workplace will inevitably cost money. Accidents mean lost production time plus time wasting inspections by government officials. They may also incur legal costs as well as the expense of correcting the situation. It has to be cheaper to do it right the first time. One of the better known environmental standards is put forth by the International Organisation for Standardisation (ISO), known as ISO 14001. Basu and Wright (2003) have established that environmental protection relates to pollution control in two stages. Conventional restraints or 'first generation pollution' controls are applied to pollution in air and water and regarding noise created in the manufacturing process. Such jurisdictions are usually regulated by legislation. There is also a 'second generation pollution', which relates to the problems caused by the usage of certain products and chemicals over a long period. The most widespread example of such 'second generation pollution' is the contamination of land that permeates ground water.

The primary focus of climate change initiatives is the reduction of greenhouse gases. Therefore each major manufacturing company is expected to have a carbon neutrality strategy that is to achieve the net-zero carbon footprints by 2050 or earlier. I propose a three-step carbon management strategy as follows:

1. Develop a Total Supply Chain Emission Chart
2. Follow a Carbon Management Action Plan
3. Coordinate and share carbon management actions with key stakeholders

A typical Total Supply Chain Emission Chart is shown in Figure 8.3. This chart is the starting point of measuring and

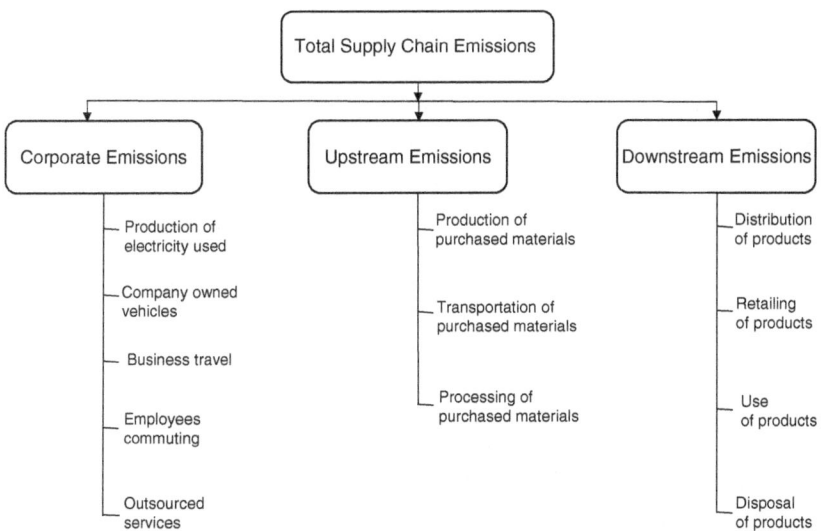

Figure 8.3   Total Supply Chain Emission Chart

monitoring carbon footprints and initiating Carbon Management Action Plan.

A Carbon Management Action Plan should follow the following hierarchy as proposed by Watt (2012):

- Avoid
- Reduce
- Replace
- Offset

Here are some tips to follow a Carbon Management Action Plan. Avoid carbon intensive materials (e.g. steel and cement) and activities (e.g. air travel). Reduce waste and do whatever you do more efficiently (e.g. apply Green Six Sigma tools). Replace high-carbon energy sources with low carbon energy ones (e.g. substitute plastics packaging). Offset those emissions that cannot be eliminated by the above. Unfortunately, the process of offsetting is rather less straightforward. A carbon offset is used to reduce greenhouse gas emissions in order to compensate for the emissions made elsewhere. Businesses can buy carbon credits generated by projects that are cleaning up our atmosphere.

We are still left with the environmental challenge with three major materials for the industry – steel, cement and plastic. When we produce steel or cement tonnes of carbon dioxide are released, but when we make plastic around half of the carbon stays in the plastic. However, plastics can take hundreds of years to degrade. Additional research is needed specifically for these three heavily used materials beyond the scope of Green Six Sigma. The following Case Example 8.1 shows that some progress has been made in manufacturing 'fossil-free steel'.

Case Example 8.1   SSAB Delivers 'First Fossil-Free Steel'

Sweden SSAB announced in August 2021 that its 'Hybrit technology' produced 'the world's first fossil-free steel', and started delivering it to the Volvo Group. The idea underpinning this 'Hybrit technology' is the use of fossil-free hydrogen rather than coal in steel production. The cost effectiveness of the 'Hybrit technology' is not known but the goal of SSAB is to market the technology on an industrial scale as early as 2026.

At this stage we can also follow the hierarchy of Avoid, Reduce, Replace and Offset. If we encourage companies to share their climate change initiatives with their key stakeholders up and down the supply chain then we are likely to get radical responses. For example, Marks & Spencer may correctly decide to work with agricultural suppliers to ensure a future supply of low carbon products, and Unilever may correctly decide to influence consumer habits to use low carbon ethically sourced products.

8.5.   Green Initiatives by Retailers

Global retail giants Walmart and Carrefour, as well as other supermarkets all over the world, are responding to the pressures on packaging waste reduction and the additional environmental issues involved in the green supply chain. It is important to consider replacing all non-recyclable packaging materials as far as possible. PET, which stands for polyethylene terephthalate, is a form of polyester and is recyclable.

Recent media reports are loaded with announcements on 'greening the supply chain' from large retail groups. Walmart, a US company and the world's largest retailer, unveiled its packaging scorecard to major suppliers such as Proctor & Gamble, Unilever and Nestle, which was designed to cut packaging. Walmart hopes that the scheme will reduce packaging across its global supply chain by 5% by 2013.

British supermarkets have taken the initiative in becoming more environmentally aware. ASDA supermarket, a subsidiary of Walmart in the UK, claimed, as an example, that taking pizzas out of cardboard boxes saved 747 tonnes of cardboard in a year. UK supermarket Sainsbury announced in October 2006 that 500 of its own-brand goods would be presented in compostable packaging. 'Friends of the Earth', a non-profit organisation in the UK, gave a cautious welcome to Tesco's new environment fund of $100 million but said the supermarket giant still had a very long way to go if it was serious about greening its operations. Tesco would need to address a number of key areas if it was serious about reducing its environmental impacts. These include moving away from car-dependent stores, switching from its global supply chain, radically improving energy efficiency in its stores and cleaning up its supply chains.

Perhaps the best example of a company devoting itself to acting upon environmental issues is the British retailer Marks and Spencer. Their website (marksandspencer.com/about) detailed the evolution of their 'Plan A' scheme, and M&S launched Plan A in January 2007, which listed 100 commitments that the firm aimed to achieve within a five-year timeframe. Since then, M&S have extended this commitment to encompass 180 goals that they wished to attain by 2015. Their proudly stated aspirations included 'working with our customers and our suppliers to combat climate change, reduce waste, use sustainable raw materials, trade ethically, and help our customers to lead healthier lifestyles' and that they have 'the ultimate goal of becoming the world's most sustainable major retailer.'

Even the airlines, the biggest polluters with their CO_2 emissions, have joined the green bandwagon. Richard Branson committed the next 10 years of profits for Virgin – around \$3 billion – to fighting global warming.

There has been stronger emphasis to introduce ethical, fair trade, organic and bio products to the consumer. The following case example of 'Carrefour Bio Coffee' illustrates that, by promoting unbranded 500 g/1 kg coffee in bags as 'organic coffee to support fair trading' in 1997, sales increased by 80% in four years.

Such is the importance of a company displaying its eco credentials that there is a growing awareness that communicating their efforts to the consumer leads to favourable publicity and an enhanced reputation of the brand. Indeed, close perusal of any paper media advertising will reveal how many companies actually seem to be using newspapers and magazines to broadcast their environmentally conscious efforts instead of boasting about their products. In today's climate, ecological issues are such a current and hot topic that firms realise that they can tap into the public consciousness and portray themselves as 'green', thus superseding the traditional tenets of advertising, the focus on the goods themselves. This method is used not only by supermarkets but by manufacturers of white goods or motor cars (emphasis on energy efficiency of products), petroleum firms, energy companies and so on. The reader can also examine everyday objects to see this principle in action; the covers of recently published books (which inform us of their use of paper from sustainable forests) or the packaging of almost any food or cosmetic item to see details of the sustainability of their source materials.

8.6. Green Initiatives by Consumers

Consumers have both the power and responsibility to enhance the activities and effectiveness of the green supply chain. It is the consumer who pays for the end product or service, and it is the consumer who ultimately suffers or benefits from the result-ant impact on the environment. Green initiatives from consumers could be manifested in three ways:

- Make your home green
- Feedback to retailers
- Reverse supply chain

'Make you home green' is becoming a conscious target of many consumers. This is effected in two paths. Firstly, consumers are attempting to minimise 'carbon emission' by making houses and household appliances more energy efficient and also by mov-ing towards eco-friendly transport. Secondly, encouraged by local authorities, consumers are making commendable efforts in the recycling of household wastes by the provision of green (composta-ble) waste, paper and glass bins for the home, use of local recycling centres, etc. The retrofitting of homes to 'make your home green' will be discussed further in Chapter 10.

A reverse supply chain is a process of getting goods from the customers back to the manufacturers. This is a relatively new trend in supply chain management that focuses on 'green manufacturing' to target recycling, recovery and remanufacturing systems. In these reverse networks, consumers bring products to a retailer or a col-lection centre. For example, supermarkets in Germany have a bin where customers leave used batteries. Depending on the particular product, it can be refurbished, remanufactured or recycled, mak-ing sure the physical flow is efficient. It is estimated that 63 mil-lion personal computers worldwide became obsolete during 2003 and about 10 million electric waste products are dumped per year in Japan. By 2030, the obsolete PCs from developing regions will reach 400–700 million units, far more than from developed regions at 200–300 million units. The principle of the 'circular economy', i.e. reuse, repair, refurbish and recycle, is appropriate for domes-tic appliances, minimising the use of new ones and the creation of wastes (Yu et al., 2010).

Mobile phones can be returned to the store where the new one is purchased. From there, the phones are resold and reused in other countries where the very technology that is being phased out in developed countries are being introduced. Many other products have the potential for second use, including computers, auto parts, printer cartridges, refillable containers and a host of other possibilities. In remanufacturing, reverse logistics introduces additional challenges to planning for a closed-loop supply chain. The planning, sourcing, making and delivery of the products are affected by the reverse flow of used products and materials for subsequent consumption in the manufacturing of new products. Reverse logistics play a key role as retail organisations tend to look at their reverse supply chains more closely to enhance customer satisfaction, cost/time efficiencies and supplier performance.

8.7.   Green Initiatives by Farmers

Agriculture and land is a primary link of green supply chain, and farmers are its major stakeholders, although it is unreasonable to make the farmers alone responsible for this sector. This sector, accounting for 24% of the total greenhouse emissions, covers a large range of human activities, from raising animals to growing crops and harvesting trees. With agriculture the main emission is not carbon dioxide but methane and nitrous oxide. Methane causes 28 times more warming than carbon dioxide and nitrous oxide, and though low in its share of all greenhouse gases, causes 265 times more warming. Scientists estimate that the emission from agriculture and animal farming is more than 7 billion tonnes of carbon dioxide equivalent per year. Another big challenge is deforestation and other uses of the land, which together is adding about 1.6 billion tonnes of carbon dioxide every year and destroying essential biodiversity.

The agriculture and land sectors offer more challenges but there are not many breakthrough solutions. Let us address some of these challenges. The first challenge is our food habits and the rapid growth in population. The world population has more than doubled within the last 50 years to the current level of 7.9 billion people. As people are getting richer they eat more meat and dairy products. Although there is little growth in meat consumption per person in the USA, Europe and Latin America, it is climbing rapidly in China. The supply of meat and dairy is coming from cows, sheep and pigs. The enteric fermentation in cattle is emitting methane equivalent to 4% of all greenhouse gas emissions. The excrements from farm animals also release a mix of powerful greenhouse gases – mostly nitrous oxide and some methane.

There is some progress with a compound that has to be administered to the cattle every day to reduce methane emissions by about 30%. This is not a winning area. We could try by applying the principle of the circular economy, which is to replace and reduce. There is an active 'vegan movement' that we should just stop raising livestock for food only. There are some successful developments of plant-based meat and lab cultivated meat. There is another way we can reduce emissions from the meat that we eat by wasting less of it. In the USA more than 40% of food is wasted. One good news is that the productivity of grain farming (e.g. rice, wheat and corn) has increased many-fold by two main factors – innovation (e.g. Borlaug's semi-dwarf wheat), mechanisation and fertilizers. However, a fertilizer is also a mixed blessing. The nitrogen from the fertilizer escapes into the air as nitrous oxide.

A large contributor (30%) of greenhouse gases in the agriculture and land sector is 'deforestation'. For example, Brazil's forests have shrunk by at least 10% since 1990 to clear it for pastureland for cattle. When a tree is removed the stored carbon gets released into the atmosphere as carbon dioxide, while a tree in the rainforest can absorb 4 tonnes of carbon dioxide over 40 years. A popular process of carbon offsetting is the planting of trees. However, scientists have estimated that to offset the life-long emissions of one person we would need around 20 hectares worth of trees. Trees with a higher carbon absorption capacity (e.g. American Sweetgum tree, European Beech tree, Silver Maple tree, seagrass) should be preferred for new plantation.

8.8.   How Green Six Sigma Can Help the Green Supply Chain

The tools, techniques and processes of Green Six Sigma can provide an effective framework to implement the initiatives in all three dimensions of Green Thinking, viz. Efficiency, Environment and Ethics.

8.8.1.   FIT SIGMA in Efficiency

The fundamentals of Lean Thinking are embedded in Green Six Sigma and are underpinned by:

1. Elimination of waste
2. Smooth operation flow
3. High level of efficiency
4. Quality assurance

The lean methodology as laid out by Womack and Jones (1998) is sharply focused on the identification and elimination of 'mudas' or waste; indeed their first two principles (Value and Value Stream) are centered around the eradication of waste. One important area of waste in processes is excess inventory. The cycle time or lead time reduction is another target area of waste reduction. Environmental misuses – including squandered energy – can cost companies thousands of dollars a year. Green Six Sigma tools (such as Value Stream Mapping and the Flow Diagram) are there to analyse processes and identify wastes and non-value-added activities. The additional impact of Green Six Sigma on Efficiency is ensuring the sustainability of that efficiency by quality assurance and well-structured training programmes for Black Belts and Green Belts.

The elimination of waste through Lean Thinking in any entity or form of consumption, whether products, processes, materials or utilities, is de facto in the domain of Green Thinking. Lean Thinking is also a key component of Green Six Sigma and thus Green Six Sigma can be a major driver of the 'Efficiency' leg of Green Thinking.

Case Example 8.2   GE Jet Engine Testing

A facility of General Electrics in Peebles, Ohio (where GE runs jet engine tests in the open air), is a leader within the company in applying Lean to address greenhouse gas (GHG) emissions. The quantity of testing conducted is directly related to the amount of business the airlines are doing. More engine testing means more jet fuel consumption and more GHG emissions. These reductions have also resulted in significant cost savings.

Before Lean events, the engine had to be turned on three times in order to complete the balancing process. Lean methods helped Peebles develop a new balancing process that only required the engine to be turned on once, which reduced both fuel consumption and GHG emissions. While the facility's old troubleshooting process required the engine to be running, the new procedure allowed troubleshooting to occur while the engine was not running. Through these changes the company reduced its use of fuel from 20,000 gallons to 10,000 gallons. There was also an overall cost savings of over a million dollars a year.

Source: US Environment Protection Agency (2019).

In the well-known Toyota Production System (TPS), the forerunner of Lean Thinking, Toyota has developed a 5R programme (see Table 8.1) to reduce polluting wastes in order to maintain production with Green Thinking (Black and Phillips, 2010).

It is evident from the 5R programme that eliminating waste at the source by using Lean and related Green Six Sigma techniques helps the process of achieving zero waste as part of Green Thinking in Efficiency.

8.8.2.   Green Six Sigma in the Environment

The impact of Green Six Sigma in the Environment is achieved by identifying and prioritising environmentally related projects as part of Black Belt/Green Belt training programmes. There are five areas

Table 8.1 Toyota's 5R for Green Thinking

5R	Measures	Responsibility
Refine	Expansion to reduce, reuse and recycle by changing the design and raw materials	Operations Departments
Reduce	Reduction of amount of waste generated at source	Operations Departments
Reuse	Reuse within operations processes	Operations Departments
Recycle	In-plant and outside use of generated waste	Operations Departments
Retrieve energy	Recovery of energy from waste materials that cannot be refined, reduced, reused or recycled	Environment Technology Department

under which environmental issues are addressed in identifying Green Six Sigma projects, namely:

1. Green procurement
2. Energy conservation
3. Resource conversation
4. Elimination of hazardous waste
5. Risk management

　　Green procurement is the selection of products and services that minimise environmental impacts. The rationalisation of the supply chain to significantly reduce delivery vehicle movements is such an example. Green procurement is part of Green Logistics of Efficiency but its focus on Environment is more significant in Green Six Sigma projects. Energy conservation is achieved through efficient energy use – in other words, energy use is reduced while achieving a similar outcome. In addition to industrial facilities, domestic housing and road transport are also two major areas of concern. The Resource Conservation Challenge (RCC) is a national effort to protect natural resources (including energy) by managing materials more efficiently. 3M is a pioneer in the use of Lean Six Sigma methods and tools to minimize hazardous waste and improve operations and quality. The famous 3P programme (Pollution Prevention Pays) of the 3M Company brought about major savings including $2 million from the elimination of hydrocarbon wastes from a reactive casting process.

Case Example 8.3   3M Company: Environmental Health and Safety

When 3M instigated its 3P programme several years ago, the approach was to capture and control pollution and emissions before they could damage the environment. This tactic, although effective, has been altered to a philosophy of prevention rather than containment. The 3P programme now aims to prevent pollution at source by using different materials, changing the process, redesigning the plant and equipment, and recycling waste.

Since 2001, 3M's Environmental, Health and Safety Operations (EHS) organisation has deployed Lean Six Sigma to improve corporate EHS services and activities. EHS team members receive two weeks of Lean Six Sigma Green Belt training, and coaching is provided by Black Belts.

There are specific tools and processes of Green Six Sigma to contribute to the environment and sustainable climate change initiatives. In addition to the sustainability tools of Green Six Sigma, the rigour of Six Sigma and Green Six Sigma can be applied to verify the issues of the broader climate change debate. There are many Green Six Sigma tools in the book that are highly relevant for climate change projects. For example, Control Charts can help analyse the range of variability in climate change or the Cause and Effect Diagram can articulate the different causes of global warming. At a more advanced level of analysis, Six Sigma tools like DOE (Design of Experiments), MSA (Measurement Systems Analysis) and SPC (Statistical Process Control) can contribute a data-driven rigour to the debate of climate change. As a specific example, SPC analysis of global temperature pinpointed special causes of variation affecting the temperature data (Dale, 1999). In this example, three special causes are identified and analysed as the 'heat island' effect (urbanization), CO_2 emission due to human activity and the sunspot cycle.

Green Six Sigma is not the 'holy grail' to environmental challenges or the climate change debate but it can contribute as a systematic and proven methodology in these challenges. There are many other initiatives from all stakeholders that are required, as discussed earlier. There are many such initiatives in progress, such as the Renewable Energy Directive (EU target to produce 22% of electricity from renewable sources), Climate Change Levy (tax on greenhouse gases) and Carbon Reduction Commitment (UK target to achieve 78% reduction of carbon emission by 2035). There are more legislations in the pipeline, including the regulation of waste in portable batteries and widening the scope of the Hazardous Waste Regulation. It is a good start but it has a long way to go.

8.8.3. Green Six Sigma in Ethics

There are three key aspects of Ethics that could be supported and enhanced by Green Six Sigma, namely:

1. Product and occupational safety
2. Carbon footprint
3. Corporate social responsibility

A major incident in product safety, particularly in consumer and food products, can seriously damage the brand and business. Accidents in the workplace mean lost production time and are often accompanied by paying out both compensation to employees and legal costs. A carbon footprint is 'the total set of GHG (greenhouse gas) emissions caused directly and indirectly by an individual, organisation, event or product' (UK Carbon Trust, 2008). An individual organisation's carbon footprint is measured by undertaking a GHG emissions assessment. Corporate social responsibility (CSR) is a self-regulating mechanism whereby organisations would monitor and ensure their adherence to the law, public interests and ethical standards. CSR also embraces the concept of the 'triple bottom line', covering environmental, social and economic bottom lines. A key role that Green Six Sigma can play in Ethics is by bringing together the specialists in HSE (health, safety and environment) and other operations in Black Belt/Green Belt training.

Case Example 8.4   Carrefour Bio Coffee

Carrefour is a global hypermarket retail chain organisation from France with a turnover of more than €100 billion, making it second only to Walmart, the largest retail company in the world.

The first shipment of coffee beans was delivered in 10 kg sacks to Vitrolles, France, in 1970. The beans were roasted in store and sold in 500 g and 1 kg bags. In April 1997 Carrefour launched the 'organic' coffee brand under the name 'Carrefour Bio' to promote organic products and support fair trading. In 2001 it was decided to establish a 'green supply chain' for 'Carrefour Bio'.

The organic coffee marketed under the name 'Carrefour Bio' is not indexed on the world coffee market. The purchase price is approximately 30% higher than the average cost in Mexico. The supplier is contracted to pay a guaranteed minimum price to producers. Thus producers can obtain up to 60% of the value of the coffee at current international rates. Some 3,000 producers from 37 Mexican communities cultivate coffee using organic methods. A local infrastructure has been introduced to transport people between towns and villages (a two hour bus ride replacing what was previously a two-day walk). A health scheme has been introduced, providing free medicine and healthcare and a consortium has been set up to buy basic foodstuffs at cost price.

The coffee is cultivated by small farmers working for the Uciri cooperative in Mexico using an organic method of farming. Such cultivation helps prevent the land becoming impoverished. The cultivation is carried out in accordance with French Organic Society standards without the use of organofluiridated fertilisers or chemical pesticides for tropical forest conditions. An organic fertiliser comprising sun-dried and hand-picked stoned cherries

(continued)

(continued)

and animal waste is spread over the plants. This is the only plant treatment used by the farmers.

Cultivation methods are monitored by an organic certification body. An agricultural education centre has also been established, catering for organic farming, animal breeding and bio culture.

The 'Carrefour Bio' coffee project appears to constitute a win–win initiative for the green supply chain. For Carrefour, sales for the product increased from 29.5 tonnes in 1997 to 54 tonnes in 2001. The fertility of the land has been protected. The average income per family of producers increased from €53 per year in 1985 to €1,524 per year in 2000. The local communities benefitted from the infrastructure and facilities for transport, healthcare and education. Finally, consumers are happy with an organic product at an affordable price.

In addition to implementing environment management systems such as ISO 1401 or EMAS (Eco-Management and Audit Scheme), the adherence to a strong ethical culture by continuous training means the executive board of an organization can be confident that brands or the business would not be tainted by prosecution or negative press. The training on environment, safety and ethics can be embedded in Green Six Sigma training workshops.

8.9.   Summary

'The scientific evidence is now overwhelming: climate change is a serious global threat, and it demands an urgent global response,' concludes Nicholas Stern (2006).

It should be noted that this view has been disputed, especially by fossil fuel lobbyists. However, irrespective of what we believe, the pressure is on for industry and nations to adopt a green approach to the supply chain. In this chapter we have attempted to present a balanced view of various initiatives adopted by manufacturers and suppliers, farmers, retailers and also consumers. Every stakeholder has a role and responsibility in 'greening' the supply chain. We have shown that there are commercial benefits in reducing wastes (e.g. excessive packaging). Large retailers like Walmart, Carrefour and Tesco are probably facing disproportionate demands from environmental pressure groups and regulatory bodies but nonetheless are displaying visible efforts to respond to these demands.

Quality as a whole can play a major role in raising the awareness of Green Thinking and sustainable developments. In this chapter, mainly the impact of Green Six Sigma and Six Sigma programmes (which are part of the quality movement) are touched upon. Learning from the proactive focus on Green Thinking in the Six Sigma programmes of leading organisations like GE and 3M, the adaptive tools and processes of Green Six Sigma could be appropriately applied by all organisations in their Green Thinking initiatives. Edward de Bono of Indigo Businesses Services (de Bono, 2016) also suggests the inclusion of 'Green Hat' in his concept of 'Green Thinking Hats of Six Sigma'. In addition to following the fundamental tenets of Six Sigma the additional features of Green Six Sigma should bolster the sustainable climate change initiatives of the stakeholders of the green supply chain.

Green Tips

- Lean Six Sigma has been effective in improving the performance of green supply chain. Green Six Sigma will add more value by ensuring sustainable processes and environmental standards.
- The amount of methane emitted by cows and sheep account for 4% of global emissions.
- Each stakeholder of the supply chain has a role to play in reducing carbon dioxide emissions.
- Every organisation should have a Carbon Management Action Plan and follow a hierarchy as avoid, reduce, replace and offset.
- Toyota's 5R for Green Thinking is in alignment with the principles of the circular economy in Green Six Sigma.

Chapter 9
Green Six Sigma and Green Transport

'Global warming is causing the loss of living species at a level compa-
rable to the extinction event that wiped out the dinosaurs 65 million
years ago.'

– Al Gore

9.1. Introduction

The various forms of transport that we use daily contribute only
14% of the total global greenhouse gas transmissions (emissions?).
Thus, this sector ranks fourth behind energy, land and industry.
However, if you were to ask a random person which activities pol-
lute most, he or she probably would say burning coal for energy,
driving cars and travelling by plane. Although transportation is not
the biggest cause of emissions worldwide it is high on the list in the
USA and Europe, where people drive and fly a great deal. In 2020,
as the Covid-19 pandemic led to a sudden and drastic reduction in
transport activities, it was noticeable that carbon dioxide transmissions also fell by 2.4%.

If we are going to attain net-zero emissions we will have to minimise all the greenhouse gases caused by transportation around the world.

9.2.   Guiding Factors of Clean Transports

We cannot leave without transport, unless we plan to go everywhere on foot. Even if we reduce our non-essential travel we will still need transportation by land, sea or air to move goods for our survival. Farmers need to get their crops to the market. The benefits of globalisation cannot be realised without the movement of goods and people, both between nations and within countries. Therefore, in order to enjoy the benefits of transportation and travel without making our climate unlivable, we need to adopt green or eco-friendly solutions urgently.

In order to find such green solutions for transport-related emissions, we need to analyse where these emissions are coming from. Although at present the USA and Europe are responsible for a major part of such transport-related greenhouse gas emissions, these countries reached their peak in the past decade and in fact their emission rates have started to decline. At present, most of the growth in transport-related emissions can be traced to emerging economies as their growing populations are getting richer and buying more cars. For example, in China, transport-related emissions have doubled over the past decade.

Table 9.1 shows the share of emissions from different types of transport, such as cars, planes, ships, etc. Passenger vehicles

Table 9.1   Emissions from transports

Types of Transport	Share of Emissions (%)
Passenger vehicles	47
Trucks and buses	30
Cargo and cruise ships	10
Airplanes	10
Trains	3

(cars, SUVs and motor cycles) constitute the biggest portion at 47%, and trucks and buses contribute another 30%. Airplanes then add another 10%, as do cargo and container ships. Finally, trains account for the last 3%. As a whole, every year all forms of transports are emitting over 7 billion tonnes of carbon dioxide equivalent to the atmosphere. Our goal is quite simply to get every source of these transportation emissions to net zero.

There is also pollution from particulate matter or PM2.5. Inhalation of particulate pollution can have severe longer-term health impacts such as the age-specific mortality risk, particularly from cardiovascular causes. However, its damaging effects can be fatal, regardless of age; in December 2020 a coroner ruled that the death of nine-year-old Ella Adoo-Kissi-Debrah, who lived very close to the South Circular Road in Lewisham, south-east London, was in part attributable to high levels of air pollution. This landmark ruling meant that Ella became the first person in the UK to have 'air pollution' recorded as a cause of death. In addition to it naturally occurring (e.g. volcanic eruptions and wild fires), PM2.5 is also produced by human activities (e.g. emissions from car exhausts). Therefore, clean energy initiatives for passenger vehicles will also eliminate the man-made emission of PM2.5.

There are a number of methods that can be implemented to reduce greenhouse gas emissions from transportation. These include:

- Do less moving around by transports. This requires less driving and reduced travel by air and sea. We should encourage more walking, cycling and working from home. During the Covid-19 pandemic a 'new normal' way of working, by using technology for virtual communication tools, has been established and proven to be effective.
- Use fewer carbon-intensive materials (e.g. steel and plastics) in making cars, trucks, buses, planes and ships. The less we use these materials in a car, the smaller its carbon footprint will be.
- Use fuels more efficiently by setting fuel efficiency standards. Cars have been designed with innovative components (e.g. catalytic converters) and more efficient engines to meet these standards.

The above methods are all on the right track and will reduce the amount of carbon dioxide in the atmosphere – but they will not get us to zero emissions. The key way in which we can move towards net zero is by switching to electric vehicles (EV) or using alternative fuels. These alternative fuels (e.g. ethanol for petrol and biodiesel for diesel) contain carbon, albeit in a negligible proportion. EV is the cleaner and greener option.

9.3.   How Clean Transport Solutions Reduce Greenhouse Gas Emissions

Let us address in more detail how the above methods of carbon reductions are being applied to the different types of transport listed in Table 9.1.

9.3.1.   Passenger Cars

Top of the list is passenger cars, contributing 47% of emissions by all types of transports. We now have two recognised solutions to this issue – electric alternatives and biofuels.

Fortunately, we have the proven engineering and technology of making, using and maintaining electric cars (EVs) today. There are about one billion cars on the road currently and about 5% of these are electric. From Audi through to Volkswagen, all car manufacturers are delivering all-electric or hybrid cars. Hybrid vehicles are powered by an internal combustion engine and an electric motor driven energy stored in batteries. The battery is charged through the internal combustion engine. However, as these cars also use petrol they are not the preferred solutions for net zero carbon emissions. Instead, we should go for all electric plug-in solutions.

The fastest EV sales have been in Europe. As shown in Table 9.2, nearly three-quarters of the cars sold in 2020 in Norway and more than half in Iceland were electric. In 10 other European countries the share of electric vehicles was between 11% and 32%. Both in the UK and France the share of EVs was 11.3% in the same year. EVs in

Table 9.2   Electric vehicles (EVs) in Europe

Country	EV Shares of Total Cars (%)
Norway	74.8
Iceland	52.4
Sweden	32.3
Netherlands	25.0
Finland	18.1
Denmark	16.4
Switzerland	14.3
Portugal	13.8
Germany	13.5
UK	11.3

SOURCE: Pew Research Center Report, Washington (2021).

Europe as a whole experienced a compound growth rate of 60% per annum from 2016 to 2020. By contrast, the share of the EVs in the USA was only 2% and in China a little higher at 5.7%. The growth in EVs could be even greater but for three main reasons – higher costs, lack of battery charging points and a shortage of microchips. The elevated cost is due to the price of batteries. Fortunately for the consumer, the cost of batteries is coming down, with an 87% drop since 2010. Lithium is the preferred choice of battery production for EVs due to its light weight and its excellent electricity conductance. These batteries can withstand higher temperatures and have longer battery lives compared to traditional lead–acid batteries.

There are some government directives to encourage the use of EVs on the road. For example, the Mayor of London has introduced congestion charges for passenger vehicles and EVs are exempted. All diesel and petrol vehicles will be gradually phased out by 2030.

It is estimated that as at July 2021, the cost of running an EV for an average family in the UK driving about 10,000 miles per year is approximately £1,000 more compared to a similar diesel or petrol car. If the price of petrol rises then the extra cost for an EV will be less. The higher expense is negligible but with government incentives for road tax and congestion charges, EVs are an attractive option and are likely to persuade many car buyers.

As indicated earlier, another method of moving towards meeting the net-zero emission target is the use of alternative biofuels. There are traces of carbon in alternative fuels but it is argued that these fuels use carbons that are already present in the atmosphere. The common form of alternative biofuel is ethanol. Ethanol fuel is actually ethyl alcohol made from sugar cane, corn or beet sugar. Fiat was the first car company to introduce a passenger car running only on ethanol in Brazil in 1978. However, ethanol poses a few problems. First it is less efficient than gasoline. Ethanol needs 1.5 times the volume of gasoline to produce the same energy. Therefore, the cost per litre for both petrol and ethanol fuel is in the same range, although it varies from one country to another. However, the major challenge is that the amount of land needed to grow sugar cane or corn to produce a sufficient quantity of biofuel is so vast that it could impact the biodiversity of our environment. In spite of these problems, scientists are optimistic about alternative fuels and are working on converting biomass, such as trees, and leftovers from other processes (e.g. paper making) into carbon-free fuels.

9.3.2. Trucks and Buses

Medium-sized vans and city buses are reasonably lightweight and generally travel shorter routes. The advantage is that these vehicles can work on electric power. China has already electrified the local government fleet of some of its cities such as Shenzhen. Unfortunately, electrification is a less practical option for long-distance trucks and buses because they would need too many powerful batteries to travel over longer journeys without recharging enroute. An expensive Tesla EV may travel 300 miles without charging but to cover the same distance an electric truck would need to carry many batteries. In order to compensate for this crucial extra weight, it would have to lose a quarter of its loads. To obtain the same amount of energy as that from a litre of gasoline requires batteries 35 times heavier than a litre of gasoline. All in all, batteries for long-distance buses or trucks do not seem practical.

One possible solution under trial is so-called 'electrofuels' produced by combining the hydrogen in water and the carbon obtained from carbon dioxide. But 'electrofuels' are at the moment four times more expensive and need electricity (which should be clean energy) to make them. Large organisations like Siemens Energy can see a huge potential for what they call the 'hydrogen economy'. Dr Armin Schnettler of Siemens Energy has commented, 'I strongly believe that the next step of the global energy transition will be based on the hydrogen economy – transforming "green electrons" to "green molecules" via water electrolysis' (Whitlock, 2020). It is expected that by using renewable electrical energy like wind or solar power for 'green electrons' from the power sector this will unlock enormous environmental and business benefits across all sectors. However, we will also need the infrastructure of special refuelling stations along the highways in order to make this work.

9.3.3.   Airplanes and Ships

Batteries are unlikely to be powerful enough to move long-haul ships or planes. 'The best all-electric plane on the market can carry two passengers, reach a top speed of 210 miles per hour, and fly for three hours before recharging' (Gates, 2021, p. 143). The Airbus A350 is already carrying 350 passengers and flying 15,000 km non-stop for nearly 19 hours from New York to Singapore. Batteries are improving but it is hard to see their practical application in airplanes or ships in the near future. A possible solution for planes and ships (applicable to both cargos and cruises) could be to replace fossil fuels with electrofuels or advanced biofuels. Major oil companies, such as Exxon, are also serious about the future of biofuels and developing scalable biofuels derived from cellulose and algae.

Ship operators are now experimenting with available and affordable biodiesel. This is being seen as a 'drop-in' (with no major changes in ships' fuel storage and delivery systems) interim solution for reducing carbon emissions. The following Case Example 9.1 illustrates a successful trial of biodiesel on the Hurtigruten cruise line.

Case Example 9.1　Norwegian Cruise Line Hurtigruten Trials Biofuel on a Cruise Ship

Hurtigruten AS is a Norwegian cruise line headquartered in Tromso, Norway. It also operates as a ferry service along the coast of Norway. This company claimed to be the first to test biofuels to power its 12,000 tonnes cruise ship MS *Polarlys* in 2019. The fuel for the test was a certified biodiesel that is free of palm oil.

Commenting on the development, CEO Daniel Skjeldam said: 'Biodiesel can in the long run potentially give a carbon dioxide reduction of as much as 95% compared to traditional marine fuels' (Warner, 2019).

The shipping industry consumes more than 330 million tonnes of fuel every year, and is responsible for nearly 2% of global carbon dioxide emissions. By using biodiesel, which is sourced from waste cooking oil, corn, soya, wheat, tallow or palm, the industry can begin to reduce its carbon footprint. The move to biodiesel is in its infancy but it has the potential to grow quickly and therefore transform the shipping industry.

9.3.4.　*Trains*

Trains are gradually moving towards being all electric. Today, three-quarters of passenger rail transport activity takes place on electric trains and the electrification of railways is on the rise although it varies between different countries. In China, Russia, Japan and India over 70% of trains are electrified, while in the USA, which has the largest rail network in the world, a mere 1% of trains are electric. At present in Europe only Switzerland can boast a 100% electric train network, while larger European countries are behind with electrification schemes, as shown by Table 9.3.

There are great opportunities for going green in the realm of rail transportation. Airplane and motor transport passengers should be encouraged to travel instead by green railways. Led by Japan, high-speed trains are cutting down the proportion of travel undertaken by

Table 9.3   Rail electrification in larger European countries

Larger European Countries	Electrification (%)
Italy	72
Spain	64
France	58
Germany	53
UK	38

SOURCE: Statistica Research Department, Hamburg (2021).

airplanes and buses. The high-speed train network under construction in the UK (HS2) is expected to reduce carbon dioxide emissions by 400,000 tonnes per year. Each country should consider inter-city high-speed rail networks, with key routes such as Los Angeles to San Francisco and Washington to New York in the USA, St Petersburg to Moscow in Russia, Mumbai to Delhi in India, or Melbourne to Sydney in Australia being ripe for such a change.

9.4.   How Six Sigma Is Helping Green Transports Initiatives

The biggest player in green transports is Electric Cars or EVs. Car manufacturers already have all the requirements to benefit from high-level Six Sigma methodology. The industry produces complex products requiring very high-quality standards. The organisations are global, big and have many talented full-time employees. The largest car manufacturer, Toyota, constitutes the 'temple' of Lean Thinking or Toyota Production System (TPS), which is the integral part of Lean Six Sigma. Ford Motors has already demonstrated its commitment to Six Sigma by training its 350 senior executives, including its CEO and more than 10,000 employees, in various aspects of Six Sigma, producing both Black Belts and Green Belts. The application of Lean Six Sigma techniques has enabled multinational companies to eliminate more than US $2.19 billion in waste over the last fifteen years. However, it must be said that there were also some obstacles for implementation. These were an initial lack of commitment, finding time and money, and data needs. In spite of these impediments, Ford has completed about 10,000 Six Sigma projects since the early 2000s.

Toyota Production System (TPS) has been blended with Six Sigma methodology to create a potent Lean Six Sigma programme. The outcome of such an effective programme has led to a high-performance culture and enabled the company to hold the position of being the top profitable car manufacturer. Toyota has revolutionised the hybrid car market over the last two decades. During this period, according to Toyota, hybrid cars saved over 120 million tonnes of carbon dioxide compared to equivalent petrol cars. In 2022, Toyota is going to join the line-up of full electric vehicles. It is a given that Toyota has applied TPS/Lean Six Sigma principles to manufacture and supply its Yaris or Corolla hybrid models and will also apply the methodology to bZ4X models.

There is evidence (Chaurasia et al., 2019) that car manufacturers in India and nearly all car manufacturers in Europe (e.g. Audi, BMW, Daimler-Benz, Volkswagen, Nissan) are engaged in delivering EVs or hybrid cars and also have applied some form of Lean Six Sigma to improve productivity and reduce waste.

Tesla Inc. has made a powerful brand name for itself under the leadership of Elon Musk. As shown in Case Example 9.2, their success was helped by the application of Lean Six Sigma in Tesla's manufacturing processes.

Case Example 9.2 Elon Musk Capitalises on Lean Six Sigma

Tesla Inc. is one of Elon Musk's three major companies, based in Palo Alto, California, manufacturing electric vehicles. The Gigafactory in Nevada from Tesla's energy division will be the biggest factory in the world for lithium ion batteries. Many are calling the Tesla Model 3 (costing around $35,000 in the USA) the Model T of our time, a breakthrough new electric vehicle. As the only dedicated electric car manufacturer, Musk has engaged in clever strategies like First Principle Thinking and Lean Six Sigma to grow his company into a globally recognised brand.

Supported by the Six Sigma principles, as advocated by Peter Peterka of 'Global Six Sigma', the company is focused on a philosophy of enhancing efficiencies in their processes. It takes Tesla three days to build a car, starting from raw materials through to finishing the very last detail. The company embraced the Lean Six Sigma core principle, 'no extra processing that doesn't add value' and also DMAIC methodology. Tesla's adaptation of DMAIC has been in three major steps:

- Identification of weakness (Define and Measure)
- Improvement of weakness (Analyse and Improve)
- Application of control measures (Control)

The success of Tesla was reflected when the company booked close to $14 billion in deposit-backed advance sales in under three weeks through the direct-to-consumer launch of the Model 3 in 2018. The Model 3 is the world's all-time best-selling plug-in electric vehicle (PEV).

There is also good evidence of the application of Six Sigma or Lean Six Sigma in rail infrastructure, as Case Example 9.3 and Case Example 9.4 illustrate.

Case Example 9.3   Lean Six Sigma at Network Rail UK

Network Rail Limited is the infrastructure manager of most of the railway network in Great Britain. It is a public body of the UK government and employs around 42,000 employees. In 2013, rail services were severely affected by regular delays in passenger trains and Bourton Consulting Group were asked to investigate.

(continued)

(continued)

Their consultants identified five areas causing over 50% of the delays: Points, Track Circuits, Signalling, Seasonal Preparedness and Operational Procedures. Working with Network Rail, senior staff consultants introduced a Lean Six Sigma programme across 1,200 selected people.

Full-time leaders were trained as Black Belts, leaders of smaller-scale projects were schooled as Green Belts while part-time project team members became Yellow Belts. All classroom training was supported by about 300 real projects. As a result, £60 million in efficiency savings were achieved by Lean Six Sigma projects. Lean Six Sigma improvements were also recognised as a key contributing factor behind the 50% reduction of train delays.

Case Example 9.4   Six Sigma in HS1

The Channel Tunnel High Speed Rail Link (HS1) is the first ever high-speed railway in the UK, capable of speeds of up to 300 kmph. It comprises 100 kilometres between London and the Channel Tunnel near Dover, with three stations and two depots. Rail Link Engineering (RLE) was appointed as Project Manager. The group was a consortium of construction companies formed between Arup, Bechtel, Halcrow and Systra. At the height of construction in 2001, the combined workforce of LCR (London and Continental Railway) and RLE was over 1,000, and at the closure stage the figure was 350. The completed £5.8 billion project opened on time and within budget and was delivered for commercial operation to Eurostar on 14 November 2007.

Bechtel was the first major engineering and construction company to adopt Six Sigma, a data-driven approach to improving efficiency and quality, for major projects. On big rail modernisation schemes in the UK, including the HS1 project, Bechtel teams used Six Sigma to minimise costly train delays caused by engineering work, and in so doing reduced the 'break in' period for the renovated high-speed tracks.

The introduction of Six Sigma to the HS1 scheme delivered both cost savings and programme benefits. The Six Sigma programme trained 23 Black Belts and around 250 Green Belts and Yellow Belts. A further 100+ senior managers were educated to act as Champions on improvement projects. In fact, over 500 such improvement projects were completed, which in turn led to a cost saving/avoidance of at least £40 million. These ventures covered and benefitted a wide range of activities across the whole HS1 undertaking, including numerous architectural, civil and railway construction endeavours. Consequently, this had the effect of ensuring timely third-party methodology approvals, facilitating procurement, accelerating drawing reviews and allowing the judicious generation of construction record documentation. It is evident that some of these improvement projects, such the reduction of lead time in methodology approvals and drawing reviews, also applied Lean Thinking concepts.

9.5. How Green Six Sigma Can Help Green Transport Initiatives Further

There is clear evidence of the application of Six Sigma/Lean Six Sigma methodology in the transport sector in Case Examples 9.2, 9.3 and 9.4. Green Six Sigma, comprising both the tool sets of Six Sigma and Lean Six Sigma, should be very effective in all new green transport projects, whether they are for passenger cars, trucks and buses, trains, ships or airplanes. Thus, any new and future green transport initiatives, especially in the manufacturing sector, should adopt the Green Six Sigma approach to ensure both cost benefits and sustainable outcomes.

As indicated in Chapter 7, the distinctive additional contributions of Green Six Sigma include:

- A comprehensive performance management system supported by a periodic self-assessment to monitor and sustain performance levels (see Chapter 4).
- A regular senior management review (e.g. Sales and Operations Planning) to include Green Six Sigma projects (see Chapter 4).
- Application of carbon footprint tools and software (see Chapters 5 and 6).
- Application of Material Flow Account (see Chapter 5).

9.6. Summary

Although transports are not the biggest polluter compared to energy, agriculture and industry, their impact on the environment is arguably most visible. We are making good progress in electrifying passenger cars and trains, but we still face a major challenge to find zero carbon solutions for long-distance haulage by trucks and buses as well as air travel. The growth in online shopping has also increased the volume of local deliveries by vans. We can of course aim to use electric vans but green solutions for trucks and buses are still a long way from being driven by hydrogen-powered internal combustion engines. The alternative low carbon aviation fuels are still in development. A further problem is that there are not yet biofuels available in sufficient quantity suitable to run cargo ships or cruise ships.

Therefore, we need more investment and research to develop cost effective and proven solutions for longer distance transport, whether by trucks, buses, airplanes or ships.

Green Tips

- We are making good progress in electrifying passenger cars but we still do not have practical solutions for the long-haul road transport.
- The alternative low carbon aviation fuels are still in development.
- There should be further expansions of high-speed rails between neighbouring big cities in larger countries.
- Green solutions overlap each other. For example, if we find a solution in hydrogen we may not need magic batteries.
- Building on the success of Lean Six Sigma in green transports, Green Six Sigma can add the extra value of sustainability.

Chapter 10

Green Six Sigma and Retrofitting Buildings

'I have spent a fortune to distant shores and looked at lofty mountains and boundless oceans, and yet I haven't found time to take a few steps from my house to look at a single dew drop on a single blade of grass.'

– Rabindranath Tagore

10.1.   Introduction

Buildings contribute only 6% of total global greenhouse gas transmissions, thus ranking last of all sectors. Some reports (RIBA, 2021) have estimated that the contribution of buildings to greenhouse gas emissions is in fact much higher. Regardless, the important point is that this is one area where we as individuals can start to do something – now.

The term 'buildings' covers both industrial and residential structures. Residential building operations account for 72% of the total emissions from this sector. This chapter focuses on the retrofitting of buildings, i.e. the addition or replacement of new features to improve energy efficiency and reduce carbon emissions.

As with other sectors, if we are going to attain net-zero emissions we will have to minimise all the greenhouse gases caused by building operations around the world.

10.2. Guiding Factors of Retrofitting Buildings

In building operations the main areas of energy consumption are heating, cooling, lighting and cooking. When considering lighting I have included the electricity used to run television, radio, computers and other home appliances. Energy consumption for lighting is higher in advanced economies compared to poorer countries.

Heating and cooling is an interesting area. In general, in hot countries in the tropics region we need more cooling devices (with electric fans and air conditioners) and in colder countries, naturally, we need more heating. However, many nations in the subtropical region (e.g. USA, Japan, China, Australia) spend huge amounts of energy on both heating **and** cooling. Air conditioning is also essential in some industries, including for cooling server centres containing thousands of computers. Table 10.1 shows the proportion of houses fitted with air conditioning in the top five countries.

It is likely that people will be adding to this global number of air conditioning units as the population grows and heat waves become more frequent. However, these A/C units not only consume a large amount of electricity, they also contain fluorine (F-gas), which is a powerful contributor to global warming.

Table 10.1   Air conditioning in households in the top five countries

Country	Households with A/C (%)
Japan	85
USA	84
South Korea	83
Saudi Arabia	62
China	60

SOURCE: Gates (2021).

Domestic boilers and water heaters account for about a third of all emissions that come from domestic buildings. A/C units run on electricity, which may also come from renewable sources, but boilers and water heaters in our households mostly run on fossil fuels. Fortunately, we have some proven technology already available to decarbonise our homes by retrofitting existing equipment. For example, we already have heat pumps, electric water heaters and heating systems and solar panels to provide domestic electricity.

10.3. How Retrofitting Buildings Provides Solutions for Reducing Greenhouse Gas Emissions

The path to a net-zero carbon strategy for domestic dwellings is likely to comprise the following steps that everyone can try to take:

1. Reduce energy losses and energy consumption
2. Replace fossil fuel boilers and water heaters
3. Seek to use renewable energy
4. Apply a circular economy

Let's look at each solution in more detail.

10.3.1. Reduce Energy Losses and Energy Consumption

There are many ways in which we can insulate our homes but first we should consider how to minimise heat loss from our buildings. In poorly constructed homes, the amount of heat loss varies according to the source of exit from the structure. For example, we are squandering heat through external walls (40%), the roof (25%), windows and doors (20%), the ground floor (10%) and finally via draughts (5%).

To draught-proof our home, we should block up any unwanted gaps (with the exception of ventilators) that let cold air in and warm air out. This is the cheapest and most effective approach to save energy. There are various inexpensive ways of preventing draughts, e.g. self-adhesive foam strips for doors and windows, a letter box brush, chimney cap and silicone fillers around pipework. It is also important to make the house airtight as far as possible by replacing glass windows and external glass doors with double glazed units.

It is easy to follow a number of energy saving, common sense actions including the following suggestions:

- Install a smart thermostat and set it at the desired temperature and timings.
- Install a smart meter to monitor energy consumption.
- Use energy efficient appliances.
- Choose energy saving LED electric bulbs.
- Turn off standby appliances and computers when not in use.
- Be smarter about hot water usage, for example, shower rather than running a long bath.

Most newly built homes are fitted with loft insulation and older homes can save up to 25% of potential heat losses by investing in loft insulation. This insulation will last over 40 years and the payback period is about two years. Mineral and wool sold in rolls like a blanket is the most common loft insulation material.

The most effective method allowing protection against heat loss from walls is so-called cavity wall insulation. This involves injecting an insulation material into the void between the inner and outer layers of brickwork. It works in the same way in which a thermos flask keeps a drink hot, by creating a layer around the house. Most newly built homes have cavity wall insulation as standard but older houses (such as those built before 1920 in the UK) do not have cavity walls. Here a possible solution is external solid wall insulation. There are many insulation materials (such as aluminium composite panel or rain screen cladding) which can be used for cladding external walls. However, following a number of fire tragedies (e.g. Grenfell Tower, UK, 2017), it is an essential prerequisite that cladding materials conform to building regulatory standards.

Appropriate floor insulation materials (e.g. expanded polystyrene sheets, polyurethane spray) can be used to insulate floorboards on the ground level of houses and to seal the gaps between floors and skirting boards. It is also important to insulate water tanks by using approved cylinder jackets and water pipes by polyethylene foam insulation.

10.3.2. Replace Fossil Fuel Boilers and Water Heaters

Heating systems in residential homes come in two parts – one section is for the supply of hot water to bathrooms, the kitchen and washing machines, while the other aspect is for hot water radiators. Many homes in the UK and rich countries are provided with a central heating system, which serves both hot water and heating. The supply of energy in this system comes from fossil fuel boilers. There are two types of fossil fuel boilers. Firstly, combination or 'combi' boilers provide hot water on demand for domestic use as well as central heating, and are a good choice for smaller homes. With the second type, a heat-only boiler (also known as a conventional boiler system), the hot water is stored in a hot water cylinder or storage tank. This system is suitable for a larger home with greater demand, where several people frequently need to use hot water at the same time. They also require space for a cold water feed tank, usually housed in the loft.

During July 2021 I interviewed 12 UK suppliers specialising in replacing fossil fuel boilers to find cost estimates for different possible scenarios. It should be noted that the figures that follow are indicative only.

In order to replace fossil fuel boilers and water heaters we have different options depending on the type and size of households. If the household is a one- or two-bedroom apartment then a simple solution could be to install a stand-alone electric water heater with a hot water cylinder for domestic hot water supply and plug-in electric convector heaters or electric storage heaters. A typical cost for this solution for a small apartment is around £3,000 in the UK.

For a medium-sized household with three or four bedrooms fitted with a fossil fuel central heating system, an energy saving alternative could be to replace the fossil fuel boiler with an appropriate

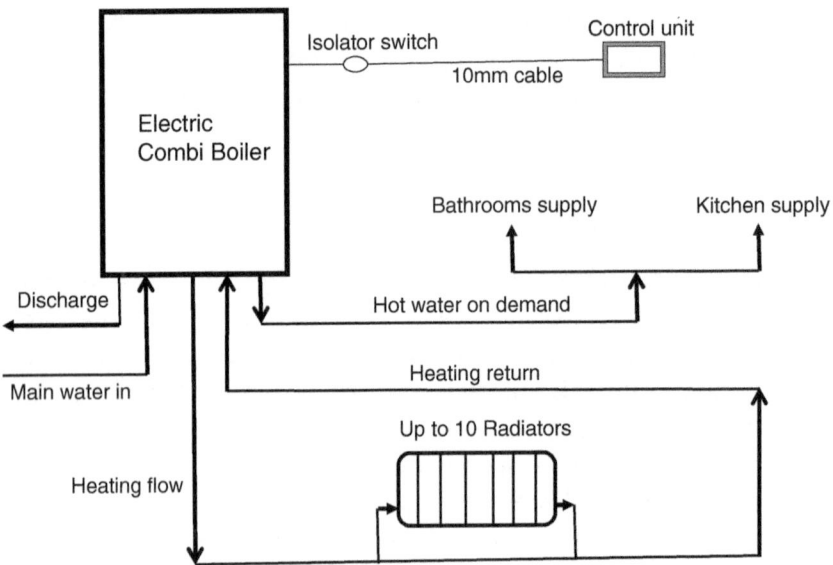

Figure 10.1 Electric combi boiler solution

electric combi boiler. As shown in Figure 10.1, this solution has the advantage that it will retain the existing radiators and can be retro-fitted in the existing space. The cost of this type of solution could be £4,000 to £8,000 in the UK.

Retrofitting an electric combi boiler is a simpler solution but it is limited to smaller properties and at present the running cost of a gas boiler is more economical. It is envisaged that a longer-term green energy solution for households is likely to be electric heat pumps.

A heat pump is either air sourced or ground sourced. As shown in the schematic diagram in Figure 10.2, an air source heat pump works rather like a reverse fridge. The heat pump is installed outside and outside particles of air are blown over a network of tubes filled with a refrigerant to turn it into gas. The gas then passes through a compressor. The compressed hot gases pass into a heat exchanger surrounded by cool water in order to heat this water. This is circulated around the house to provide heating and hot water. Then the refrigerant condenses into cool liquid and starts the cycle again.

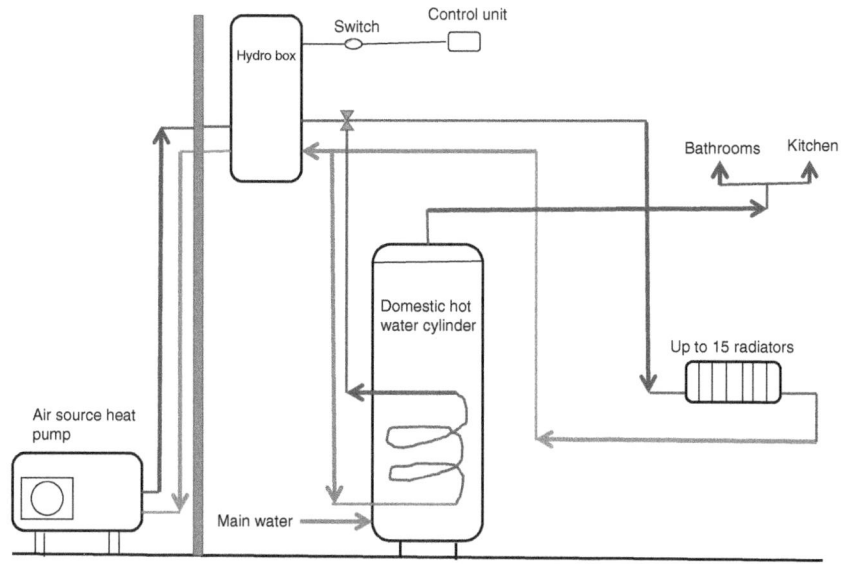

Figure 10.2 Air source heat pump: a schematic diagram

An air source heat pump (ASHP) costs from £8,000 to £18,000 to install in the UK. A Renewable Energy Incentive scheme is also operational in some countries including the UK. It works both as a heater or an air cooler. Air source heat pumps have key advantages: energy bills are lower than comparable gas heating systems, and they are known to work efficiently in severely cold countries such as Canada. However, an ASHP also poses drawbacks, including its noisy operation and a requirement for larger radiators.

Ground source heat pumps (GSHP) are also good low carbon heating systems, and they have higher efficiency rates and lower running costs than ASHPs. A GSHP makes use of the ground's constant temperature and uses that to both heat up homes and supply domestic hot water. A GSHP absorbs low-grade surrounding energy from the ground and then compresses and condenses this energy to a higher temperature. Heat is transferred to the heating and hot water system of the house, as shown in a schematic diagram in Figure 10.3. The fluid from the heat exchanger then continues its circuit back to the submerged pipework to commence the cycle all over again.

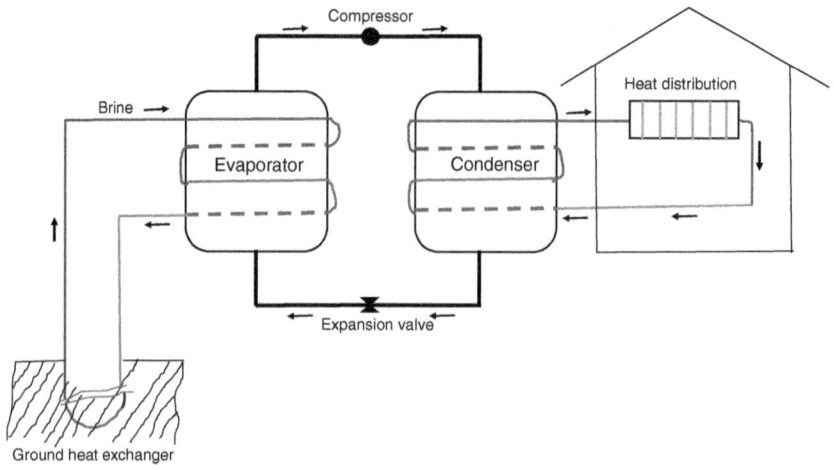

Figure 10.3   Ground source heat pump: a schematic diagram

By comparison with an ASHP, a GSHP has several advantages as it is not noisy and is both more energy efficient and cheaper to run. However, the main disadvantage of a GSHP is it very expensive to install (in the region of between £20,000 to £40,000 in the UK) and it requires a lot of ground space. Households in the UK would also require planning permission. Thus, an ASHP could be considered for a medium-sized house and a GSHP is more suitable for a larger property with available land. Heat pumps are more attractive in countries requiring both heating and air conditioning (e.g. USA, Canada, Japan).

10.3.3.   Seek to Use Renewable Energy

A steady forward approach for a household aiming to attain lower carbon emissions is to switch to a renewable energy supplier. However, herein lies the problem. Some major suppliers in the UK (for instance, E-On, Centrica, Pure Planet) are claiming to be renewable suppliers, but while this may be true, their approach at present is likely to be offsetting carbon by planting trees all over the world. There are some suppliers (e.g. Octopus Energy, Ecotricity) who have a better reputation as truly renewable energy suppliers. Centrica have invested in EDF Energy's existing and future nuclear plants (e.g. at Hinkley Point and Sizewell in the UK) and aim to increase their share of nuclear source electricity.

The most genuine method of using a source of renewable energy for a household is to consider domestic solar energy. As explained in Chapter 7, solar panels, also known as photovoltaic systems (PV systems), covert the sun's energy into electricity that can power our households. The system uses semiconductor technology to convert energy from sunlight into direct current (DC) electricity. This current is then passed through an inverter to convert it into alternating current (AC). As shown in Figure 10.4, the system can be either grid-connected or stand-alone.

Grid-connected systems are linked to the local utility grid to ensure a continuous supply of electricity. When the domestic solar panel system generates more electricity than the household needs, the surplus energy can be exported back to the national grid. Likewise, if more electricity is needed the grid can supply this. Stand-alone systems are not connected to the grid, but instead charge a solar battery system. These batteries store the electricity generated by solar panels. The stored electricity from these batteries will be used to operate household appliances. Stand-alone systems are operated in areas with local utility grids and are typically more

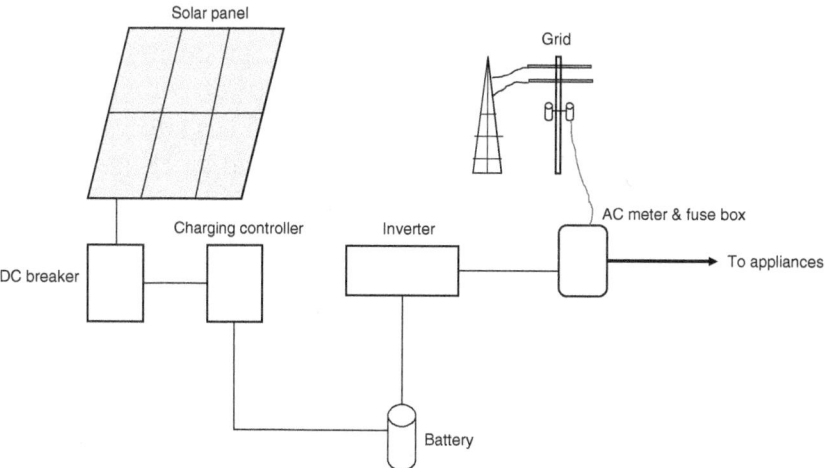

Figure 10.4 Domestic solar energy: a schematic diagram

expensive to include the cost of expensive storage batteries. The average domestic solar panel system, without storage batteries, costs between £5,000 and £10,000 in the UK.

Solar thermal collectors do not have PV cells and use sunlight directly to heat up water that is stored in a cylinder. The hot water from the cylinder can then be used for domestic heating needs. Solar thermal panels are roof-mounted, just like solar PV panels, but look slightly different, as instead of cells they have multiple pipes to heat water.

10.3.4. *Apply a Circular Economy*

As defined in Chapter 3, a circular economy is aimed at eliminating waste and the continual use of resources. The approach is to reuse resources, repair defects, refurbish facilities, rebuild products to original specifications, and recycle wastes to create a closed-loop system. The outcome is minimising the use of resource input, wastes, pollution and carbon emissions.

The application of a circular economy can benefit all sectors of our economy. In the context of retrofitting buildings two specific areas will be discussed: the construction industry and household appliances.

According to a recent report (Retro-First, 2021), every year some 50,000 buildings are demolished in the UK, producing 126 million tonnes of waste and accounting for 10% of carbon emissions. RIBA (the Royal Institute of British Architects) has advocated that the demolition of buildings should be halted and buildings should be preserved and re-purposed. Materials should be salvaged and re-used whenever possible. RIBA argues that the construction of large buildings gobbles up fossil fuel–hungry materials (e.g. steel, cement, aluminium and plastics) and hence developers ought to be more considerate and should be obliged to refurbish. The Institute has requested that it should be allowed to force firms to calculate the total carbon impact of each project they wish to undertake. The Royal Institute of Chartered Surveyors (RICS), in partnership with RIBA and other organisations, is developing the first international standard for reporting carbon emissions across all areas of construction.

The campaign by these influential professional bodies is on the same page as the principles of the circular economy. The end goal of a circular economy is to retain the value of materials and resources indefinitely with little or no residual wastes. This requires a transformational change in the way that buildings are designed, built, operated and demolished. Government intervention in both taxation and legislation should help. For example, retrofitting could be tax-exempt like new constructions and all new build proposals should indicate how much carbon will be emitted during the manufacturing and construction process.

The principles of a circular economy should also be applied to the 'replace or repair' policy of home appliances (e.g. washing machines, dishwashers, cookers, fridges). Their suppliers should be obliged to produce and supply spare parts for, say, 10 years so that appliances can be easily repaired. Suppliers should also introduce an exchange plan and offer to take the customer's old item away when delivering the new one. As shown in Figure 10.5, the cycle of the circular economy can work well and to the benefit of both suppliers and customers.

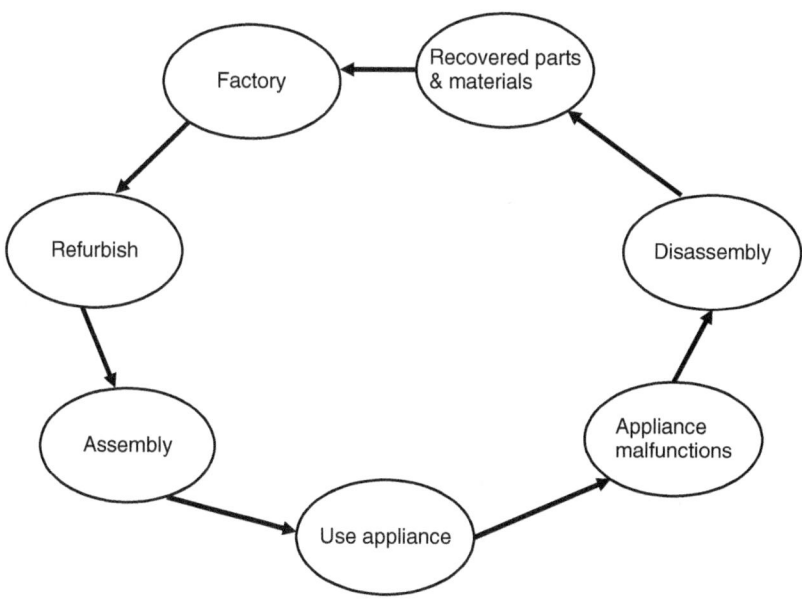

Figure 10.5 Circular economy for home appliances

The recycling of products also applies to electrical and electronic items (such as televisions or computers). The Waste Electrical and Electronic Equipment (WEEE) directive regulates the manner in which manufacturers and retailers in European countries should behave regarding recycling.

10.4. How Six Sigma Is Helping Retrofitting Buildings Initiatives

There is no significant visible evidence of the application of any type of Six Sigma methodology in the manufacture and supply of electric boilers or heat pumps. However, I have found some publications showing the application of Six Sigma research in delivering domestic solar energy, as discussed in the following examples.

Case Example 10.1   Six Sigma Approach to Optimise Solar Cell Manufacturing

Domestic solar energy systems use silicon-based photovoltaics (PV) cells in solar panels. In general, a silicon solar cell process uses either p-type or n-type doped silicon as the starting material. In a research paper (Prasad et al., 2016), boron-doped wafers were considered and phosphorus was used as the doping material. The paper describes the application of Six Sigma DMAIC methodology for improving the throughput of the phosphorous process. The optimised process was implemented in production and as a result an effective gain of 0.9 MW was reported per annum.

Case Example 10.2   Six Sigma Approach to Domestic Solar Energy Efficiency Programme

Mowris el al. (2006) argue that the increased emphasis on energy efficiency to reduce energy use and mitigate global warming requires rigorous evaluations based on the International

---

Performance Measurement and Verification Protocol (IPMVP). Increased focus on customer satisfaction and resource efficiency to improve profitability has motivated businesses worldwide to adopt Six Sigma strategies. Research data in this paper shows how Six Sigma strategies can provide a framework to measure and verify energy savings and performance metrics at critical steps in the supply chain of domestic solar energy systems (i.e. design, manufacturing, installation and service). The authors advocate a publicly funded energy efficiency programme to transform the renewable energy market, with particular reference to domestic solar energy systems, so that the cost to deliver energy efficiency products can be minimised. This research also indicates that this goal can be achieved by incorporating IPMVP and Six Sigma into programme design, implementation, and evaluation. The Six Sigma approach encompassing IPMVP is applicable to assess energy efficiency in all forms of energy systems.

10.5.   How Green Six Sigma Can Help Retrofitting Houses Initiatives Further

It is evident that Six Sigma methodology has not been effectively applied in initiatives related to retrofitting houses. Therefore, there are significant opportunities for Green Six Sigma in this virtually untapped sector. The question is, simply – is it worthwhile for manufacturers and suppliers of electric boilers, air source heat pumps, ground source heat pumps and solar energy systems to adopt Green Six Sigma tools and techniques in order to be cost effective? The answer is certainly 'yes'. The majority of these suppliers are small and medium size enterprises (SMEs) and they do not need to retain high profile and expensive Six Sigma consultants. They can train their key employees using a week-long training session for Green Belt or a three-day training session for Yellow Belt and then apply the 'fitness for purpose' Green Six Sigma approach. The available government grants and bursaries for adult learners (e.g. UK government grants) should help SMEs.

With adequate training, Green Six Sigma can show break-through results in the supply chain of retrofitting building initiatives. The data-driven and process-focussed DMAIC methodology will improve the design, performance and manufacturing costs of boilers, heat pumps, solar panels and associated components. Any outcome will be underpinned by sustainable processes and reduced carbon footprints.

Thus, the benefits of the circular economy as discussed in Section 10.3.4 are a fundamental tenet of Green Six Sigma culture.

10.6. Summary

In this chapter general principles, processes and the appropriateness of retrofitting building initiatives have been discussed. It is important to note that the success of these household-related initiatives depend on us, the customers. The majority of action points are customer driven 'pull' processes. All facilities and help are available in the marketplace now and are ready to apply. Some practical guidelines are included to manage energy economy and retrofit appropriate domestic energy systems. For example, one should consider combi electric boilers for smaller households and air source heat pumps for medium households. Ground source heat pumps should not be contemplated unless the property is large with adequate garden space. The pay-back period of a solar energy system is usually eight years. However, it is strongly advisable that professional surveys by multiple suppliers and the eligibility of government grants are properly investigated before selecting any retrofitting system for a household.

The supply chain of the retrofitting houses sector thus constitutes fertile ground for Green Six Sigma to reap sustainable rewards.

Green Tips

- Ensure the insulation of all sources of heat losses in the house, e.g. loft, walls, floor and windows.
- Consider combi electric boilers in small houses and air source heat pumps for medium-sized properties.
- Long pay-back period for total solar energy solutions.
- Hydrogen solutions for home heating is not yet feasible.
- Government grants are necessary to implement climate change initiatives for retrofitting homes.
- Green Six Sigma can be very effective for SMEs in home retrofitting supply and installations.

Chapter 11
Green Six Sigma and Climate Adaptation

'The measure of intelligence is the ability to change.'
– *Albert Einstein*

11.1. Introduction

'Climate change adaptation is the process of adjusting to current or expected climate change and its effects' (IPCC, 2014a). Even taking into account that some progress has been achieved due to present climate change initiatives, it is a certainty that we will breach 1.5 degrees centigrade of global warming in the early 2030s and may remain unprepared. The global reality of the climate crisis could hardly be more serious now. July 2021 alone saw the effects of several chaotic weather events; over 200 people perished in floods in Germany, the Netherlands and Belgium, causing unprecedented scenes of devastation in northern Europe, while at least 50 people died and a further 400,000 people were displaced in central China after heavy downpours. In western India many properties were flooded and 125 people perished in a torrential monsoon. At the same time in western Canada and the USA, a blistering set of heat

291

waves provided the tinder for wildfires to rage for months, while drought threatens areas from Algeria to Yemen.

As I write this chapter, Covid-19 has killed over 4 million people and the UK government is advising us that, in the long term, we must adjust and learn to live with the virus because we have vaccines. Many of the lessons learned from the pandemic also apply to climate change. The world has made remarkable progress by working together in developing and testing vaccines in record time. The same degree of concerted effort is needed world-wide to mitigate and adapt to the consequences of global warming. By investing in climate change initiatives and R&D we can both rescue the post pandemic economy and avoid a climate disaster.

The fundamental strategy of climate change preparation is 'Predict, Prevent and Preserve'. In terms of prediction, scientists have already forecast the longer-term causes and effects of climate change. We also need continuous prediction of climate fluctuations to prepare for events such as cyclones, floods, heavy downpours and extraordinary heat waves. Prevention is rooted in the elimination of the root causes (e.g. greenhouse gas emissions) as well as mitigation initiatives, as discussed in previous chapters. Preservation lies in dedicated adaptation to the changes to our lifestyles, health and safety caused by climate change in spite of preventative initiatives. In this chapter, climate adaptation processes and actions will be discussed under the following headings:

- Climate Adaptation in the Global Community
- Climate Adaptation in Clean Energy
- Climate Adaptation in Green Supply Chains
- Climate Adaptation in Green Transports
- Climate Adaptation in Retrofitting Houses
- Climate Adaptation and Infrastructure Projects
- Climate Adaptation and Innovation

In each section the ways in which Green Six Sigma can help by making additional contributions will also be discussed.

11.2. Climate Adaptation in the Global Community

At the time of writing there are less than 100 days until more than 190 world leaders will gather in Glasgow at the United Nations COP 26 climate conference on 31 October 2021. This is an excellent opportunity to reboot climate change targets and initiatives. The UK Government calls the summit the world's 'last best chance'. Although I will complete my manuscript before the conference, this book will be on the market after it takes place. Hence it may be presumptuous, but I will suggest that the agreed communique should include the following:

1. There will be no new oil, gas or coal exploration projects beyond the end of 2021 as recommended by the International Energy Agency (IEA).
2. An increase on the $100 billion (promised in the Paris Climate Agreement) by rich nations to support poorer countries in cutting emissions and a pledge to deliver this as soon as possible.
3. Introduce annual audits by the United Nations of top 10 greenhouse gas emitters in order to monitor the targets of the Paris Climate Agreement.
4. Set new targets for each of the signed-up countries, e.g.
   - No new diesel or petrol vehicles after 2030
   - No fossil fuel domestic heating after 2035
   - Reduction in Methane emission
5. Introduce afforestation targets for each country as it is difficult to monitor voluntary carbon offsets or 'greenwashing'.
6. Deliver $100 billion fund for climate initiatives to poorer countries ASAP.

As host, the UK is pivotal to the success of any planned objectives. This could start by committing to end all new fossil fuel projects, and rolling out a nationwide clean energy programme with grants to accelerate decarbonised domestic heating.

How Green Six Sigma Can Help

As discussed in preceding chapters, Green Six Sigma can accelerate most initiatives by its holistic approach and ensure the sustainability of both processes and the environment. In the 1950s and 1960s the United Nations rolled out its Work Study to developing countries with the proactive support of the International Labour Organisation (ILO, 1978). Bearing in mind the success of the Work Study programme, the United Nations should consider a similar global agenda designed to roll out Green Six Sigma.

11.3. Climate Adaptation in Clean Energy

As noted in Chapter 7, the biggest source of greenhouse gases is fossil fuel power stations and good progress has been made in the field of obtaining clean energy supplies from renewable sources and nuclear power. However, the current programmes in clean energy all over the world suggest that some amount of carbon dioxide from other energy sources in the future is inevitable. There are two sources of alternative fuels that can be considered and have the advantage of having processes in place for adaptation. These low carbon energy funds are biofuels and so-called 'green gases' (e.g. biogas and hydrogen produced by electricity). We may also have to live with power stations run by natural gas, which is considered to be less polluting than other fossil fuels.

We can either capture the carbon dioxide from the exhaust pipes of power plants and bury it in underground rocks or actively remove greenhouse gases from the atmosphere for storage. Major oil and gas companies (e.g. Exxon Mobile, Shell and BP) are investing heavily in carbon capture research projects. ExxonMobil has an equity share in about 20% of the world's carbon capture capacity. Shell has developed and patented carbon capture technology utilising a re-generatable amine (a nitrogen atom) that offers cutting-edge performance.

How Green Six Sigma Can Help

Unfortunately, most of the business practices carried out by big companies contribute to waste and non-renewable energy. This is where Green Six Sigma can help oil and gas corporations improve their waste management. The DMADV (Define, Measure, Analyse,

Design and Verify) programme is a modified version of DMAIC and this methodology will lead to more effective research in the realm of carbon capture technology.

11.4.   Climate Adaptation in Green Supply Chains

Green supply chains will have a central role in supporting societal adaptation to the physical impacts of climate change, especially in more directly affected sectors such as manufacturing, agriculture, forestry, construction or transportation.

The supply chain discipline has progressed towards a common understanding of resilience to adapt to changing business conditions because of the emergence of new competitors, new products and altered political, economic and legal conditions. Adaptation plans for coping with the Covid-19 pandemic and climate change are also beginning to emerge. There is a growing emphasis internationally on engaging supply chain businesses in adaptation, given their potential to develop technologies and innovative solutions, and enhancing the cost-effectiveness of certain adaptation measures. Large national and multinational corporations are among the key actors in this respect. Already, many of these corporations are purportedly taking steps to adapt their operations to climate change, as Case Example 11.1 illustrates.

Case Example 11.1   Unilever Sets Out New Actions to Adapt to Climate Change

Unilever has been leading the industry on sustainable sourcing practices for over a decade, and 90% of its forest-related commodities are certified as sustainably sourced. Unilever's climate adaptation strategy of 2020 clearly states that brands will collectively invest €1 billion over the next ten years in projects focused

(continued)

(continued)

on landscape restoration, reforestation, carbon sequestration, wildlife protection and water preservation. Unilever has been the industry leader in sustainable and ethical sourcing policies for over a decade. Unilever's ice cream brand Ben & Jerry's initiative is already underway to reduce GHG emissions from dairy farms and another brand, Knorr, is supporting farmers to grow food more sustainably.

Unilever aims to attain net-zero emissions from all its products by 2039. To achieve this goal 11 years ahead of the 2050 Paris Agreement deadline, the company prioritises building partnerships with its suppliers who have also committed to their own science-based targets. This transparency regarding corporate carbon footprint is used as an accelerator and a system is set up for all suppliers to declare, on each invoice, the carbon footprint of the goods and services provided. Unilever has also introduced a pioneering agricultural code for all suppliers, built on green farming practices. The corporation will also join the 2030 Water Resources Group, a multi-stakeholder platform hosted by the World Bank.

It is pivotal that all major organisations, both in the manufacturing and service sectors, publish their 'Net-Zero Carbon Plan' and evaluate its progress every year as part of their Annual Report. This plan will also include the systems and processes in place to adapt to the consequences of climate change. A well-designed and executed blueprint is most likely to project the organisation as a leading company of environmental sustainability and act as a competitive advantage. There are a few sustainable business awards in different sectors of the supply chain that are independently judged by an expert jury representing a cross-section of the business sector. These awards also act as a facilitator towards a more sustainable future.

A vital link in the foods supply chain is agriculture. Climate change presents significant risks for agriculture as farmers, whether in a rich country or a poor one, are certain to be adversely affected by any future changes in higher mean temperatures, drought and floods caused by climate change. Adaptation pathways planning should be in place to allow stakeholders to identify and evaluate adaptation options.

In July 2021, the Prince of Wales launched a booklet to translate 50 sustainability terms into a language that is more accessible to farmers. Bill Gates (Gates, 2021) suggested that CGIAR (the Consultative Group for International Agricultural Research) could help farmers provide a wider variety of crops and livestock so that one setback does not have the effect of wiping them out. The National Food Strategy Report of the UK, published in June 2021, recommends that the UK government should "nudge" people towards plant-based foods in an effort to cut national meat consumption in the interests of the environment and animal welfare. We should also shore up our natural defences to protect agriculture – this is discussed further in Section 11.8.

How Green Six Sigma Can Help

Because Green Six Sigma focuses on reducing wastes and increasing efficiency, major corporations have implemented a variety of Six Sigma methodologies to improve their business processes. In doing so, their actions have significantly improved their waste management and production efficiencies. As a result, fewer resources were needed to create the same products. If less energy is required to manufacture products, this in turn leads to fewer carbon emissions and a reduced dependency on fossil fuel energy. With regard to climate adaptation activities, key stakeholders of a supply chain will also benefit from the application of Green Six Sigma to reduce wastes and ensure sustainable outcomes. With a 10% reduction of wastes in the supply chain sector, 2.9 billion tonnes of greenhouse gases will be removed from the atmosphere.

11.5.   Climate Adaptation in Green Transports

The transportation industry is emitting 14% of greenhouse gases and the aviation sector is responsible for a large portion of these emissions. Research studies (Lee et al., 2021) have modelled the impact of climate change-imposed constraints on the recoverability of airline networks. The climate change adaptation activities of multinational airlines have been focused on evaluating the costs of disruptions in the form of flight delays and cancellations, as well as passenger misconnections. There is also some evidence of research in the field of aviation fuels and finding an alternative to fossil fuel-based kerosene. A study by Seyam et al. (2021) has found that the maximum overall thermal efficiencies of hybrid turbofan engines are achieved by using a fuel composed of 75% methanol and 25% hydrogen, which reduces carbon emissions by 65% compared to fossil fuels. However, there is a long way to go before we see commercial airlines running on this low carbon fuel.

Both the aviation industry and oil and gas corporations are investing in innovative fuel concepts that may provide environmental benefits. While some of these are already being produced and used regularly in aircraft operations (e.g. Sustainable Aviation Fuels or SAF), others are still under research and development, such as Lower Carbon Aviation Fuels and Hydrogen. Air BP's SAF is called BP Biojet and is currently made from used cooking oil and other wastes (such as household wastes and algae). Traditional jet fuel is blended with SAF to make it suitable for long-haul flights. Air BP claims that SAF gives an impressive reduction of up to 80% in carbon emissions over the life cycle of the fuel compared to the traditional jet fuel that it replaces. In the continuing quest for carbon-free aviation fuel, research is ongoing to evaluate hydrogen as a possible solution in the future. However, several factors are currently against the possible use of hydrogen on commercial flights, such as on-board storage, safety concerns and the high cost of producing the fuel. We need more research to mitigate these challenges.

Hydrogen combustion engines are also the most likely solution for long-distance buses and trucks. Research on hydrogen-fuelled internal combustion to replace fossil fuels has been ongoing for decades. However, hydrogen engines still have the problems of lower volumetric efficiencies and frequent pre-ignition events relative to gasoline-fuelled engines. Therefore, we have to keep faith for a breakthrough in the path towards carbon-free long-distance road transports.

The progress regarding green passenger cars is encouraging. We are gradually adapting ourselves to using plug-in electric cars and perhaps all electric adaptation could be achieved in European countries by 2030. In doing so, we need to improve the infrastructure and replace fossil fuel service stations with electric charge point (ECP) stations. In the UK Tesco have implemented the availability of free electric charging bays at some 400 stores in a collaboration with Volkswagen and Pod Point, with a variety of power chargers all using completely green energy.

How Green Six Sigma Can Help

We need extensive research in the area of developing and improving carbon-free aviation fuel. More research is required to create safe and efficient hydrogen-fuelled internal combustion engines. Green Six Sigma has broad applications in an R&D context because R&D is fundamentally a series of problem-defining and problem-solving processes and there are appropriate Green Six Sigma tools on offer. For example, DFSS (Design for Six Sigma) is a Green Six Sigma tool that scientists can effectively use to accelerate R&D projects on alternative fuels.

11.6. Climate Adaptation in Retrofitting Houses

As consumers, all of us together can have a huge impact on the demand side of climate adaptation. We can influence the market by choosing the nature of the energy supply we have, what kind of transport we use, what sort of food we eat or what type of houses we live in. If all of us make individual changes towards carbon neutral products and services then this can add up to a huge total reduction in carbon emission. Fossil fuel driven suppliers will have to change to adapt to customers' choices.

The processes for climate adaptation in retrofitting houses has an overlap with the climate mitigation processes described in Chapter 10. These mitigation processes will also apply to climate adaptation practices in every household and should include:

1. Reduce energy losses and energy consumption.
2. Replace fossil fuel boilers and water heaters.
3. Seek to use renewable energy.
4. Apply a circular economy by reducing wastes and repairing appliances rather than discarding and replacing them.

We should also prepare against frequent flooding and excessive downpours. As short-term measures, households near potentially flood affected areas should arrange houses with quick-fit flood barriers at their doors and flood pumps should be installed in the local community. However, in order to attain viable longer-term solutions, national governments should invest in flood protection schemes and agile rescue and relief resources. Some examples of flood protection schemes will be discussed in Section 11.7. There are also many examples of flood relief operations over recent years as Case Example 11.2 illustrates.

Case Example 11.2   Flood Relief in Barbados

Barbados can be affected by tropical storms, causing serious flooding. In 2018 Storm Kirk deposited between 50 and 100 mm of rain in just 24 hours. The resultant flooding forced the closure of schools, universities and other public services. Flood barriers were manufactured in the UK and shipped out within 48 hours on a direct flight. A building company based in Barbados managed the installation works on the following day. It is expected that climate change will cause sea levels to rise and will undoubtedly lead to further flooding in Barbados.

In fact, supply chain professionals are undervalued in disaster relief operations. It is important that their expertise and resources are deployed to develop and deliver a quick response logistics support, as Case Example 11.3 illustrates.

Case Example 11.3   Hurricane Katrina Disaster Relief Mastered by Supply Chain Management

Referring to the Hurricane Katrina disaster in New Orleans in 2005, Walmart responded more quickly and was more effective in providing what was required than both the Federal Emergency Management Agency and Red Cross. While their speed of response was commendable, one could argue that Walmart was only doing what it does every day. Walmart delivered 2,500 containers to the region and set up satellite links for its stores that had lost phone or Internet service so that they could stay connected to headquarters.

New design concepts for residential buildings are required to enable low carbon dioxide operations and to adapt to climate change. Furthermore, any climate adaptation strategy for dwellings must also be cognisant of building regulations, new technologies and occupant needs. The good news is that our architects and builders do know how to build green buildings. One positive example is the Bullitt Center in Seattle, which has been designed to stay naturally warm in winter and remain cool in summer. The Center is also equipped with carbon neutral energy saving technologies. Although it is too expensive to build a perfect green residential house like the Bullit Center every time, we can still ensure that our energy efficient homes are constructed at an affordable cost. Architects are already designing eco-friendly energy efficient homes for the future to adapt to climate change. Some of these design features are summarised in Table 11.1.

Table 11.1   Climate adaption for house design

Climate and Energy Causes	Building Design Responses
Heating system	Air tightness
	All electric
	Heat pumps
	Solar panels
Floods	Air bricks
	Door guards
	Solid flooring
	Community flood defence
	Sustainable drainage (SUD) system
Storms	Reinforcement of building and roofs
	Robust guttering and drain pipes
	Vigilant maintenance
Cold events	Roof insulation
	Cavity wall insulation
	Smart meters
	Double/triple glazed windows
Heat waves	Shutters
	Smart glass windows
	Heat pumps as air coolers (if installed)
	Aerated concrete

As discussed in Chapter 10, rather than demolishing large office or residential buildings to build new multi-storeyed structures, builders should refurbish existing buildings to help them adapt to the consequences of climate change.

How Green Six Sigma Can Help

Six Sigma methodology and tools are proven to be very effective in delivering the quality standards and project deliverables required of building projects. Green Six Sigma will be equally effective as Six Sigma for building projects and in addition it will ensure the sustainability of outcomes as well as the all-important sustainability of the environment. The paradigm and processes of the circular economy are embedded in Green Six Sigma and are also central to the adaptation of climate change in both household practices and refurbishing larger buildings.

11.7.   Climate Adaptation and Infrastructure Projects

The Economist published an article on 30 May 2020 about the cyclone 'Amphan' and its effect. On 16 May an anticlockwise spiral of clouds over the Bay of Bengal detected by satellite warned of an imminent disaster. Four days later Amphan made landfall, gusting at up to 185 km per hour along the coast of West Bengal and Bangladesh. The number of fatalities in Bangladesh amounted to 20 while the death tolls for earlier cyclones had been in their thousands. What was the reason for the considerable saving of lives this time?

The answer lies in the fact that Bangladesh has now developed a layered adaptation plan with an early warning system to evacuate people to concrete cyclone shelters. Seawalls were also built with international support to protect stretches of coastlines. This is an example of a successful climate adaption project to prepare for major cyclones.

The United Nations Environment Programme (UNEP) has been assisting over 70 projects on climate change adaptation in more than 50 countries. These multinational schemes are essential to enable developing countries to adapt to the consequences of climate change. I have chosen to focus upon two case examples, as described in Case Examples 11.4 and 11.5.

Case Example 11.4   Bring Back Mangroves Project

Mangroves are short trees that grow on salt waters along coast lines. UNEP research shows that mangrove ecosystems underpin global and local economies by supporting fisheries, providing

(continued)

(continued)

other food sources and protecting coastlines from flooding and erosion. However, coastlines are among the most densely populated areas on Earth and developers are clearing mangrove forests to create space for buildings.

UNEP has developed guidelines on mangrove ecosystem restoration. Following these guidelines, Kenya and Madagascar in particular have recognised the contribution of mangroves to their own livelihoods and are actively participating in carbon monitoring, re-forestation and education to ensure the incomes and quality of life of future generations. Other governments are also taking action. Cuba, Haiti, Puerto Rico, the Dominican Republic and Pakistan have all prioritised mangrove restoration.

Case Example 11.5   Eliminate Additional Marine Plastic Litter by 2050

The annual discharge of plastic into the ocean is estimated to be 11 million tonnes and at the current rate this figure is set to double by 2040. However, through an ambitious combination of interventions using known technology and established approaches, marine plastic litter entering the ocean can be reduced by 82% compared to current levels by 2040.

UNEP has launched the Osaka Blue Ocean Vision plan which voluntarily commits G20 countries to 'reduce additional pollution by marine plastic litter to zero by 2050 through a comprehensive life-cycle approach'. This vision will only be achieved by adopting more progressive policy targets. These include moving from linear to circular plastic production by incentivising re-use and designing out waste. The international trade in plastic waste would be regulated to protect both people and nature. Many countries outside the G20, though not all, have signed up to UNEP's Osaka Blue Ocean Vision and are investing in national recycling facilities. The next phase is expanding on the 'source to sea' approach, i.e. focusing on the root cause of marine plastics.

Developed nations are also investing in climate adaptation and infrastructure projects, as Case Example 11.6 illustrates.

Case Example 11.6   UK Programme for Flood Protection

In July 2020, the UK government announced a £6.2 billion programme to protect 336,000 properties from flooding by 2027. The programme includes the building of new flood and coastal defences and sustainable drainage systems (SUDs). These will support 25 areas at risk of flooding. The programme also includes investment in 'shovel-ready' flood defence schemes to benefit 22 areas across the country. In addition, the plan sets out proposed changes to the joint government and insurance industry flood compensation schemes. Longer-term projects of climate adaptation (e.g. storing water upstream to prevent flooding during heavy rainfall and then capturing this water for use during dry weather) are also included in the programme.

However, in national projects it is often found that due to changes of leadership or political systems the project deliverables are different in reality from those intended in the original project plans.

For example, spurred by the devastation of Hurricane Ike in 2008, a $10 billion flood wall scheme to protect Galveston Island and the Houston Ship Channel ballooned to a budget of $32 billion in 2019.

In another example, the 'smart city' projects in China are supposed to assist planners with urban management and safety. The system is designed to help the municipal authorities monitor water levels in real time through sensors. In spite of the merits of these 'smart city' projects, when record rainstorms battered the Henan province during July 2021, the city of Zhengzhou situated in central China with a population of 10 million people suffered at least 66 deaths, including 14 in the local subway system and six in the Jingguang Road Tunnel.

Climate adaptation projects are not part of any political paradigm – they are real and designed for saving lives and the environment. We must be both optimistic and determined to deliver project goals.

How Green Six Sigma Can Help

In this area of climate adaptation projects, the impact of Green Six Sigma will be most significant. Case examples have demonstrated that Six Sigma methodology has ensured the quality and deliverables of these large schemes comprising many stakeholders. McKesson, which is the largest pharmaceutical distribution company in the United States, proclaims on its website that it has applied Six Sigma to achieve the successful distribution of both the Pfizer and Moderna Covid vaccines. Both vaccines required ultra-cold storage and thus their distribution across the United States was an enormous undertaking. There is also evidence that Six Sigma tools were applied in the major project comprising the rollout of Covid-19 vaccines to millions of people across India.

Green Six Sigma will contribute additional values of ensuring sustainable environmental standards to large and international climate adaption projects.

11.8. Climate Adaptation and Innovation

It is evident that many climate change initiatives, both for mitigation and adaption, require new materials and breakthrough solutions that we need now but do not have. For this we require innovation supported by dedicated research and development. In energy, transport, construction, software and just about any other pursuit, innovation is not just inventing new equipment or designing a novel process. It is also offering a completely fresh way of doing things. We have sufficient demand for innovation to combat the inconvenient consequences of climate change. The essential requirements of upscaling and testing any new product or process in a larger population cannot be denied and these will follow later, but we are now hungrier and there is a greater sense of urgency for the supply side of innovation. Although we have a few affordable zero carbon or low carbon solutions today, unfortunately we do not possess all the necessary technologies or materials to meet the target of zero emissions globally. Therefore, in Table 11.2 is my list of urgently required improved technologies and materials for climate change initiatives – although environmental scientists may suggest more.

Most of the following products are not new but we do need them to be affordable and safe to use. In order to achieve this, we need more research and greater R&D investment hypothecated to climate change research initiatives. President Joe Biden's 2022 budget proposal includes around $36 billion to fight global climate change, of which only $4 billion is allocated to advancing climate research. Other rich nations should follow suit and consider a tax break for R&D investment to encourage private enterprises to invest in R&D for climate research. Large oil and gas corporations and fossil fuel-producing countries must generously support R&D initiatives for zero carbon alternatives to fossil fuels and also for carbon capture projects. The commercial future of fossil fuels as a major energy supplier is not bright in the longer term and their appropriate

Table 11.2 Improved technologies and materials for R&D

Advanced biofuels
Carbon capture and storage
Commercial grafine
Electricity storage for a long period
Geothermal energy
Green hydrogen
Hydrogen combustion engines
Plant-based meat and dairy
Tidal energy
Zero carbon aviation fuels
Zero carbon cement
Zero carbon fertilizer
Zero carbon plastics
Zero carbon steel

strategy should be to focus on advancing alternative solutions and the by-products of fractional distillation (e.g. lubricants, asphalt, naphtha, feedstocks, etc.).

How Green Six Sigma Can Help

There is evidence (Schweikhart and Dembe, 2009) that Lean Six Sigma process improvement methodologies are well suited to help research projects become more efficient and cost-effective, thus enhancing the quality of the research. There are specific tools for R&D projects (e.g. DFSS) that are also in the toolset of Green Six Sigma. It can be concluded that the application of Green Six Sigma will accelerate the quality and delivery time of much needed R&D projects for improved climate change solutions.

11.9. Summary

It is inevitable that in spite of all current mitigation plans to combat climate change, we will gradually feel the impact of global warming in the form of more frequent floods, heat waves and draughts. We will have to live with the medium-term consequences and adapt ourselves with cost-effective measures. There is a sense of optimism after the election of President Joe Biden and expectations are also very high regarding the outcomes of the 2021 United Nations Climate Change Conference, also known as COP 26.

In this chapter, some essential measures to adapt to the likely consequences of climate change in the different sectors of our lives (e.g. energy, industry, farming, transport and housing) have been outlined. These measures are based on the technologies and processes that we have already and that can be put into practice right now. Green Six Sigma tools and techniques can also help, starting from today. We also need both government and private investments in R&D to develop and innovate materials as well as suitable technology for climate change solutions that are affordable and safe to use.

Green Tips

- In spite of global, national and individual efforts to prevent the consequences of climate change we will have to prepare ourselves to adapt to more frequent floods, heat waves and droughts.
- There must be more investments, both in the public and private sectors, to develop new materials and solutions for climate change adaptations, as listed in Table 11.2.
- Green Six Sigma can play a major role in improving the effectiveness of R&D projects for climate change solutions.

Chapter 12

Implementation: Making It Happen

12.1. Introduction

When I read the summary of the UK Met Office report on climate change (Kendon et al., 2021) I was thinking of borrowing the title from Tom Clancy's novel, *Clear and Present Danger*. The report has shown that visible evidence of climate change is already here in the UK and that the twenty-first century so far has been warmer than the previous three centuries. The rate of sea level rise has been over 3 mm per year for the period 1993–2019. There can be no doubt looking at these figures that climate change is happening right now.

This is also reflected by the spate of climate-related disasters in July 2021 in geographical areas as widespread as Western Europe, North America, China and South Asia. In August 2021, a UNICEF report (Carrington, 2021) noted that of the 2.2 billion children in the world, almost half were already at "extremely high risk" from the effects of both pollution and climate change, and that nearly every child alive was at risk from at least one risk, such as disease, drought, or air pollution and extreme weather events such as cyclones, flooding and heat wave. The report highlighted the fact that for those living in the 33 countries that constitute the most endangered areas – including sub-Saharan Africa, India and the Philippines – they face the consequences of at least three events at once.

IPCC's Sixth Assessment Report (IPCC, 2021) also carries the same urgent message of the 'clear and present danger' of climate change. This report clearly states, 'Unless there are immediate, rapid and large-scale reductions in greenhouse gas emissions, limiting warming to close to 1.5 °C or even 2 °C will be beyond reach. . . . Extreme sea level events that previously occurred once in 100 years could happen every year by the end of this century.' However, it is encouraging to note that the report also suggests that 'human action has the potential to determine the future course of climate'.

In the preceding chapters I have described plans for both mitigating and adapting to the consequences of climate change. There is a Japanese proverb that says, 'Action without a plan is a nightmare and a plan without actions is a day dream'. It is clear that we need implementation plans urgently in order to avoid imminent catastrophe – we need to make it happen.

In this chapter implementation plans are presented in two parts:

- Implementation of Climate Change Initiatives
- Implementation of Green Six Sigma

As the primary domain of this book is Green Six Sigma, more details regarding implementation plans are included in the Green Six Sigma sections. This is where this book will add greater values. In the climate change initiatives section, high-level points for implementation are outlined.

12.2. Implementation of Climate Change Initiatives

Any implementation programme including climate change initiatives, whether international or national, should follow a structured plan based on the best practices of project management and change management (Basu, 2009). The implementation plan of Green Six Sigma, as described in Section 9.3, also follows the principle of change management. The success of the implementation of climate change initiatives at a national level, in particular, is linked to the way they are integrated with the economic and social policies of the national government in power. The leadership strategy/attitude to green initiatives of the national government also plays a critical role. There are many learning points that can be derived from earlier implementation projects related to climate change (de Oliviera, 2009; Sharp et al., 2011) that would be useful for other climate change initiatives. These learning points include:

- Start with an immediate and recognisable threat, such as frequent forest fires, hurricanes or flooding. It will help spur action, especially if the community has recently experienced the disaster.
- Begin with a project that can be integrated with an initiative that is already in progress to minimise the duplication of activities and resources.
- Recognise local values and be prepared to be flexible and respond to a community's needs. Reach out to the community and provide open communication.
- Involve elected officials of the local and regional governments early. Although they may not lead on climate change initially, they appreciate being involved and their support is crucial.
- Use outside resources and consultants based on their expertise and track records. Early-stage community organising is the most important skill. Later on, technical experts can help with specific needs to provide the solution.
- Recognise that mitigation can be a first step. Climate mitigation and adaptation are close cousins. If there are separate budgets for mitigation and adaptation for the same problem, combine them.
- Ensure that the project is funded adequately either from a budget or an emergency relief fund.
- Focus critically on data-driven communication, transparency and stakeholder management rather than media-driven public relations.

It is also recommended that the application of Green Six Sigma tools should be considered, and its approaches for 'fitness for purpose' and 'fitness for sustainability'.

A stakeholder is a party that has interest in the project and can influence its outcomes. It cannot be emphasised enough that stakeholder management is crucial to the success of a climate change solution – both to deliver and also to initiate. It is important that key stakeholders are proactive either to activate or influence climate change projects right now.

12.2.1. International Community

The role of the international community is arguably the most crucial driver of implementing any climate change initiatives. 2021 has been coined as a 'super year' for the environment. President Joe Biden and other G7 leaders have committed to a new partnership to build back better for the world. The upcoming summits, such as COP26 and the G20, are promising green recovery opportunities from the Covid-19 pandemic. Despite some failures of previous summits, experts are predicting tangible outcomes.

12.2.2. National and Local Governments

There are visible signs that the national, devolved and local governments of the UK have started the implementation of climate change projects. Communities across the UK are tackling the climate crisis with hundreds of local schemes ranging from neighbourhood heating to food co-ops, community land ownership projects and flood defences (*The Guardian*, 10 March 2021). In spite of the Covid-19 pandemic, major climate change projects have started in other countries as well. Political campaigns by Green parties are also driving changes.

12.2.3. Non-Governmental Organisations (NGOs)

There are tens of NGOs, including Greenpeace and Friends of the Earth, across the world. These organisations have been campaigning, often by direct action, over decades to influence the policy makers to achieve a greener planet. Now their campaign has changed from policy to actions.

12.2.4. Industry and Service Providers

This is a powerful sector to make changes happen. If the big four corporations of the oil and gas industry get together then alternative aviation fuels will be guaranteed within five years. If the largest private sector consumers of materials like steel, cement and plastics can cooperate then cleaner substitutes will soon be found. The good news is that some of the world's richest people like Bill Gates and Jeff Bezos are contributing billions of dollars to work to fix the climate crisis. Companies can also invest in their own R&D projects to develop innovative zero carbon products. Many companies around the world have already committed to using renewable energy for a large part of their operations.

12.2.5. The General Public

Every member of the general public is both a consumer and a citizen and, as such, there is much that each of us can do. As a consumer, a person can influence demand for products by fossil fuel energy and as a citizen an adult can vote to change a policy towards achieving climate change solutions. If all of us make individual adjustments in what we buy and use, as discussed in Chapter 10, it will also force the suppliers to change. We can also create demand, say, by buying electric cars and the market will respond accordingly. In a democracy, we can also use our voice to express a view and request change from those in power. As a citizen, if we write to our local elected representative demanding actions for climate change then this can have a real impact.

12.2.6. Media

The media world of newspapers, books, television, radio and social media is playing its role by influencing the mindsets of people and affecting government policies on climate change paradigms. The impact of the movie, 'An Inconvenient Truth' by Al Gore in 2006 and the 'Blue Planet II' documentary on plastics pollution by David Attenborough in 2017 have been game changers. Progressive newspapers (e.g. *The Guardian*) and television channels (such as the BBC, who showed 'Blue Planet') have been providing fact-based information to inform, educate and update the audience on both climate change challenges and possible solutions. Sky News has dedicated 30 minutes every day to broadcasting news exclusively about climate change. However, there are also some channels and social media platforms feeding 'fake news' to the deniers of climate change, and their impact and reach cannot be underestimated.

12.3. The Implementation of Green Six Sigma

The implementation of Green Six Sigma presented here is also part of the application of climate change initiatives. The implementation of Green Six Sigma, and for that matter the instigation of any change programme, is a bit like having a baby – it may be very pleasant to conceive, but the delivery of change can be a tricky process. According to Carnall (1999), 'the route to such changes lies in the behaviour: put some people in new settings within which they have to behave differently and, if properly trained, supported and rewarded, their behaviour will change. If successful, this will lead to mindset change and ultimately will impact on the culture of the organisation'. The implementation of Six Sigma and Lean Six Sigma has been going on for decades. Thus, learning from the proven pathways of both the successful and failed programmes are suggested here for consideration in implementing Green Six Sigma for climate change initiatives.

Below we outline proven pathways for implementing Green Six Sigma for organisations involved in climate change initiatives and potential organisations for climate change that are in different stages of Six Sigma awareness and development. As Green Six Sigma is an adaptation of Six Sigma and Lean Six Sigma principles, any reference to Six Sigma or Lean Six Sigma also relates to Green Six Sigma. We have categorised three stages of development:

1. New starters of Green Six Sigma.
2. Started Six Sigma, but stalled.
3. Green Six Sigma for small and medium enterprises.
4. Green Six Sigma for successful organisations.

12.4. Implementation for New Starters

There are many large climate change projects waiting to happen where Green Six Sigma can be applied right from the start. The significant projects in this category include the decommissioning of a fossil fuel power plant, building a new regeneration power supply system, a high-speed train project, setting up a new EV manufacturing plant, a major climate change research project (e.g. for carbon capture) and so on.

At the earliest stage the decision makers should understand the urgent need for a climate change initiative towards a net-zero carbon objective and the necessity for an improvement programme underpinned by a data-driven holistic process of Green Six Sigma. The main concern will be the change required to the culture of the organisation and the absence of a proven structure for transformation of a culture. Management knows what they want but how do they convince their staff that they need to or want to change and encourage to buy into the process? And how do they sell Green Six Sigma to stakeholders? You can take a horse to water – but how do you make it drink?

Here I provide a total and proven pathway for implementing a Green Six Sigma programme, from the start of the initiative via the embedding of the change, right through to a sustainable organisation-wide culture. Note that both the entry point and the emphasis on each step of the programme could vary depending on the 'state of health' of the organisation.

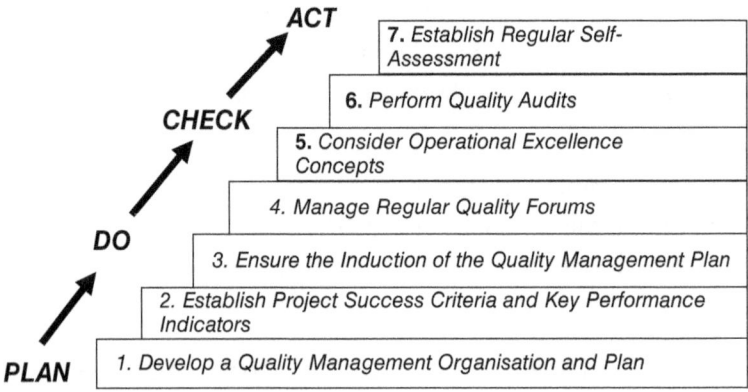

Figure 12.1   Framework of a Green Six Sigma implementation
© Ron Basu

The framework of a Green Six Sigma programme is shown in Figure 12.1 and described below.

12.4.1.   Step One: Management Awareness

A middle manager has been tasked by the CEO with leading a Green Six Sigma programme in a large organisation that has no previous experience of Six Sigma or Lean Six Sigma. The CEO has just read an article concerning Jack Welch's successes with Six Sigma at General Electric, and he is full of enthusiasm and has high expectations. The middle manager, however, is less enthused; in fact, he does not want to participate at all and has grim forebodings of failure. He realises that the CEO is a powerful member of the board, but after all he is only one member. Meanwhile, in another organisation, the Quality Manager for a medium-sized company has attended a Six Sigma conference and has mixed feelings about the task ahead – optimism as well as some doubts. So, which one of them has the correct approach? In fact, the author believes that both these managers are right to be concerned.

Learnings from previous Six Sigma and Lean Six Sigma programmes suggest that it is essential to convince the CEO and at least a third of the board regarding the scope and benefits of Green Six Sigma, prior to launching the programme. The success rate of a 'back door' approach without the endorsement of the key players cannot be guaranteed. If a programme is not company-wide and wholly supported by senior management it is simply not Green Six Sigma. It may be a departmental improvement project – but it is not Green Six Sigma. In cricketing terms, a CEO can open the batting, but a successful opening stand needs a partner at the other end.

Research by the Corporate Leadership Council (2005) revealed that through using leadership and change training programmes, companies can substantially increase the potential for change initiatives to be successful. The research also indicated that companies that initiate too much change too quickly actually negatively affect the motivation of employees and their performance.

Learnings from previous Six Sigma programmes suggest that Management Awareness has been a key factor in the successful application of Six Sigma in large organisations. Various methods have been followed including:

1. Consultants' presentation to an offsite board meeting (e.g. General Electric)
2. The participation of senior managers in another organisation's leadership workshop (e.g. GSK and Raytheon)
3. Study visits by senior managers to an 'experienced' organisation (e.g. Noranda's visit to General Electric, DuPont and Alcoa)

Popular Six Sigma literature has advocated that Six Sigma cannot be implemented successfully without top management commitment (Pyzdek, 2003; Ladhar, 2007; Breyfogle, 2008). Moreover, Basu (2009) further argues that if the chief executive does not have a passion for quality and continuous improvement, and if that passion cannot be transmitted down through the organisation, then paradoxically the ongoing driving force will be from the bottom up. It can be argued that the apparent lack of total commitment but tacit support of management has empowered the middle management and acted as an incentive to demonstrate tangible results.

Small- and medium-sized firms can learn from the experience of larger organisations, and indeed there can be mutual benefits for the larger organisation through an exchange of fact-finding missions. A service industry organisation could well benefit by exchanging these sorts of visits with successful Six Sigma companies in the finance sector such as American Express, Lloyds TSB and Egg plc.

During the development of the management awareness phase it is useful to produce a board report or 'white paper' summarising the findings and benefits. This account has to be well written and concise, but it should not be rushed. It is recommended that you allow between four and twelve weeks for fact finding, including visits, and the writing of the 'white paper'.

12.4.2.   Step Two: Initial Assessment

Once the agreement in principle from the board is achieved, it is recommended that an initial 'health check' should be carried out at the organisation to develop a 'fitness for purpose' approach. There are many good reasons for conducting an initial assessment before formalising a Green Six Sigma programme. These include:

1. Having a destination in mind and knowing which road to take are not helpful until you find out where you are to start.
2. You should get to know the organisation's needs through analysis and measurement of the initial size and shape of the business and its problems/concerns or threats. Once these are ascertained, then the techniques of Green Six Sigma can be tailored to meet these needs.
3. The initial assessment acts as a spring board by bringing together a cross-functional team and reinforces the 'buy in' at the middle management level.
4. It is likely that most organisations will have pockets of excellence along with many areas where improvement is obviously needed. The initial assessment process highlights these at an early stage.

5. The health check must take into account the overall vision/ mission and strategy of the organisation, so as to link Green Six Sigma to the key strategy of the board. Thus, the health check will serve to reinforce or redefine the key strategy of the organisation.

There are two essential requirements leading to the success of the assessment (health check) process:

1. The criteria of assessment (checklist) must be holistic, covering all aspects of the business and specifically addressing the key objectives of the organisation.
2. The assessing team must be competent and 'trained' in the assessment process. (Whether they are internal or external is not a critical issue.)

It is sensible that the assessment team be trained and conversant with basic fact-finding methods, such as those used by industrial engineers. Some knowledge of the European Foundation for Quality Management (EFQM, 2003) would be most useful.

Once the health check assessment is completed a short report covering strengths and areas for improvement is required. It is emphasised that this report should be short (not the 75 page detailed account required for the EFQM). In writing the document the company might require the assistance of a Six Sigma consultant. The typical time needed for the health check is two to six weeks.

12.4.3.   Step Three: Programme Brief and Organisation

This is the organisation phase of the programme requiring a clear project brief, the appointment of a project team and the development of a project plan. All elements are essential since 'major, panic driven changes can destroy a company; poorly planned change is worse than no change' (Basu and Wright, 1997).

The brief must clearly state the purpose, scope objectives, benefits, costs and risks associated with the programme. A Green

Six Sigma syllabus is a combination of Total Quality Management, Lean Management, Six Sigma and culture change supervision. It is a huge undertaking and requires the disciplined approach of project management. 'Programme management is a portfolio of projects that change organisations to achieve benefits that are of strategic importance' (MSP, 2007).

One risk at this stage is that management might query the budget for the programme, and there might be some reluctance to proceed. If this is the case, then it is obvious that management has not fully understood the need for change. This is why the importance of the first step, 'Management Awareness', is stressed. However, reinforcement could be needed during step three, underpinned with informed assumptions and data including a cost/benefit/risk analysis. Unless management is fully committed there is little point in proceeding.

There is no rigid model for the configuration of the Green Six Sigma team. Basic elements of a project structure for a major change programme can be found in Basu and Wright (1997). A tested Green Six Sigma model is shown in Figure 12.2.

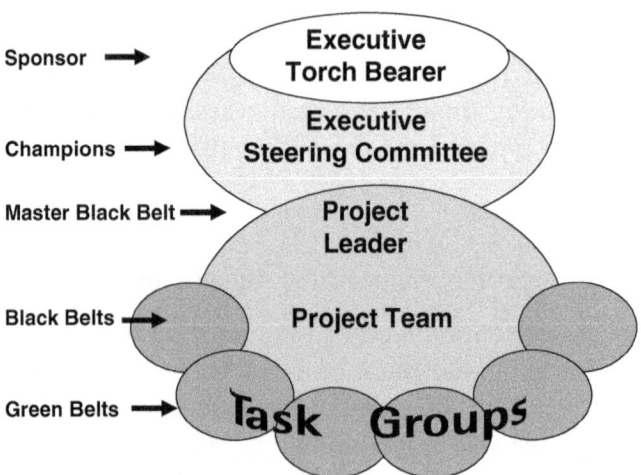

Figure 12.2   Green Six Sigma programme organisation
© Ron Basu

Executive Torch Bearer

Figure 12.2 shows an Executive Torch Bearer, who ideally will be the chief executive officer (CEO) and will be the official sponsor for Green Six Sigma. There is a correlation between the higher up the organisation the Torch Bearer is and the greater the success of the programme. The role of the Torch Bearer is to be the top management focal point for the entire programme and to chair the meetings of the Executive Steering Committee. Being a Torch Bearer may not be a time-consuming function, but it is certainly a very important role to give the programme a high focus, to expedite resources and to eliminate bottlenecks.

Executive Steering Committee

To ensure a high level of commitment and ownership to the project, the steering committee should be drawn from members of the board plus senior management. Their role is to provide support and resources, to define the scope of the programme consistent with corporate goals, to set priorities and consider and approve the programme team recommendations. In Six Sigma terminology they are the champions of processes and functional disciplines.

Programme Leader

The Programme Leader should be a person of high stature in the company – a senior manager with broad knowledge of all aspects of the business and possessing good communication skills. He or she is the focal point of the project and also the main communication link between the Executive Steering Committee and the programme team. Often the Programme Leader will report direct to the Torch Bearer.

The Programme Leader's role can be likened to that of a consultant. The function of the Leader is to a great extent similar to

Hammer and Champy's 'czar' in *Re-Engineering the Corporation* (1993). In other words, the Programme Leader's task is to:

- Provide necessary awareness and training for the project team, especially regarding multi-functional issues,
- Facilitate the work of various project groups and help them develop and design changes and
- Interface across functional departments.

In addition to the careful selection of the Programme Leader, two other factors are important in forming the team. Firstly, the membership size should be kept within manageable limits. Secondly, the members should bring with them not only analytical skills but also an in-depth knowledge of the total business covering marketing, finance, logistics, technical and human resources. The minimum number of team members should be three, with a maximum of seven. Any more than even this figure can lead to a series of practical difficulties such as arranging meetings, communicating and keeping to deadlines. The dynamics within a group of more than seven people allows a pecking order to develop and for sub-groups to emerge. The team should function as an action group, rather than as a committee that deliberates and makes decisions. Their role is to:

- Provide objective input into the areas of their expertise during the health check stage
- To lead activities when changes are made

For the Programme Leader the stages of the project include:

- Education of all the people in the company
- Gathering the data
- Analysis of the data
- Recommending changes
- Regular reporting to the Executive Steering Committee and to the Torch Bearer

Obviously, the Programme Leaders cannot do all the work themselves. A Programme Leader has to be the type of person who knows how to make things happen and who can motivate and galvanize other people to help achieve this aim.

Programme Team

The members of the Programme Team represent all functions across the organisation and they are the key agents for making changes. Members are carefully selected from both line management and a functional background. They will undergo extensive training to achieve Black Belt standards. Our experience suggests that a good mix of practical managers and enquiring 'high flyers' will make a successful project team. They are very often the process owners of the programme. Most of the members of the Programme Team are part time. As a rule of thumb, no less than one percent of the total workforce should form the Programme Team. In smaller organisations the percentage will of necessity be higher so that each function or key process is represented.

Task Groups

Task Groups are spin-off sets formed on an ad hoc basis to prevent the Programme Team getting bogged down in detail. A Task Group is typically created to address a specific issue. The topic could be relatively major, such as the Balanced Score Card, or comparatively minor, such as the investigation of losses in a particular process. By nature, the Task Group members are employed directly on to the programme on a temporary basis. However, by supplying basic information for the programme, they gain experience and Green Belt training. Their individual improved understanding and 'ownership' of the solution provide a good foundation for sustaining future changes and ongoing improvements.

Time Frame

A preliminary time plan with dates for milestones is usually included in the Programme Brief.

The 'Do' Steps

In Figure 12.1 we can see that after the 'Plan' phase there comes the 'Do' phase.

Once the programme and project plan have been agreed by the Executive Steering Committee it should receive a formal launch.

It is critical that all stakeholders, including managers, employees, unions, key suppliers and important customers are clearly identified. A high-profile programme launch targeted at stakeholders such as these is desirable.

12.4.4.   Step Four: Leadership Workshop

All board members and senior managers of the company need to learn about the Green Six Sigma programme before they can be expected to give their full support and input into the scheme. Leadership training is a critical success factor. Leadership Workshops can begin simultaneously with Step One, but should be completed before Step Five (see Figure 12.1). Workshops will last between two and five days and will cover the following issues:

1. What are Six Sigma and Green Six Sigma?
2. Why do we need Green Six Sigma?
3. What will it cost and what resources will be required?
4. What will it save, and what other benefits will accrue?
5. Will it interrupt the normal business?
6. What is the role of the Programme Leader and the Executive Committee?

12.4.5.   Step Five: Training Deployment

The training programme, especially for the team members, is rigorous. One might question whether it is really necessary to train in order to achieve Black Belt certification. Indeed, formal certification might not be essential. However, there is no doubt that without the in-depth training of key members of the programme, little value will be added in the short term, and certainly not over a longer period. The training/learning deployment creates a team of experts. It is presupposed that programme members will be experts in their own departments and processes as they are currently being run. It is expected that they will have the capability of appreciating how the business as a whole will be organised in the future. Green Six Sigma will equip them with the tools for the business overall in order to achieve world class performance.

Apart from the rigorous education in techniques and tools, it is emphasised that the training will change how the members will look at things. Training is an enabler, not only to understand the strategy and purpose of change but – as evidenced by the experience of American Express – it will help members to identify:

Project replication opportunities

Leveraging the results of the programme

Identification and elimination of areas of rework

Drivers for customer satisfaction

Leverage of Green Six Sigma principles into new products and services

Smaller organisations are very often concerned about the cost of training, especially the money paid out to consultants and for courses. In a Green Six Sigma programme teaching costs can be minimised by the careful selection of specialist consultants and through the development of own in-house training programmes.

12.4.6.   Step Six: Project Selection and Delivery

The Project Selection process usually begins during the Training Deployment Step.

Project selection, and subsequent delivery, is the visible aspect of the programme. A popular practice is to begin by having easy, and well publicised, successes (known as 'harvesting low hanging fruit'). We recommend that 'quick wins' should be aimed for (or 'just do it' projects).

In a similar fashion, Ericsson AB applied a simplified 'Business Impact' model for larger schemes. They categorise ventures under three headings:

Cost Takeout

Productivity

Cost Avoidance

Table 12.1   Categories of savings

Level	Cost Takeout	Productivity and Growth	Cost Avoidance
Definition	'Hard' savings - Recurring expense prior to Six Sigma - Direct costs	'Soft' savings Increase in process capacity so you can 'do more with less', 'do the same with less', 'do more with the same'	Avoidance of anticipated cost or investment that is not in today's budget
Example	• Less people to perform activity • Less $ required for same item	• Less time required for an activity • Improved machine efficiency	• Avoiding purchase of additional equipment • Avoiding hiring contractors
Impact	Whole unit	Partial unit	Not in today's cost
Weighting	100%	50%	20%

Business impact = cost takeout + 0.5 productivity

$$+ \, 0.2 \text{ cost avoidance} - \text{implementation cost}$$

A variable weighting is allocated to each category, as shown in Table 12.1.

For smaller, 'just do it' projects, it is a good practice to establish an 'Ideas Factory' to encourage Task Groups and all employees to contribute to savings and improvement. Very often small projects from the 'Ideas Factory' require negligible funding.

Project Review and Feedback

One important point of the Project Selection and Delivery Step is to monitor the progress of each task and to control the effects of the changes so that expected benefits are achieved. The Programme Leader should maintain a progress register supported by a Gantt Chart, defining the change, expected benefits, resources, time scale, and expenditure (to budget), and showing the people who are responsible for each of the identified actions.

This phase of review and feedback involves a continuous need to sustain what has been achieved and to identify further opportunities for improvement. It is good practice to set fixed dates for review meetings as follows:

Milestone Review (at least Quarterly)

> = Executive Steering Committee,
>
> Torch Bearer, and
>
> Programme Leader

Programme Review (Monthly)

> = Programme Leader and Team,
>
> with a short report to Torch Bearer

The problems/hold-ups experienced during projects are identified during the Programme Review with the aim of the project team taking action to resolve sticking points. If necessary, requests are made to the Executive Steering Committee for additional resources.

12.4.7.   Step Seven: Measurement of Success

The fundamental characteristic of a Six Sigma or Green Six Sigma programme that differentiates it from a traditional quality curriculum is that it is results orientated. Effective measurement is the key to understanding the operation of the process, and this forms the basis of all analysis and improvement work. In a construction project the milestones are both tangible and physically obvious, but in a change programme such as Green Six Sigma the modifications are not always apparent. It is essential to measure, display and celebrate the achievement of milestones in a Green Six Sigma programme, and in order to improve and sustain its results, the importance of performance management is strongly emphasised. The process and culture of measurement must start during the implementation of changes.

The components of measurement of success should include:

Project tracking

Green Six Sigma metrics

Balanced Score Card

Self-assessment review (e.g. EFQM or Baldridge).

There are useful software tools available such as Minitab (www.minitab.com) for carrying out detailed tracking of larger Six Sigma projects. However, in most programmes the progress of savings generated by each project can be monitored on an Excel spreadsheet. It is recommended that summaries of results are reported and displayed each month. Examples of forms of displays are shown in Figures 12.3 and 12.4.

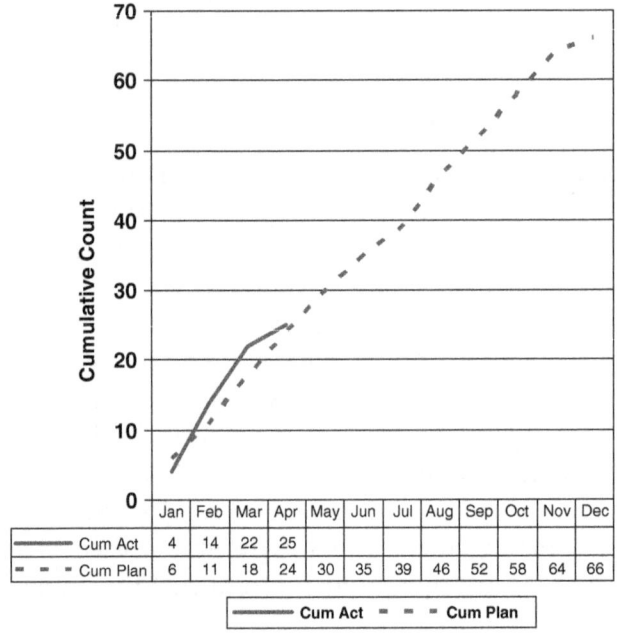

	Jan	Feb	Mar	Apr	May	Jun	Jul	Aug	Sep	Oct	Nov	Dec
Cum Act	4	14	22	25								
Cum Plan	6	11	18	24	30	35	39	46	52	58	64	66

Cum Act — — — Cum Plan

Figure 12.3 Project planned and completed
© Ron Basu

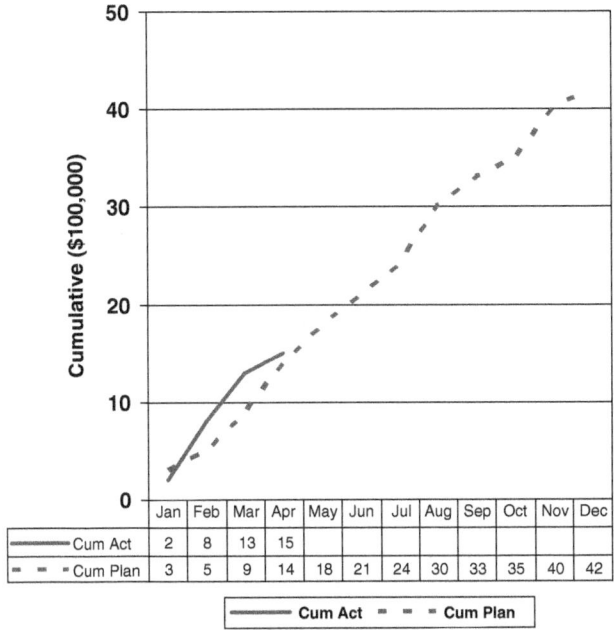

Figure 12.4   Value of planned and completed projects
© Ron Basu

Green Six Sigma Metrics

Green Six Sigma metrics are required to analyse the reduction in process variance and the reduction in the rate of defects resulting from the appropriate tools and methodology.

A word of caution: Black Belts can get caught up with the elegance of statistical methods and this preoccupation can lead to the development of a statistical cult. Extensive use of variance analysis is not recommended.

The following Green Six Sigma metrics are useful, easy to understand and easy to apply:

Cost of Poor Quality = COPQ ratio

Defects per Million Opportunities = DPMO and

First Pass Yield = FPY

Carbon Footprint

COPQ

$$\text{Internal failure \$} + \text{External failure \$} + \text{Appraisal and prevention \$}$$
$$+ \text{Lost Opportunity\$ Monthly Sales\$}$$

DPMO

Total number of defects $\times$ 1,000,000

Total units and opportunities per unit

FPY

Number of units completed without defects and rework

Number of units started

Carbon Footprint

A carbon footprint is the total amount of greenhouse gas emissions caused by an individual, event, organisation or process expressed as a carbon dioxide equivalent. There are digital tools available (e.g. Emitwise, emitwise.com) for automatic calculations of carbon footprints.

By measuring and monitoring Green Six Sigma metrics each month, opportunities for further improvement will be identified.

As has already been emphasised in Chapter 5, a carefully designed Balanced Score Card is essential for improving and sustaining business performance. It is generally agreed that the Balanced Score Card is applicable for a stable process and thus should be appropriate after completion of the Green Six Sigma programme. This may be so, but unless the measures of the Balanced Score Card are properly defined and designed for the purpose at an early stage, its effectiveness will be limited. Therefore, it is strongly recommended that during the Green Six Sigma programme the basics of the Balanced Score Card should be established in order to manage the company-wide performance system.

The fourth component of measurement is the 'self-assessment and review' process. There are two options to monitor the progress of the business resulting from the Green Six Sigma programme, and either of the following can be used:

1. A simple checklist to assess the overall progress of the programme or
2. A proven self-assessment process such as the European Foundation of Quality Management (EFQM) or the American Malcolm Baldridge system.

In the initial health check appraisal stage, the use of EFQM is advocated; thus the methodology will already have been applied. Additionally, it gives further experience in the self-assessment process, which will enable future sustainability. Finally, it will provide the foundation should the organisation wish at a later stage to apply for an EFQM or Baldridge award.

12.4.8. Step Eight: Culture Change and Sustainability

A culture change must **not** begin by replacing middle management by imported 'Black Belts'. Winning over as opposed to losing middle management is essential to the success of Green Six Sigma, or for that matter any quality initiative.

What is required is that the all-important middle management, and everyone else in the organisation, understands what Green Six Sigma is and possesses the culture of quality.

The Green Six Sigma Culture is shown in Table 12.4.

Green Six Sigma requires a balanced culture comprising the key characteristics of the above four categories. If an organisation is predominantly one type, then some cultural change will be required. Training Deployment, see Step Five of Figure 12.5, includes preparation for culture change, but education alone will not transform the mindset required for Green Six Sigma.

Table 12.4   Green Six Sigma Culture

1. Total vision and commitment of top management throughout the programme.
2. Emphasis on measured results and the rigour of project management.
3. Focus on training with short-term projects and results, and long-term people development.
4. Use of simple and practical tools.
5. Total approach across the whole organisation (holistic).
6. Leverage of results by sharing best practice with business partners (suppliers and customers).
7. Sustaining improvement by knowledge management, regular self-assessment and senior management reviews.
8. Sustaining environmental requirements by monitoring the carbon footprints of solutions.

Communication

Finally, the key to sustaining a Green Six Sigma culture is the process of good communication. Methods of communication include:

- A Green Six Sigma website, specifically developed, or clearly visible on the corporate website
- Specially produced videos
- A Green Six Sigma monthly newsletter
- Internal emails, voicemails, memos with updated key messages – **not** slogans such as 'work smarter not harder' and other tired clichés
- Milestone celebrations
- Staff get-togethers, such as special morning teas, a Friday afternoon social hour or 'town hall' type meetings
- An 'ideas factory' or 'think tank' to encourage suggestions and involvement from employees

12.4.9.   Step Nine: Improve and Sustain

'Improve and sustain' is the cornerstone of a Green Six Sigma programme. This is similar to Tuckman's (1965) fifth stage of team dynamics for project teams ('Forming, Storming, Norming, Performing and Mourning'). During the Mourning step the project team disbands and members move onto other ventures or activities. They typically regret the end of the project and the breakup of the group, and the effectiveness or maintenance of the new method and results gradually diminish. In Chapter 5 we have discussed in some detail that, in order to achieve sustainability, four key processes must be in place:

1. Performance management
2. Senior management review
3. Self-assessment and certification
4. Knowledge management

The 'end game' scenario should be carefully developed long before the completion of the programme. There may not be a sharp cut-off point like a project handover and the success of the scenario lies in the making of a smooth transition without disruption to the ongoing operation of the business.

As part of the performance management, improvement targets should be gradually, and continuously, stretched and more advanced tools considered for introduction. For example, the DFSS (Design for Six Sigma) is resource hungry (Basu, 2009) and can be considered at a later stage in a Green Six Sigma programme. With Six Sigma, the aim is to satisfy customers with robust 'zero defect' manufactured products. In order to do so, DFSS is fully deployed covering all elements of Manufacturing, Design, Marketing, Finance, Human Resources, Suppliers and Key Customers (including the supplier's suppliers and the customer's customers).

At an advanced stage of the programme, a milestone review should be included in senior management operational review team meetings (such as the sales review meetings and operational planning meetings/committees). In other words, a milestone review should occur not only within the Green Six Sigma Executive Steering Committee.

It is recommended that a pure play EFQM (or other form of self-assessment) should be incorporated as a six-month feature of the Green Six Sigma programme. Even if the company gains an accolade, such as an EFQM or Baldridge award, the process must still continue indefinitely.

Two specific features of knowledge management need to be emphasised. Firstly, it is essential that the company seek leverage from Green Six Sigma results by rolling out the process to other business units and main suppliers. Secondly, it is equally important to ensure that career development and reward schemes are firmly in place to retain the highly trained and motivated Black Belts. The success of the sustainability of Green Six Sigma occurs when the culture becomes simply an undisputed case of 'this is the way we do things'.

Time Scale

The time scale of Green Six Sigma implementation will last several months and is, of course, variable. The duration not only depends upon the nature or size of the organisation but also on the business environment and the resources available. Four factors can favourably affect the time scale:

1. Full commitment of top management and the board
2. Sound financial position
3. Correct culture (workforce receptive to change)
4. A competitive niche in the marketplace

It is good practice to prepare a Gantt Chart containing the key stages of the programme and to use it to monitor progress. Figure 12.5 shows a typical timetable for a Green Six Sigma agenda in a single-site medium-sized company. The diagram shows an order of magnitude only, and the sequence could well vary. The time line is not linear, stages overlap and frequent retrospection should occur in order to learn from past events and work towards future progress.

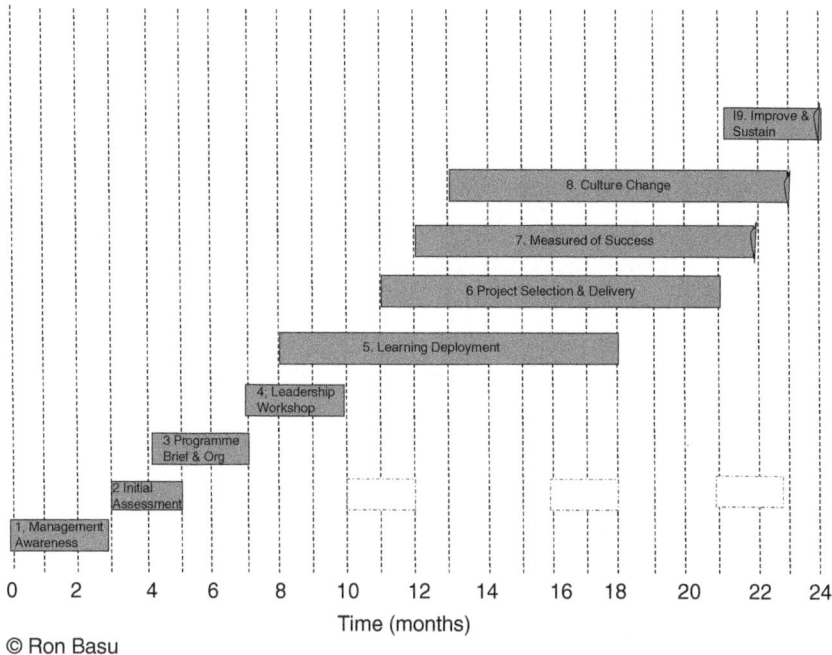

Figure 12.5 A typical time plan for a Green Six Sigma programme

12.5.   Green Six Sigma for 'Stalled' Six Sigma

Some organisations have already attempted to implement a Six Sigma (or a TQM) programme, but the process has stalled. Results are not being achieved and enthusiasm is waning; in some cases the programme has effectively been abandoned. The reasons for stalling are various but often progression has ground to a halt due to an economic downturn (such as that experienced in the Telecommunications industry in 2001), a change in top management or a merger or takeover.

There are some organisations in this category who applied Lean Six Sigma for a specific project but not across the whole organisation, e.g. Network Rail in Case Example 9.3. These organisations will benefit by focusing on a net-zero carbon strategy supported by an organisation-wide Green Six Sigma approach.

Green Six Sigma: Not a 'Quick Fix'

During restructuring, or if the company is in survival mode, the implementation of Green Six Sigma is not appropriate. Green Six Sigma is not simply a 'quick fix', a plaster hastily stuck over gaping wounds, and in such cases it is not sufficient. Instead, the underlying, more serious, issues must be addressed. After applying the short-term cost saving measures of a survival strategy, when the business has stabilised and a new management team is in place, *then* Six Sigma can be restarted. However, this time it should be done correctly, and using the Green Six Sigma approach.

It is likely when restarting that many of the steps will not need to be repeated, including Training/Learning Deployment. However, in a restart there is one big issue that makes life more difficult, and that is credibility. How do you convince all the necessary people that it will work the second time around, when things did not come together at the first attempt? This will put special pressure on Step Eight, Culture Change. The employees could well be tired of excessive statistics and complex Six Sigma tools. Thus the selection of appropriate tools is a strong feature of Green Six Sigma.

The Green Six Sigma programme for a re-starter will naturally vary according to the condition of the organisation, but the programme can be adapted within the framework shown in Figure 12.1. The guidelines for each step are:

1. Management Awareness. If there is none, then you cannot re-start.
2. Initial Assessment. This has to be the re-start point. Where are we, where do we want to go?
3. Programme Brief and Organisation. The programme will need to be re-scoped and new teams formed.
4. Leadership Workshop. This will be essential, even if management has not changed.
5. Training/Learning Deployment. Appropriate tools should be selected. If past team members, in particular Black Belts, are not happy with the terminology of the old programme, then new expressions should be used. The title 'Black Belt' in itself

is not sacrosanct and might be changed. If the 'old' experts are still in the organisation, then training time might be reduced; for example, a workshop of only one week's duration might be sufficient.

6. Project Selection and Delivery. This is the same as the full Green Six Sigma programme; harvest the 'low hanging fruit'.

7. Measurement of Success Review. This involves looking at the old measures, ascertaining what worked and what did not, and following the full Green Six Sigma programme.

8. Culture Change. This will be critical. Top management support must be extremely evident. Reward and appraisal systems will have to be aligned to Green Six Sigma.

9. Improve and Sustain. Same as for Green Six Sigma.

12.6. Green Six Sigma for Small and Medium Enterprises

There are many small and medium enterprises (SMEs) which are delivering products and services for climate change initiatives, especially for retrofitting buildings. These are the companies engaging in the manufacture of heat pumps, home insulation and the circular economy.

The organisation structure of the programme will vary according to the nature and size of the organisation. For small and medium enterprises (SMEs) a typical structure is as shown in Figure 12.6. In small enterprises the Programme Leader might be part time. In all other cases the Programme Leader will be full time.

Small and Medium Enterprises may follow the DMAIC Lite process (Basu, 2011). Similar to the full DMAIC process, the DMAIC Lite procedure has three structured steps (viz. Define, Measure and Analyse and Improve and Control). However, the boundaries between 'Measure' and 'Analyse' and also between 'Improve' and 'Control' are more flexible in the DMAIC Lite version. DMAIC Lite should be followed by the sustainability tools of Green Six Sigma.

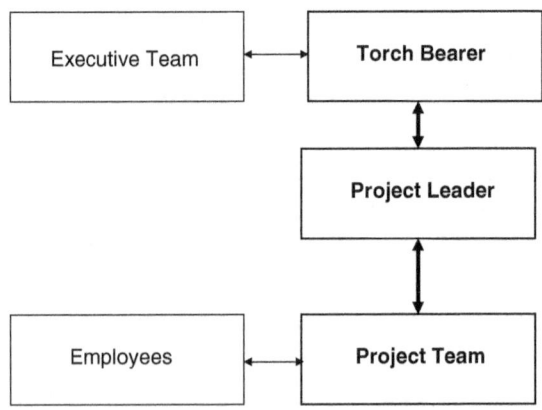

Figure 12.6   Green Six Sigma structure for SMEs
© Ron Basu

12.7.   Green Six Sigma for Successful Organisations

There are some organisations that have been consciously engaged in successful Lean Six Sigma projects to achieve clean energy or green transports. The examples in this category include Ivanpah Solar Electric Generating System (Case Example 7.1) and Tesla Electric Vehicles (Case Example 9.2). The approach for these projects should be to focus on the sustainability tools of Green Six Sigma. This is also a case for 'we've completed Six Sigma, but where to now?'

William Stavropoulos, the CEO of Dow Chemical, is reported to have once said, 'The most difficult thing to do is to change a successful company.' It is true that employees of firms enjoying a high profit margin with some dominance in the market are likely to be complacent and to feel comfortable with the status quo. Perhaps it is even more difficult to remain at the top or to sustain success if the existing strategy and processes are not adaptable to change. Darwin famously observed, 'It is not the strongest species that survive, nor the most intelligent, but the ones most responsive to change.' It is possible for the management of some companies, after the completion of a highly successful Six Sigma programme, to find their attention diverted to another major initiative such as e-business or Business to Business Alliances. Certainly, new schemes must be pursued, but at the same time the long-term benefits that could be achieved from Six Sigma should not be lost. Green Six Sigma for sustainability – staying healthy – is the answer.

If a company has succeeded with Six Sigma, then the time is now right to move onto Green Six Sigma to achieve Step Nine: Improve and Sustain.

12.8. External Consultants

Many businesses, especially SMEs, are often concerned with the cost of consultants for a Six Sigma programme. Large consulting firms and academies for Six Sigma could well expect high front-end fees. However, with Green Six Sigma the recommended approach is to be selective in the use of outside consultants. We advocate that you should use outside consultants to train your own experts, and to supplement your own expertise and resources when necessary. No consultant will know your own company as well as your own people. For this reason, the use of external consultants is not favoured in the role of the Programme Leader.

In a Green Six Sigma programme the best use of consultants is in:

Step Two: Initial Assessment. Here one would use a Six Sigma expert or an EFQM consultant to train and guide your team

Steps Four and Five: Leadership Workshop, and Training/ Learning Deployment. Outside consultants will be needed to facilitate the Leadership Workshops, and to tutor your own 'Black Belts'. Once trained, your own 'Black Belts' will in turn train 'Green Belts' and develop new 'Black Belts'.

Step Eight: Culture Change. An outside consultant is best suited to develop a change management plan for a change of culture.

12.9. Summary

Chapter 12 provides practical guidelines for selecting appropriate tools and techniques and 'making it all happen' in a quality programme like Green Six Sigma. Many a Six Sigma exercise started with high expectations and looked good on paper. Many an organisation has been impressed by success stories of Six Sigma, but unsure of how to start. The implementation plan shown here will enable any organisation at any stage of a Green Six Sigma initiative to follow a proven path to success and to sustain benefits. The implementation plan has nine steps, beginning with Management Awareness right through to the ongoing process of Improve and Sustain. There is no end to the process of striving for and measuring improvement.

In the spirit of Green Six Sigma, fit for purpose, this framework can be adjusted and customised to the specific needs of any organisation. Explicit comments have been included in this chapter for the implementation of Green Six Sigma in small and medium enterprises (SMEs) where resources are constrained (see Sections 12.4.1 and 12.4.3). Instead of all nine steps in Figure 12.1, SMEs should focus primarily on steps 1, 3, 5, 6 and 9.

At all stages of the programme, it is essential not only that the Executive Steering Committee and the Torch Bearer are kept informed (and in turn the Torch Bearer will keep the board up to date), but that there is open communication with all members of the organisation, so that everyone is aware of the aims, activities and successes of the programme.

As a final thought, with the 'clear and present danger' of climate change upon us, it is hard to be optimistic about the future. However, it is also possible that we have a fact-based worldview of climate change and when we all work together we can hope for and look to achieve a greener world for our future generations.

Green Tips

- United Nations, with the support of national governments, should sponsor the global rollout of Green Six Sigma as they did for Work Study in 1960s.
- Universities should include courses to train and certify Green Six Sigma Black Belts as part of their undergraduate curriculums.
- Green Six Sigma should be appropriately applied to all climate change initiatives, whether they are new starters, completed projects or stalled projects, to accelerate the process and ensure sustainability of outcomes.
- Green Six Sigma can be tailored to apply to SMEs engaged in the supply and installation of home retrofitting projects.
- Green Six Sigma can be a catalyst to deliver climate change initiatives.

Appendix 1
Carbon Footprint Factsheet

Carbon Footprint

'A carbon footprint is the total greenhouse gas (GHG) emissions caused directly and indirectly by an individual, organization, event or product.' It is calculated by summing the emissions resulting from every stage of a product or service's lifetime (material production, manufacturing, use, and end-of-life). Throughout a product's lifetime, or life cycle, different greenhouse gases GHGs may be emitted, such as carbon dioxide (CO_2), methane (CH_4) and nitrous oxide (N_2O), each with a greater or lesser ability to trap heat in the atmosphere. These differences are accounted for by calculating the global warming potential (GWP) of each gas in units of carbon dioxide equivalents (CO_2e), giving carbon footprints a single unit for easy comparison.

Sources of Emissions

FOOD

- Food accounts for 10–30% of a household's carbon footprint, typically a higher portion in lower-income households. Production accounts for 68% of food emissions, while transportation accounts for 5%.
- Food production emissions consist mainly of CO_2, N_2O and CH_4, which result primarily from agricultural practices.
- Meat products have larger carbon footprints per calorie than grain or vegetable products because of the inefficient transformation of plant energy to animal energy, and are due to the methane released from manure management and enteric fermentation in ruminants.
- Ruminants such as cattle, sheep and goats produced 178 million metric tons CO_2e of enteric methane in the US in 2018.
- Eliminating the transport of food for one year could save the GHG equivalent of driving 1,000 miles, while shifting to a vegetarian meal one day a week could save the equivalent of driving 1,160 miles.
- A vegetarian diet greatly reduces an individual's carbon footprint, but switching to less carbon intensive meats can have a major impact as well. For example, beef's GHG emissions per kilogram are 7.2 times greater than those of chicken.

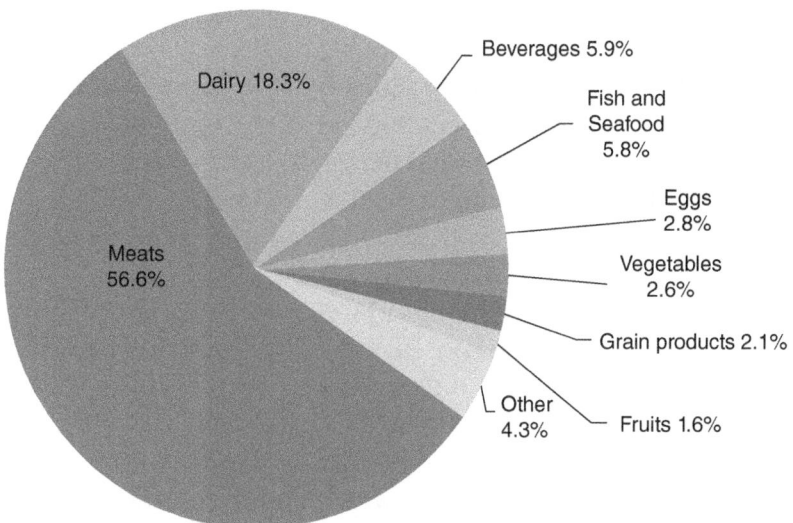

Greenhouse gases contribution by food type in average diet pounds of CO_2e per serving

HOUSEHOLD EMISSIONS

- For each kilowatt hour generated in the US, an average of 0.953 pounds of CO_2e is released at the power plant. Coal releases 2.2 pounds, petroleum releases 1.9 pounds, and natural gas releases 0.9 pounds. Nuclear, solar, wind, and hydroelectric release no CO_2 when they produce electricity, but emissions are released during upstream production activities (e.g. solar cells, nuclear fuels, cement production).
- Residential electricity use in 2018 emitted 666.5 metric million tonnes of CO_2e, 10% of the US total.
- Residential space heating and cooling are estimated to account for 44% of energy in US homes in 2020.
- Refrigerators are one of the largest users of household appliance energy; in 2015, an average of 720.5 lb of CO_2e per household was due to refrigeration.
- 26 metric million tonnes of CO_2e are released in the US each year from washing clothes. Switching to a cold water wash once per week, a household can reduce its GHG emissions by over 70 lb annually.

PERSONAL TRANSPORTATION

- US fuel economy (mpg) declined by 12% from 1987 to 2004, then improved by 30% from 2004 to 2018, reaching an average of 25.1 mpg in 2018. Annual per capita miles driven increased 9% since 1995 to 9,919 miles in 2018.
- Cars and light trucks emitted 1.1 billion metric tonnes of CO_2e or 17% of the total US GHG emissions in 2018.
- Of the roughly 66,000 pounds of CO_2e emitted over the lifetime of an internal combustion engine car (assuming 93,000 miles driven), 84% come from the use phase.
- Gasoline releases 19.6 pounds of CO_2 per gallon when burned, compared to 22.4 pounds per gallon for diesel. However, diesel has 11% more BTU per gallon, which improves its fuel economy.
- The average passenger car emits 0.78 pounds of CO_2 per mile driven.
- Automobile fuel economy can improve by 7–14% by simply observing the speed limit. Every 5 mph increase in vehicle speed over 50 mph is equivalent to paying an extra \$0.13–\$0.25 per gallon.
- Commercial aircraft GHG emissions vary according to aircraft type, trip length, occupancy rates, and passenger and cargo weight, and totalled 130.8 million metric tonnes of CO_2e in 2018. In 2018, the average domestic commercial flight emitted 0.39 pounds of CO_2e per passenger mile.
- Domestic air travel fuel efficiency (passenger miles per gallon) rose by 118% from 1990 to 2018, largely due to increased occupancy. Emissions per domestic passenger mile decreased 44% from 1990 to 2018, due to increased occupancy and fuel efficiency.
- In 2018, rail transportation emitted 42.9 million metric tonnes of CO_2e, accounting for 2% of transportation emissions in the US.

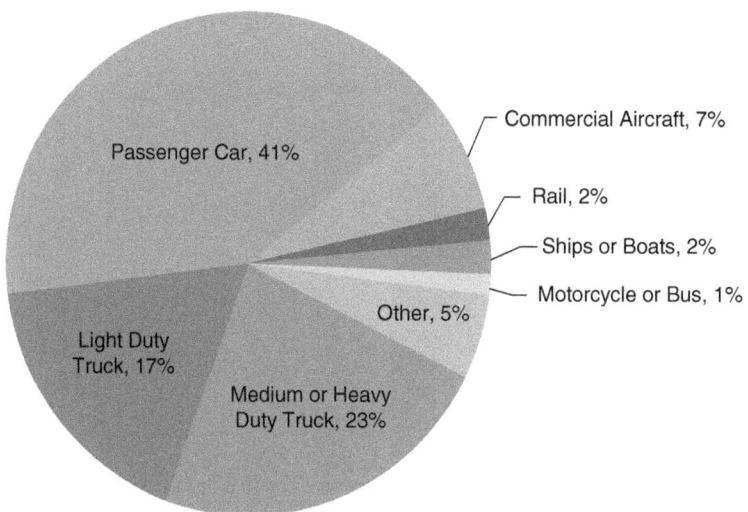

SOURCE: University of Michigan (2021).

Appendix 2
Yield Conversion Table

These are estimates of log-term sigma values. Subtract 1.5 from these values to obtain actual sigma values.

Sigma	DPMO	Yield %	Sigma	DPMO	Yield %
6.0	3.4	99.99966	2.9	80757	91.9
5.9	5.4	99.99946	2.6	90801	90.3
5.8	8.5	99.99915	2.7	155070	88.5
5.7	13	99.99866	2.6	135666	86.4
5.6	21	99.9979	2.5	158655	84.1
5.5	32	99.9968	2.4	184060	81.6
5.4	48	99.9952	2.3	211855	78.8
5.3	72	99.9928	2.2	241964	75.8
5.2	108	99.9892	2.1	374253	72.6
5.2	159	99.984	2.0	308538	69.1
5.0	233	99.977	1.9	344578	65.5
4.9	337	99.966	1.8	382089	61.8
4.8	483	99.952	1.7	420740	57.9
4.7	687	99.931	1.6	460172	54.0
4.6	968	99.90	1.5	500000	50.0
4.5	1350	99.87	1.4	539828	46.0
4.4	1866	99.81	1.3	579260	42.1
4.3	2555	99.74	1.2	617911	38.2
4.2	3467	99.65	1.1	665422	34.5

Sigma	DPMO	Yield %	Sigma	DPMO	Yield %
4.1	661	99.53	1.0	691482	30.9
4.0	6210	99.38	0.9	725747	27.4
3.9	198	99.18	0.8	758036	24.2
3.8	10724	98.9	0.7	788145	21.2
3.7	13903	98.6	0.6	815940	18.4
3.6	17864	98.2	0.5	841345	15.9
3.5	22750	97.7	0.4	864334	13.6
3.4	28716	97.1	0.3	884930	11.5
3.3	35930	96.4	0.2	903199	9.7
3.2	44565	95.5	0.1	919243	8.1
3.1	54799	94.5			
3.0	66897	93.3			

References

Apak, S., Atay, E. and Tuncer, G. (2017), 'Renewable hydrogen energy and energy efficiency in Turkey in the 21st century', *International Journal of Hydrogen Energy*, Vol. 42, No. 4, pp. 2446–2452.

Barth, H. and Melin, M. (2018), 'A Green Lean approach to global competition and climate change in the agricultural sector – A Swedish case study', *Journal of Cleaner Production*, Vol. 204, pp. 183–192.

Bassard, M. and Ritter, D. (1994), *Memory Jogger*, Methuen, Massachusetts.

Basu, R. (2002), *Measuring e-Business in the Pharmaceutical Sector; A strategic assessment of new business opportunities*, Reuters, London.

Basu, R. (2004), 'Six Sigma in operational excellence: Role of tools and techniques', *International Journal of Six Sigma and Competitive Advantage*, Vol. 1, No.1, pp. 44–64.

Basu, R. (2009), *Implementing Six Sigma and Lean*, Elsevier, Oxford.

Basu, R. (2011), *FIT SIGMA: A Lean Approach to Building Sustainable Quality Beyond Six Sigma*, John Wiley & Sons, Chichester, UK.

Basu, R. (2012), *Managing Quality in Projects*, Gower Publications, Routledge, Abingdon, UK.

Basu, R. and Wright, J.N. (1997), *Total Manufacturing Solutions*, Butterworth and Heinemann, Oxford, UK.

Basu, R. and Wright, J.N. (2003), *Quality Beyond Six Sigma*, Butterworth and Heinemann, Oxford, UK.

Basu, R. and Wright, J.N. (2017), *Managing Global Supply Chains*, Routledge, Abingdon, UK.

Belhadi, A., Kamble, S., Cherafi, Z.A. and Touriki, F.E. (2020), 'The integrated effect of Big Data Analytics, Lean Six Sigma and Green Manufacturing on the environmental performance of manufacturing companies: The case of North Africa', *Journal of Cleaner Production*, Vol. 252.

Black, J.T. and Phillips, D.T. (2010), 'The lean to green evolution', *Industrial Engineer*, Vol. 42, No. 7, pp. 46–51.

BP (2020), 'BP Statistical Review of World Energy', BP Plc, St James's Square, London.

Breyfogle III, Forrest W. (2008), 'Better Fostering Innovation: 9 steps hat Improve Lean Six Sigma', *Business Performance Management,* September 2008.

British Quality Foundations (BQF) (1999), *The European Foundation of Quality Management (EFQM) Model*, London.

BSI (2009), 'BS EN ISO 9004:2009. Managing for sustained success of an organisation. A quality management approach', British Standards Institution, London.

Carnall, C. (1999), *Managing Change in Organisations*, Prentice Hall, London.

Carrington, D. (2021), 'A billion children at "extreme risk" from climate impacts – Unicef', *The Guardian*, August 20, 2021.

Chaurasia, B., Garg, D. and Agarwal A (2019), 'Lean Six Sigma Approach: A strategy to enhance performance of first through time and scrap reduction in the automotive industry', *International Journal Business Excellence*, Vol. 17, No. 1, pp. 42–57.

Cherrafi, A., Elfezazi, S. and Govindan, K. (2017), 'A framework for the integration of Green and Lean Six Sigma for superior sustainability performance', *International Journal of Production Research*, Vol. 55, No. 15, pp. 4481–4515.

Coppola, D, Online share of retail sales in the United Kingdom (UK) from 2011 to 2020, statista, October 21, 2021. https://www.statista.com/statistics/315520/online-share-of-retail-sales-in-the-uk/.

Corporate Leadership Council (2005), 'Leadership competencies in a Lean environment', Corporate Executive Board, August 2005, Catalog No. CLC13TKO7X, London.

Dale, B.G. (1999), *Managing Quality*, Blackwell Publishers, Oxford, Chapter 18, pp. 366–389.

de Bono (2016), *Six Thinking Hats*, Penguin Books, London.

De Carlo, N. (2007), *Lean Six Sigma*, Alpha Books, New York.

Deming, W.E. (1986), *Out of the Crisis,* MIT Centre for Advanced Research, Cambridge, Boston.

De Oliviera, J.A.P. (2009), 'The implementation of climate change related policies at subnational level: An analysis of three countries', *Habitat International*, Vol. 33, No.3, pp. 253–259.

Earth Systems Science Data (2020), *A Comprehensive and Systematic Dataset for Global, Regional and National Greenhouse Gas Emissions by Sector*, Edited by K. Elger, D. Carlson, J. Kemp and G. Peng, Copernicus Publications, Gottingen, Germany.

Easton, G. and Jarrell, S. (1998), 'The effects of total quality management on corporate performance', *Journal of Business*, Vol. 71, No. 3, pp. 253–307.

Eckes, G. (2001), *Making Six Sigma Last*, John Wiley & Sons Ltd, Chichester, UK.

Elkington, J. (1994), 'Towards the sustainable corporation: Win-win-win business strategies for sustainable development.' *California Management Review*, Vol. 36, No. 2, pp. 90–100.

Erwin, J. and Douglas, P.C. (2000), 'It is difficult to change company culture', *Journal of Supervision*, Vol. 51, No. 11.

European Foundation of Quality Management (2003), *The EFQM Excellence Model*, Brussels.

EY Global Renewables (2020), *Global Renewable Outlook: Energy Transformation 2020*, IRENA, Abu Dhabi.

Fiedler, T., Pitman, A.J., Mackenzie, K., et al. (2021), 'Business risk and the emergence of climate analytics', *Nature Climate Change*, Vol. 11, pp. 87–94.

Finkelstein, S. (2006), 'Why smart executives fail: Four case histories of how people learn the wrong lesson from history', *Business History*, Vol. 48, No.2, pp. 153–170

Gates, B. (2021), *How to Avoid a Climate Disaster*, Penguin Random House, UK.

George, M.L. (2002), *Lean Six Sigma: Combining Six Sigma Quality with Lean Production Speed*. McGraw-Hill, New York.

George, G., Merrill, R.K. and Schillebeeckx, J.D. (2020), *Digital Sustainability and Entrepreneurship: How Digital Innovations Are Helping Tackle Climate Change and Sustainable Development*, Sage Publications; also *Entrepreneurship Theory and Practice*, Vol. 45, No. 4, pp. 1–28.

Gernaat, D.E.H.J., de Boer, H.S., Daioglou, V., et al. (2021), 'Climate change impacts on renewable energy supply', *Nature Climate Change*, Vol. 11, pp. 119–125.

Gijo, E.V. and Sarkar, A. (2013). 'Application of Six Sigma to improve the quality of the road for wind turbine installation', *The TQM Journal*, Vol. 25, No. 3, pp. 244–258.

Global Carbon Project (2019), *Global Carbon Budget 2021,* Edited by P. Jittrapirom, and P. Canadell, Global Carbon Project, Canberra.

Goel, S. and Chen, V. (2008), 'Integrating the global enterprise using Six Sigma: Business Process Reengineering at General Electric Wind Energy', *International Journal of Production Economics*, Vol. 113, No. 2, pp. 914–927.

Goldratt, E.M. (1999), *The Theory of Constraints*, North River Press, New York.

Hammer, M. and Champy, J. (1993), *Re-Engineering the Corporation*, Nicholas Brealey Publishing, London.

Hartman, E. (1991), 'How to install TPM in your plant', *8th International Maintenance Conference*, Dallas, 12–14 November 1991.

ICAP (2021). Emissions Trading Worldwide: Status Report 2021, International Carbon Action Partnership, Berlin.

ILO (1978), 'Work Study (Third Edition)', International Labour Organisation, Geneva.

IPCC (2014a), 'AR5 Climate Change: Mitigation of Climate Change, IPCC's Fifth Assessment Report', Intergovernmental Panel of Climate Change.

IPCC (2014b), 'Glossary', Intergovernmental Panel of Climate Change.

IPCC (2021), 'AR6 Climate Change 2021: The Physical Science Basis', 2021 Intergovernmental Panel of Climate Change.

Juran, J.M. (1999), *Juran on Leadership for Quality: An Executive Handbook*, Free Press, New York.

Kalkar, P., Phule, D. and Chittanand, A. (2018), 'Dealing with the sustainability challenge with Lean Six Sigma framework', *International Journal of Management*, Vol. 9, No. 3, pp. 21–31.

Kaplan, R.S. and Norton, D.P. (1996), 'Linking balanced scorecard to strategy', *California Management Review*, Vol. 39, No. 1, pp. 53–79.

Kaplan, R.S. and Norton, D.P. (2004), 'Measuring the strategic readiness of intangible assets', *Harvard Business Review*, February, Vol. 82, No. 2, pp. 52–64.

Kaswan, M.S. and Rathi, R. (2020), 'Green Lean Six Sigma for sustainable development: Integration and framework', *Environmental Impact and Assessment Review*, Vol. 83.

Kendon, M., et al. (2021), 'State of the UK Climate 2020', *International Journal of Climatology*, Vol. 41, No. S2, pp. 1–76

Khadri, S. (2013), 'Six Sigma Methodology for the environment sustainable development', *Mechanism Design for Sustainability*, pp. 61–76, Palgrave McMillan, New York.

Kharub, M., Sharma, G. and Sahoo, S.K. (2018), 'Investigating the cause of poor efficiency in thermal power plant – A Six Sigma based case study', *CVR Journal of Science & Technology*, Vol. 14.

Kotabe, M. and Helsen, K. (2000), *Global Marketing Management*, John Wiley & Sons Ltd, New York.

Ladhar, Harjinder (2007), 'Effective Lean Six Sigma deployment in a global EMS environment', Circuits Assembly, March 2007.

Lewin, K. (1951), *Field Theory in Social Science: Selected Theoretical Papers*, Harper-Collins, New York.

Ledolter, J. and Burnhill, C.W. (1999), *Achieving Quality Through Continual Improvement*, John Wiley & Sons Ltd, Chichester, UK.

Lee, J., Maria, L. and Vaishnav, P. (2021), 'The impact of climate change on the recoverability of airlines network', *Transport and Environment*, Vol. 95, Elsevier.

Lemos, M., Kirchhoff, C. and Ramprasad, V. (2012), 'Narrowing the climate information usability gap', *Nature Climate Change*, Vol. 2, pp. 789–794.

Liker, J.K. (2004), *The Toyota Way*, McGraw-Hill, New York.

Ling, R.C. and Goddard, W.E. (1988), *Orchestrating Success*, John Wiley & Sons Ltd, Chichester, UK.

Matsushita, K. (2020), '*Japan's response to the issue of climate change*', Sasakawa Peace Foundation, USA.

Mengel, T. (2008), 'Outcome-based project management education for emerging leaders – A case study of teaching and learning project management', *International Journal of Project Management*, Vol. 26, No. 3, pp. 275–285.

Moroney, M.J. (1973), *Facts from Figures*, Penguin Books, London.

Mowris, R.J., Jones, E. and Jones, A. (2006), 'Incorporating IPMVP and Six Sigma Strategies into Energy Efficiency Program Design, Implementation, and Evaluation', *2006 ACEEE Summer Study on Energy Efficiency in Buildings*.

MSP (2007), *Managing Successful Programme*, 3rd edition, The Office of Government Commerce, London.

Negroponte, N. (1995), *Being Digital*, Hodder and Stoughton, London.

Ninerola, A., Ferrer-Ruler, R. and Vidal-Sune, A. (2020), 'Climate change mitigation: Application of management production philosophies for energy saving in industrial processes', *Lean Manufacturing, Operational Excellence and Sustainability* (special edition), Universitat Rovira i Virgili, Spain.

Oakland, J.S. (2003), *TQM: Text with Cases*, Butterworth Heinemann, Oxford.

Ohno, T. (1988), *Toyota Production Systems*, Productivity Press, Cambridge, Boston.

Pallant, J. (2010), *SPSS Survival Manual*, Open University Press, Maidenhead, UK.

Pearce, I. (1992), 'Thinking Green', *Environmental Management and Health*, Vol. 3, No. 2, pp. 6–12

Pew Research Center (2021), 'European electric vehicle industry, 2021–2024', Pew Research Center, Washington, DC.

Prasad, A.G., Saravanan, S., Gijo, E.V., Dasari, S.M., Tatachar, R. and Suratkar, P. (2016), 'Six Sigma-based approach to optimise the diffusion process of crystalline silicon solar cell manufacturing', *International Journal of Sustainable Energy*, Vol. 35, No. 2, pp. 190–204.

Pyzdek, T. (2003), *The Six Sigma Handbook*, McGraw-Hill, New York.

RIBA (2021), 'RIBA 2030 Climate Challenge. Version 2', Royal Institute of British Architects, London.

Retro-first (2021), '*The Big Zero Report*', *Architects' Journal*, London.

Ruggles, R. (1998), 'The state of notions: Knowledge management in practice', *California Management Review*, Vol. 40, No.3, pp. 80–89.

Schmidt, S.R., Kiemele, M.J. and Bardine, R.J. (1999), *Knowledge Based Management*, Academy Press, Colorado Springs, USA.

Schweikhart, S.A. and Dembe, A. (2009), 'Applicability of Lean and Six Sigma techniques to clinical and translational research', *Journal of Investigative Medicine*, Vol. 57, No. 7, pp. 748–755.

Seyam, S., Dincer, I. and Chaab, M.A. (2021), 'Novel hybrid aircraft propulsion system using hydrogen, methanol, ethanol and dimethyl ether as alternative fuels', *Energy Conversion and Management*, Vol. 238, Elsevier.

Sharp, E.B., Dailey, D.M. and Lynch, M. (2011), 'Understanding local adoption and implementation of climate change integration policy', *Sage Journals*, Vol. 47, No. 3, pp. 433–457.

Shingo, S. (1985), *Non-Stock Production*, Productivity Press, Cambridge, Massachusetts.

Shirose, K. (1992), *TPM for Workshop Learners*, Productivity Press, Cambridge, Massachusetts.

Skinner, S. (2001), 'Mastering basic tenets of Lean Manufacturing – Five Ss', *Manufacturing News*, Vol. 8, No. 11.

Slack, N., Barndon-Jone, A., Johnson, R. and Betts, A. (2012), *Operations and Process Management*, Pearson Education, Harlow, UK.

Stamatis, D.H. (1999), *Six Sigma and Beyond*, St Lucie Press, New York.

Statistica Research Department (2021), 'Share of electrified railroad routes in European Countries', Editor E.B. Salas, Statistica Research Department, Hamburg.

Sterman, J., Repenning, N.P. and Kofman, F. (1997), 'Unanticipated side effects of successfull quality programmes: Exploring a paradox of organizational improvement', *Management Science*, Vol. 43, No. 4, pp. 503–521.

Stern, N. (2006), 'Stern Review: The Economics of Climate Change', HM Treasury.

Sujova, A., Simanova, L. and Marcinekova, K. (2016), 'Sustainable process performance by application of Six Sigma concepts: The research study of two industrial cases'. *Sustainability*, Vol. 8, No. 3.

The Economic Times (2009). 'Vestas saves $10 million through lean six sigma initiative', *The Economic Times*, Mumbai, August 18, 2009.

The Guardian (2021), 'UK weather: Met Office issues strong wind warnings', *The Guardian*, March 10, 2021.

Treacy, M. and Wiersema, F. (1993), 'Customer intimacy and other value disciplines', *Harvard Business Review*, January/February 1993, pp. 84–93.

Tuckman, B.W. (1965), 'Development sequence in small groups', *Psychological Bulletin*, Vol. 63, pp. 384–399.

Turner, J.R. and Simister, S.J. (2000), *Gower Handbook of Project Management*, Gower Publishing, Aldershot, UK.

UK Carbon Trust (2008), *Carbon Trust Standard 2008*, Carbon Trust, London.

UNEP (2019), 'Emissions Gap Report 2019', *United Nations Environment Programme*, New York.

United Nations (1987), *Report of the World Commission on Environment and Development,* UN General Assembly Resolution, 11 December 1987, New York.

United Nations Foundation (2020), 'Key findings of the Sustainable Development Goals Report in 2020', United Nations, New York, NY 10017.

University of Michigan (2021), '2021 Factsheets Collection', School of Environment & Sustainability, University of Michigan, Ann Arbor.

US EPA (2019), 'Global Greenhouse Emission Data', United States Environment Protection Agency, Washington, DC.

Warner, P. (2019). 'Norwegian cruise line Hurtigruten trials biodiesel on cruise ship', *Biofuels International*, London, October 31, 2019.

Watt, I. (2012), 'Lessons from corporate claims of carbon neutrality', Forum for the Future, November 7, 2012, Major Projects Association, London.

Wei, Y.M., Kang, J.N., Liu, L.C., et al. (2021), 'A proposed global layout of carbon capture and storage in line with a 2 °C climate target', *Nature Climate Change*, Vol. 11, pp. 112–118.

Weinstein, L.B., Castellano, J., Petrick, J. and Vokurka, R.J. (2008), 'Integrating Six Sigma concepts in an MBA Quality Management Class', *Journal of Education for Business*, Vol. 83, No. 4, pp. 233–238.

Welch, J. (2001), *Jack: What I Have Learned Leading a Great Company and Great People*, Headline Book Publishing, London.

Whitlock, R. (2020), 'What place for hydrogen? An interview with Professor Armin Schnettler of Siemens', *Renewable Energy Magazine*, London, April 2020.

Wild, R. (2002), *Operations Management*, Continuum, London.

Womack, J.P. and Jones, D.T. (1998), *Lean Thinking*, Touchstone Books, London.

Yu, J., Williams, E., Ju, M. and Yang, Y. (2010), 'Forecasting global generation of obsolete personal computers', *Environmental Science and Technology*, Vol. 44, No. 9, pp. 3232–3237.

Glossary

ABC Analysis   This is based on a Pareto Analysis, grouping units usually according to the share of annual cost. Units having an 80% annual cost are considered in the 'A' classification, units with the bottom 5% share are 'C' items and units with costs in between are in the 'B' category.

Activity Network Diagram   This is a network analysis technique to allow a team to find the most efficient path and realistic schedule of a project by graphically showing the completion time and sequence of each task.

Affinity Diagram   This is used to generate a number of ideas by a team and then organise natural groupings among them to understand the essence of a problem.

AI   Artificial Intelligence is demonstrated by technology as opposed to natural intelligence displayed by living creatures.

ASHP   Air source heat pump.

Bar Chart   This is also known as a Gantt Chart and indicates scheduling activities. Horizontal bars show the various activities with the length of the bar proportional to the duration of a particular activity.

Benchmarking This is the rating of an organisation's products, processes and performances with other organisations in the same or another business. The objective is to identify the gaps with competitors and the areas for improvement.

Best Practice Best practice refers to any organisation that performs as well or better than the competition in quality, timeliness, flexibility and innovation. Best practice should lead to a world class performance.

Big Data Analytics Big Data Analytics involve complex applications with predictive models and what-if analysis by the analytics system.

Black Belts These are experts in Six Sigma methods and tools. Tools include statistical analysis. Black Belts are project leaders for Six Sigma initiatives and also train other staff members in Six Sigma techniques.

Blockchain This is a type of database of information structured in table format to allow for easier searching for specific information.

BPR Business Process Re-engineering has been described as a manifesto for revolution. The approach is similar to taking a clean piece of paper and starting all over again by identifying what is really needed to make the mission of the organisation happen.

Brainstorming This is a free-wheeling group session for generating ideas. Typically, a group meeting of about seven people will be presented with a problem. Each member will be encouraged to make suggestions without fear of criticism. One suggestion will lead to another. All suggestions, no matter how seemingly fanciful, are recorded and subsequently analysed.

BWR This is a Boiling Water Reactor in a nuclear power plant.

Carbon Dioxide Equivalent Also expressed as CO_2e, this is a metric measure of greenhouse gases as carbon dioxide tonnes to compare the global warming potential from various greenhouse gases.

Carbon Footprint A carbon footprint is the total set of greenhouse gas (GHG) emissions caused by an organization, event or product. For simplicity of reporting, it is often expressed in terms of the amount of carbon dioxide or its equivalent of other GHG emissions. A carbon footprint can be measured by undertaking a GHG emissions assessment of an individual, organisation or a country.

Cause and Effect Diagram The cause and effect, fishbone or Ishikawa diagram was developed by Kaoru Ishikawa. The premise is that generally when a problem occurs the effect is very obvious, and the temptation is to treat the effect. With the Ishikawa approach the causes of the effect are sought. Once the cause is known and eliminated the effect will not be seen again.

CCS Carbon Capture and Storage is another version of Direct Air Capture.

CGIAR Consultative Group of International Agricultural Research.

Check Sheet This is a method of systematically recording data from historical sources or observations as they happen. The patterns and trends can be clearly detected and shown.

CIM Computer-integrated Manufacturing.

Circular Economy It aims for a world without waste by recycling and reusing. It is also an important tenet of Green Six Sigma.

Cloud Computing This is the on-demand availability of computer system resources, especially data storage and computing power.

Continuous Improvement This is always looking for ways to improve a process or a product, but not necessarily making radical step changes. If the basic idea is sound then building on it will improve quality. In Japan this is known as Kaizen.

Control Chart This is a tool in Statistical Process Control to monitor the number of defects found in a product or a process over time and study the variation and its source.

COP Conference of Parties organised every year to review the progress of climate change initiatives.

COPQ   The cost of poor quality is made up of costs arising from internal failures, external failures, appraisal, prevention and lost opportunity costs – in other words, all the costs that arise from non-conformance to a standard. Chapter 3 discusses COPQ in some detail.

CO_2 ppm   This is the measurement of CO_2 concentration expressed as parts per million per unit volume of water.

CPFR   Collaborative Planning Forecasting and Replenishment aims to enhance supply chain integration of stakeholders through joint visibility and replenishment of products.

CRM   Customer relationship management is the development of the database and strategies necessary to have the maximum client relationships in terms of quality, cost, reliability and responsiveness.

CSR   Corporate social responsibility.

CTQs   In Six Sigma CTQs are referred to as critical to quality. This simply means the identification of factors that are critical for the achievement of a level of quality.

Cycle Time   This is the elapsed time between two successive operations or the time required to complete an operation.

DAC   Direct Air Capture is a device that absorbs CO_2 and the output is stored.

DFSS   Design for Six Sigma; see Chapter 9 for a detailed discussion. The steps are Define, Measure, Analyse, Design and Validate.

Digital Six Sigma (DSS)   This is reported to be a revitalization of Six Sigma methodology by Motorola through the following improvements:

- Leveraging new digital tools to drive project success
- Digitizing business processes to 'permanently' enforce optimal process compliance
- Tracking vital processes through digital databases
- 'Permanently' and proactively eliminating sources of variation that cause defects

DMADV   Define, Measure, Analyse, Design and Verify. It is a modified version of DMAIC for Research and Development.

DMAIC   This is the cycle of Define, Measure, Analyse, Improve and Control. It is an integral part of a Six Sigma or Lean Six Sigma initiative.

DMAIC Lite   This is the DAMAIC process for SMEs.

DMAICS   This is the cycle of DMAIC with an additional for Sustainability. It is an integral part of a Green Six Sigma initiative.

DOE   This is the process of examining options in the design of a product or service. Controlled changes of input factors are made and the resulting changes to outputs noted. Losses from poor design include not only direct loss to the company from reworking and scrap, but includes for the user downtime due to equipment failure, poor performance and unreliability.

DPMO   Defects per million opportunities. This is the basic measure of Six Sigma. It is the number of defects per unit divided by the number of opportunities for defects multiplied by 1,000,000. This number can be converted into a Sigma value. For example, Six Sigma = 3.4 per million opportunities.

E-business   Electronic-business is more than the transfer of information using information technology. E-business is the complex mix of processes, applications and organizational structures.

EDE   Electronic Data Exchange.

EFQM   The European Foundation for Quality Management is derived from the American Malcom Baldridge Quality award. It is an award for organisations that achieve world class performance as judged by independent auditors against a checklist.

Electrofuel   Net-zero carbon-free fuel produced by combining the hydrogen in water and the carbon from CO_2.

EPA   Environment Protection Agency in the USA.

ERP   Enterprise Resource Planning is the extension of MRPII systems to the management of complete business functions including finance and human resources.

ETS   Emission Testing System.

EV   Electric vehicle.

Failure Mode and Effect Analysis   FMEA was developed in the aerospace and defence industries. It is a systematic and analytical quality planning tool for identifying new products or services, at the design stage, what could go wrong during manufactures, or when in use by the customer. It is also a tool for risk analysis.

First Pass Yield   FPY, also known as Rolled Throughput Yield (RTY), is the ratio of the number of completely defects free without any kind of rework during the process units at the end of a process and the total number of units at the start of a process. The theoretical throughput rate is often regarded as the number of units at the start of the process. RTY/FPY is used as a key performance indicator to measure overall process effectiveness.

Fishbone Diagram   The fishbone, Ishikawa, or cause and effect diagram, was developed by Kaoru Ishikawa. The premise is that generally when a problem occurs the effect is very obvious and the temptation is to treat the effect. With the Ishikawa approach the causes of the effect are sought. Once the cause is known and eliminated the effect will not be seen again.

Fit Sigma   Also see Total Quality Management (TQM), Six Sigma and Lean Sigma. Fit Sigma incorporates all the advantages and tools of TQM, Six Sigma and Lean Sigma. The aim is to get an organisation healthy (fit) by using appropriate tools for the size and nature of the business (fitness for purpose) and to sustain a level of fitness. Fit Sigma is a holistic approach.

Flow Process Chart   A flow process chart sets out the sequence of the flow of a product or a procedure by recording all the activities in a process. The chart can be used to identify steps in the process, value adding activities and non-value adding activities.

Gantt Chart   See Bar Chart.

GCP   The Global Carbon Projects established in 2001 as a global research project on carbon emissions.

GEF The Global Environmental Faculty set up in 1992 at the Rio Earth Summit.

Green Belts These are staff trained to be Six Sigma project leaders. They work under the guidance of Black Belts (see Black Belts).

Greenhouse Gases Polluting gases in the environment causing global warming. These are carbon dioxide, methane, nitrous oxide, water vapour and ozone.

Green Premium This is the difference between the cost of a green solution and the existing option.

Green Six Sigma This is an adaptation of Lean Six Sigma and FIT SIGMA for climate change initiatives.

GSHP Ground source heat pump.

Histogram A histogram is a descriptive and easy to understand chart of the frequency of occurrences. It is a vertical bar chart with the height of each bar representing the frequency of an occurrence.

ICAP International Carbon Action Partnership.

IEA International Energy Agency.

IoT Internet of Things to describe a network of physical objects connected by sensors with the Internet.

IPCC The Intergovernmental Panel of Climate Change is the most effective body of international scientists to monitor climate change activities.

IPMVP The International Performance Measurement and Verification Protocol.

IPO (Input Process Output) Diagram All operations or processes have inputs and outputs. The process is the conversion of inputs into outputs. Analysis of inputs should be made to determine factors that influence the process, for example input materials from suppliers meeting specification, delivery on time and so on.

Ishikawa The Ishikawa, or fishbone, or cause and effect diagram was developed by Kaoru Ishikawa. The premise is that generally when a problem occurs the effect is very obvious, and the temptation is to treat the effect. With the Ishikawa approach the causes of the effect are sought. Once the cause is known and eliminated the effect will not be seen again.

ISO 9000   To gain ISO 9000 accreditation an organisation has to demonstrate to an accredited auditor that they have a well-documented standard and consistent process in place that achieves a defined level of quality or performance.

JIT   Just in Time was initially a manufacturing approach where materials are ordered to arrive just when required in the process, no output or buffer stocks are held and the finished product is delivered direct to the customer. Lean Six Sigma incorporates the principals of JIT.

Kaizen   Kaizen is a Japanese word derived from a philosophy of gradual day by day betterment of life and spiritual enlightenment. This approach has been adopted in industry and means gradual and unending improvement in efficiency and/or customer satisfaction. The philosophy is doing little things better so as to achieve a long-term objective.

Kanban   Kanban is the Japanese word for card. The basic kanban system is to use cards to trigger movements of materials between operations in production so that a customer order flows through the system.

KPIs   Key performance indicators include measurement of performance such as asset utilisation, customer satisfaction, cycle time from order to delivery, inventory turnover, operations costs, productivity, and financial results (return on assets and return on investment).

Kyoto Protocol   The Kyoto Protocol was adopted in Kyoto in December 1997 by 192 countries. It extends the 1992 UNFCCC objective to reduce greenhouse gas emissions based on the scientific consensus on global warming.

Lean Six Sigma   Also see Just in Time (JIT). Lean Six Sigma was initially a manufacturing approach where materials are ordered to arrive just when required in the process, no output or buffer stocks are held and the finished product is delivered direct to the customer. Lean Six Sigma incorporates the principals of Six Sigma and is related to the supply chain from supplier and supplier's supplier through the process to the customer and the customer's customer.

MFA Material Flow Analysis is an analytical method to quantify and balance the flow of materials in a well-defined system.

Minitab This is a statistical package developed at the Pennsylvania State University and distributed by Minitab Inc. Today, Minitab is often used in conjunction with the implementation of Six Sigma and other statistics-based process improvement methods.

Mistake Proofing Refers to making each step of production mistake free. This is also known as Poka Yoke, which was developed by Shingo (also see SMED) and has two main steps: (1) preventing the occurrence of a defect and (2) detecting the defect.

Monte Carlo Technique This is a simulation process. It uses random numbers as an approach to model the waiting times and queue lengths and also to examine the overall uncertainty in projects.

MRP (II) Manufacturing resource planning is an integrated computer-based procedure for dealing with all of the planning and scheduling activities for manufacturing, and includes procedures for stock re-order, purchasing, inventory records, cost accounting and plant maintenance.

MRV Monitoring Reporting and Verification standards are used to monitor progress as part of the Paris Climate Agreement.

Mudas Muda is the Japanese for waste or non-value adding. The seven activities that are considered are:

Excess production, Waiting, Conveyance, Motion, Process, Inventory and Defects.

NDC Nationally determined contributions are plans and targets for the participating countries of the Paris Climate Agreement.

NGO Non-governmental Organisation.

NLGCC The National Leading Group on Climate Change in China.

Nominal Group Technique This is a brainstorming tool for a team to come to a consensus on the relative importance of ideas by completing importance rankings into a team's final priorities.

Normal Distribution Normal distribution, or Gaussian Distribution, is a graph of the frequency of occurrence of a random variable. The distribution is continuous, symmetrical, bell shaped and the two tails extend indefinitely.

OEE Overall Equipment Effectiveness is the real output of a machine. It is given by the ratio of the good output and the maximum output of the machine for the time it is planned to operate.

Pareto Wilfredo Pareto was a nineteenth century Italian economist who observed that 80% of the wealth was held by 20% of the population. The same phenomenon can often be found in quality problems. This is also known as the 80/20 rule.

Paris Climate Agreement The Paris Climate Agreement (also known as the Paris Accord) is an international treaty on the climate crisis. Its stated aim is to radically reduce global carbon emissions and restrict the rise in the Earth's temperature to less than 2 degrees centigrade. This treaty was signed by all 189 participating countries in Paris in December 2015 at COP 21.

PDCA The Plan-Do-Check-Act cycle was developed by Dr W.E. Deming. It refers to: Planning the change and setting standards; Doing, making the change happen; Checking that what is happening is what was intended (standards are being met); and Act, taking action to correct back to the standard.

Performance Charts These show that upper control limits (UCL) and lower control limits (LCL) are used to show variations from the specification. Within the control limits performance will be deemed to be acceptable. The aim should be over time to reduce the control limits.

PESTLE Political, Economic, Social, Technical, Legal and Environmental is an analytical tool for assessing the impact of external contexts on a project or a major operation and also the impact of a project on its external contexts. There are several possible contexts.

PET This stands for polyethylene terephthalate. It is a form of polyester that is recyclable.

PEV Plug-in electric vehicle.

PM 2.5 Pollution for particulate matter.

Poka Yoke This refers to making each step of production mistake-free. This is known as mistake proofing. Poka Yoke was developed by Shingo (also see SMED) and has two main steps: (1) preventing the occurrence of a defect and (2) detecting the defect.

Process Capability Process capability is the statistically measured inherent reproducibility of the output (product) turned out by a process that is within the design specifications of the product.

Process Mapping Process Mapping is a tool to represent a process by a diagram containing a series of linked tasks or activities that produce an output.

Project A project is a unique item of work for which there is a financial budget and a defined schedule.

Project Charter A Project Charter is a working document for defining the terms of reference of each Six Sigma project. The charter can make a successful project by specifying necessary resources and boundaries that will in turn ensure success.

Project Management This involves the planning, scheduling, budgeting and control of a project using an integrated team of workers and specialists.

PV System Photovoltaic System in solar energy.

QFD Quality Function Deployment is a systematic approach of determining customer needs and designing the product or service so that it meets the customer's needs first time and every time.

Quality Circles Quality circles are teams of staff who are volunteers. The team selects issues or areas to investigate for improvement. To work properly teams have to be trained, firstly in how to work as a team (group dynamics) and secondly in problem-solving techniques.

Quality Project Teams   Quality project teams are a top-down approach to solving a quality problem. Management determines a problem area and selects a team to solve the problem. The advantage over a quality circle is that this is a focused approach, but the disadvantage might be that members are conscripted rather than volunteers.

Regression Analysis   This is a tool to establish the 'best fit' linear relationship between two variables. The knowledge provided by the scatter diagram is enhanced with the use of regression.

Rolled Throughput Yield   Rolled Throughput Yield (RTY), aka First Pass Yield (FPY), is the ratio of the number of completely defects free without any kind of rework during the process units at the end of a process and the total number of units at the start of a process. The theoretical throughput rate is often regarded as the number of units at the start of the process. RTY/FPY is used as a key performance indicator to measure overall process effectiveness.

RU/CS   Resource Utilisation (RU) and Customer Service (CS) Analysis is a simple tool to establish the relative importance of the key parameters of both Resource Utilisation and Customer Service and to identify their conflicts.

Run Chart   This is a graphical tool to study observed data for trends or patterns over a specific period of time.

5 S's   These represent a set of Japanese words for excellent house keeping (Sein – Sort, Seiton – Set in place, Seiso – Shine, Seiketso – Standardise and Sitsuke – Sustain).

SaaS   Software as a Service is a software licensing model in which software is licensed on a subscription or rental basis.

SAF   Sustainable Aviation Fuel.

S & OP   Sales and Operations Planning is derived from MRP and includes new product planning, demand planning, supply review, to provide weekly and daily manufacturing schedules, and financial information.

Scatter Diagrams These diagrams are used to examine the relationship between two variables. Changes are made to each and the results of changes are plotted on a graph to determine cause and effect.

SCM Supply chain management.

Sigma Sigma is the sign used for standard deviation from the arithmetic mean. If a normal distribution curve exists one sigma represents one standard deviation either side of the mean and accounts for 68.27% of the population. This is more fully explained in Chapter 3.

SIPOC This is a high level map of a process to view how a company goes about satisfying a particular customer requirement in the overall supply chain. SIPOC stands for supplier, input, process, output and customer.

Six Sigma Six Sigma is a quality system that in effect aims for zero defects. Six sigma in statistical terms means six deviations from the arithmetic mean. This equates to 99.99966% of the total population, or 3.4 defects per million opportunities.

SME Small and medium enterprise with a staff headcount of less than 250.

SMED The Single Minute Exchange of Dies was developed for the Japanese automobile industry by Shigeo Shingo in the eighties and involves the reduction of a changeover of production by an intensive work study to determine in-process and out-process activities and then to systematically improve the planning, tooling and operations of the changeover process.

SoQ The Signature of Quality is a self-assessment process supported by a checklist covering:

Customer focus, Innovation, Personnel and Organisational Leadership, use of Technology and Environment and Safety issues. It is useful in Fit Sigma for establishing a company 'health' report.

SPC Statistical Process Control (SPC) uses statistical sampling to determine if the outputs of a stage or stages of a process are conforming to a standard. Upper and lower limits are set and sampling is used to determine if the process is operating within the defined limits.

SPSS The Statistical Process for the Social Sciences is a software used for interactive statistical analysis.

SUD Sustainable Drainage System.

SUV A sport utility vehicle combines features of road-going passengers and raised ground clearance with a four-wheel drive.

SWOT SWOT (Strengths, Weaknesses, Opportunities and Threats) is a tool for analysing an organisation's competitive position in relation to its competitors.

The Seven Wastes Also see Mudas. Muda is the Japanese for waste or non-value adding. The seven activities that are considered are:

Excess production, Waiting, Conveyance, Motion, Process, Inventory and Defects.

Tolerance Charts Upper control limit (UCL) and lower control limit (LCL) are used to show variations from specification. Within the control limits performance will be deemed to be acceptable.

TPM Total Productive Maintenance requires factory management to improve asset utilisation by the systematic study and elimination of major obstacles – known as the 'six big losses' – to efficiency. The 'six big losses' in manufacturing are breakdown, set-up and adjustment, minor stoppages, reduced speed, quality defects and start-up and shut-down.

TPS Toyota Production System.

TQM Total Quality Management is not a system it is a philosophy embracing the total culture of an organization. TQM goes far beyond conformance to a standard, it requires a culture where every member of the organisation believes that not a single day should go by without the organisation in some way improving its efficiency and/or improving customer satisfaction.

UCL/LCL Upper control and lower control limits are used to show variations from a specification. Within the control limits performance will be deemed to be acceptable. The aim should be over time to reduce the control limits.

UNEP United Nations Environment Programme.

UNFCCC United Nations Framework Convention of Climate Change.

Value Analysis Very often a practice in purchasing is the evaluation of the expected performance of a product relative to its price.

Value Chain Also known as Porter's Value Chain for, according to Michael Porter, the competitive advantage of a company can be assessed only by seeing the company as a total system. This 'total system' comprises both primary and secondary activities.

Value Stream Mapping Value Stream Mapping (VSM) is a visual illustration of all activities required to bring a product through the main flow, from raw material to the stage of reaching the customer.

World Class World class is the term used to describe any organisation that is making rapid and continuous improvement in performance and who is considered to be using 'best practice' to achieve world class standards.

Zero Defects Philip Crosby made this term popular in the late seventies. The approach is right thing, right time, right place and every time. The assumption is that it is cheaper to do things right the first time.

Index

3M Company, Environmental, Health and Safety (EHS) case example, 253

A

ABC Analysis, 126f
Activity Network Diagram, 167, 170–173, 172f
Air conditioning, usage (country ranking/percentage), 276t
Airplanes/ships, clean transport solution, 265
Air source heat pump (ASHP), schematic diagram, 281f
Analysis of Variance (ANOVA), 213
Application software modules, 202f
Artificial Intelligence, 198, 209–212

B

Balanced Scorecard (BSC) (Kaplan/ Norton), 77f, 180–183
hierarchy, 83f

Barbados, flood relief (case example), 300
Big Data, 198, 209–212, 210f
Black Belts, 40–43, 43t
Brainstorming, 149, 159–161
Buildings (retrofitting)
circular economy, application, 277, 284–286
energy losses/consumption, reduction, 277–279
fossil fuel boilers/water heaters, replacement, 277, 279–282
greenhouse gas emission reductions, 277–286
Green Six Sigma, impact, 275
guiding factors, 276–277
initiatives, Six Sigma (impact), 286
renewable energy, usage, 277, 282–284

C

Carbon dioxide, 2
   country emission rates/percentages,
      6f, 7t, 8f
   emissions, 3f, 5f, 194t
Carbon footprint, 332–333, 345, 349
Carbon Footprint Tool, 180, 192–195
Car pool, data points/individual
      data, 116t
Carrefour Bio Coffee, case
      example, 255–256
Cause and Effect Diagram, 112,
      118–122, 121f
Certification, 75, 84–89
Channel Tunnel High Speed
      Rail Link (HS1), Six Sigma
      usage (case example), 270–271
China, climate change
      initiatives, 22–23
Circular economy, application,
      277, 284–286
Clean energy
   climate adaptation, 292, 294–295
   Green Six Sigma, relationship, 219
   guiding factors, 220–223
   share, 224t
   solutions, impact, 223–228
Clean energy initiatives
   Green Six Sigma, impact, 232–233
   Six Sigma, impact, 228
Clean transports
   guiding factors, 260–262
   solutions, impact, 262–267
Climate adaptation, Green Six Sigma
      (relationship), 291
Climate change
   digital applications, 198
   digital revolution, relationship, 197
   digital technology
      applications, 214–215
   initiative, Green Thinking
      (relationship), 238–240
   urgency, 1–2
Climate change initiatives
   implementation, 312–316

Coin tosses, results, 37t, 38f
Cola cans
   quantitative data, 99t
   value stream, 98f
Company performance, continuous
      improvement/sustainability,
      82
Conference of Parties (COP), 14, 18–19
Consumers, Green Initiatives,
      238, 246–248
Control Charts, 112, 126–131,
      129f, 130f
COP26, 314
Critical to Quality (CTQ) Tree, 96,
      105–107, 107f
Customer Relationships Management
      (CRM) solutions, 204

D

Define, Measure, Analyse, Improve,
      Control (DMAIC), 34, 42,
      48t, 95
   extension, 50, 241
   methodology, 60, 62
   problem-solving technique,
      32, 39
   replacement, 93
   stages, 62
   steps, 339
Define, Measure, Analyse, Improve,
      Control and Sustainability
      (DMAICS), 93, 241
Define, Measure, Design, and Verify
      (DMADV), 294–295
Deployment plan, outline, 63t
Design of Experiments, 213
Digital revolution, climate change
      (relationship), 197
Digital sustainability activities, 214
Digital technology applications,
      214–215
Domestic solar energy efficiency
      program, Six Sigma
      approach (case example),
      286–287

Domestic solar energy, schematic
diagram, 283f
Dow Chemical Company, Six Sigma
project (case example),
69–70
Dupont Teijin Films (Six Sigma
programme), performance
monitoring (case example),
79–80

E
Earth, temperature (increase),
3–5, 4f, 5f
E-Business, 198, 207–209, 208f
E-Commerce solutions, 208–209
Efficiency, 45, 46–47
FIT SIGMA, 250–251
Electric combi boiler solution, 280f
Electric vehicles (Europe),
percentage, 263t
Emissions, sources, 346–349
Energy sources, power density, 222
Enterprise Resource Planning (ERP)
applications, 204
Environment
Green Six Sigma, impact, 251–254
sustainability, 93, 240–241, 296
Equipment Time Analysis, 163f
Ethics, Green Six Sigma, 254–256
European countries, rail
electrification, 267t
European Foundation of Quality
Management (EFQM), 86,
87f, 180, 183–186, 186t
Executive Steering Committee, Green
Six Sigma
implementation, 323
Executive Torch Bearer, Green Six
Sigma implementation, 323

F
Farmers, Green Initiatives,
238, 248–249
Fitness for Sustainability, 50, 56,
72–92, 313

Fitness for the Purpose, 56–60, 60f
FIT SIGMA (Fit Sigma) (FIT Σ), 29,
32–34, 49–50, 53
efficiency, 250–251
elements, 56
fundamentals, 55f
Learning Deployment programme,
options, 63–64
programme, self-assessment
methodology, 88
FIT Σ process logic, 66f
Five S (Seiri, Seiton, Seiso,
Seiketson, Shitsuke),
149, 152–156
Five Whys, 131, 144–146
Flood protection, UK programme
(case example), 305
Flow Diagram (Flow Chart), 96,
102–105, 104f
Food, emissions, 346, 347f
Force Field Analysis (diagram), 131,
135–138, 137f

G
Gantt Chart, 167, 168–169, 169f
General Electric Capital, Best
Practice sharing (case
example), 92–93
General Electric (GE), case
examples, 231, 251
General public, climate change
implementation, 315
Global Carbon Project (GCP),
establishment, 19
Global community, climate
adaptation, 292, 293–294
Global Environmental Facility
(GAF), setup, 19
Global warming, term (usage), 2
Government, Green Initiatives, 238
Greenhouse gases
country emission rates/
percentages, 6–9
emission rates, economic sector
ranking, 9–10, 9t

Greenhouse gases (*continued*)
  emission reduction, clean
    energy solutions (impact),
    223–228
  emission reduction, clean transport
    solutions (impact), 262–267
  percentages, 2t
Green Six Sigma, 27, 32–34, 53
  carbon footprint, 332–333
  clean energy, relationship, 219
  communication, 334
  culture change/
    sustainability, 333, 334t
  defining, 50–51
  digital tools, 198, 212–214
  Do Steps, 325–326
  economic sector analysis, 220t
  external consultants, usage, 341
  green supply chain,
    relationship, 235
  green transport, relationship, 259
  impact, 250–256, 287–288, 337–339
  implementation, 311, 316, 318f
  improvement/sustaining, 334–336
  initial assessment, 320–321
  leadership workshop, 326
  management awareness, 318–320
  metrics, 331–332
  programme brief/organisation,
    321–326, 322f
  programme time plan, 337f
  project planned/completed,
    330f, 331f
  project review/feedback, 328–329
  project selection/delivery, 327–328
  success, measurement, 329–330
  sustainability, success, 336
  time frame, 3225
  time scale, 336
  tools, 60–61, 61t, 95, 96
  training deployment, 326–327
Green Supply Chain, Green Six Sigma
  impact, 238, 250–256
  relevance, reasons, 238, 240–242

Green supply chains, climate
    adaptation, 292, 295–297
Green Thinking
  climate change initiative,
    relationship, 238–240
  concept, 239f
  Toyota (5R), 252t
Green transport initiatives
  Green Six Sigma, impact, 271–272
  Six Sigma, impact, 267–269
Green transports
  climate adaptation, 292, 298–299
  Green Six Sigma, relationship, 259
Ground source heat pump (GSHP),
    schematic diagram, 282f
GSK Turkey (sustainable
    performance), S&OP usage
    (case example), 83–84

H
Histograms, 112, 114–117, 117f
Home appliances, circular
    economy, 285f
Househould emissions, 347
Houses (retrofitting)
  climate adaptation, 292, 299–303
  initiatives, Green Six Sigma
    (impact), 287–288
Houses (design), climate
    adaptation, 302t
Hurricane Katrina disaster
    relief, supply chain
    management/logistics
    resources (case example), 301
Hurtigruten AS cruise line, biofuel
    trials (case example), 266
Hydropower, output, 225

I
Implementation strategy,
    205–206
India, climate change initiatives, 23
Industry/service providers, climate
    change implementation, 315

Information and communication technology (ICT), 198
Information systems, 198–206
Information technology (IT), 198–206
hardware strategy, 200–201
software strategy, 201–203
strategy, 200f
Infrastructure projects, climate adaptation, 292, 303–306
Innovation, climate adaptation (relationship), 292, 306–308
Integrated Circuit Boards (ICBs), manufacture defects (identification), 125t
Intergovernmental Panel on Climate Change (IPCC), 14, 19
International Carbon Action Partnership (ICAP), 14, 16
International climate change initiatives, 13, 14–19
Interrelationship Diagram (ID), 131, 146–149, 148f
Ivanpah Solar Electric Generating system, Six Sigma (usage, case example), 229

J
Janssen-Cilag (continuous self-improvement), Signature of Quality (application case example), 89–90
Japan, climate change initiatives, 24
Just in Time (JIT), 44, 46

K
Kanban system, 44
Knowledge management, 75, 91–92
Kyoto Protocol, 14, 15–16

L
Lean Six Sigma, 27, 30–34, 47–48
defining, 43–47
Lean Thinking, application, 45
Learning deployment, 60, 62–66

M
Mangroves project, usage/return (case example), 303–304
Manufacturers, Green Initiatives, 238, 242–244
Manufacturing correctness profile, 89f
Marine plastic litter, elimination (case example), 304
Market making applications, types, 204
Master Black Belts (MBBs), 40–43
Material Flow Account, 180, 189–191, 191f
Media, climate change implementation, 315–316
Methane, global warming (impact), 2
Minitab output, areas, 212–213
Mistake Proofing, 149, 156–159

N
National climate change initiatives, 13, 20–24
National/local governments, climate change implementation, 314
Network Rail Limited, Lean Six Sigma usage (case example), 269–270
Net-zero carbon emissions, 23
Net-zero emissions, 18, 24
Net-zero targets, 19
New starters, climate change implementation, 317–318
Non-governmental organisations (NGOs), climate change implementation, 314–315
Non-profit Organisations, Green Initiatives, 238
Noranda Inc. Six Sigma training deployment (case example), 64–65
Normal distribution curve, 38f
Nuclear power capacity, ranking, 227t

O

Operational efficiency, example, 113t
Operational excellence, roadmap, 33f
Organisations, Green Six Sigma
  (usage), 340–341
Outcomes, sustainability
  (ensuring), 302
Overall Equipment Effectiveness
  (OEE), 149, 162–167

P

Pareto Charts, 112, 122–126, 125f
Paris Climate Agreement (Paris
  Accord), 14, 17–18
Passengers cars, clean transport
  solution, 262–264
Performance, fitness for the
  sustainability processes, 74, 75
Performance management, 75–78
  stages, 78f
Personal transportation,
  emissions, 348
Plan-Do-Check-Act (PDCA) Cycle,
  167, 177–179, 179f
Plants/animals, temperature increase
  (impact), 5
Political, Economic, Social, Technical
  Legal, and Environmental
  (PESTLE) Analysis, 131,
  141–144, 143f
Power
  density, 222t
  need, 221t
Primary energy, fuel share, 221t
Programme Leader, Green Six Sigma
  implementation, 323–324
Programme Team, Green Six Sigma
  implementation, 325
Project Charter, 96, 108–111, 110f–111f
Project management, outcome, 73f
Project organisation, two-way commu-
  nication process, 67f
Project plan/delivery, 60, 66–69

Q

Quality assurance, 45, 47
Quality Function
  Deployment (QFD), 95
Quality improvement
  annual plan, 30
  impact, 108
  initiatives, development, 183
  processes, 28–29
  programme, 122, 138, 173
  programmes, 183–184
  tool, 118
Quality management. *See* Total
  Quality Management
  evolution, 51
  tools, 160
Quality movement, barriers, 54f
Quality tools, 213

R

Radar Chart, 167, 173–176, 175f
Regression Analysis, 131–135, 134f
Renewable energy, usage, 277, 282–284
Renewable hydrogen energy,
  Six Sigma usage (case
  example), 231–232
Research and development (R&D),
  technology/materials
  improvement, 307t
Retailers, Green Initiatives,
  238, 244–246
Run Chart, 112–114, 113f
Russia, climate change
  initiatives, 23–24

S

Sales and Operations Planning
  (S&OP), 81–82, 81f,
  180, 186–189
Savings
  categories, 328t
  projects, identification
  sources, 68–69

SCORE, 48t
Seagate (lean/supply chain integration), Six Sigma (usage case example), 71–72
Self-assessment, 75, 84–89, 85t
Senior management review, 75, 80–82, 81f
Shift from variation (σ) to integration (Σ), 60, 70–71
Sigma (Σ) for Improvement and Integration, 56, 60–72
Single Minute Exchange of Dies (SMED), 149–152, 152f
SIPOC Diagram, 96, 100–102, 101f
Six Sigma, 27, 34–36
    defining, 36–40
    deployment, 41–42
    impact, 228, 286
    Project Charter, 110f–111f
    SME case example, 58–59
    structured approach, 40–42
    tasks, accomplishment, 41
Small and Medium Enterprises (SMEs), Green Six Sigma (usage), 339, 340f
Smooth operational flow, 45, 46
Soap
    packing line data, 166t
    production line, 165f
Software development strategy, 2032f
Solar cell manufacturing optimisation, Six Sigma approach (case example), 286
Solar power, output, 226t
Source materials, sustainability, 246
SSAB, first fossil-free steel delivery (case example), 244
Stalled Six Sigma, Green Six Sigma (usage), 337–339
Statistics, 212–213, 214
Strengths, Weaknesses, Opportunities, and Threats (SWOT) Analysis, 131, 138–140, 140t

Suppliers
    Green Initiatives, 238, 242–244
    performance/customer expectation, 176t
Supply chain
    characteristics/objectives, 45
    green supply chain, Green Six Sigma (relationship), 235
    management, 236f
    total supply chain emission chart, 243f
Supply Chain Management (SCM) solutions, 205
Sustainability, 51–52, 94, 333–334, 341
    achievement, 335
    culture, 185, 187
    development, defining, 238
    digital sustainability activities, addition, 214
    ensuring/enabling, 250, 293, 302, 333, 343
    fitness for sustainability, 50, 56, 72–92, 313
    focus, 11, 340
    success, 336
    sustainability of processes/performance levels, creation, 241
    targeting, 178
    terms, translation, 297
    tools, 96, 180, 195, 253, 339, 340
Sustainable development, defining, 238

T
Task Groups, Green Six Sigma implementation, 325
Technical book production, project activities list, 172t
Tesla Inc., Lean Six Sigma usage (case example), 368–369
Tools for Analysis, 131
Tools for Control, 167
Tools for Improve, 149

Tools for Measure, 112
Tools for Sustain, 180
Total Quality Management (TQM),
    28–32
Total solutions, self-analysis approach,
    86, 87f, 88–89
Total supply chain emission chart, 243f
Trains, clean transport solution,
    266–267
Transports, emissions, 260t
Trucks/buses, clean transport
    solution, 264–265

U
Unilever, climate change adaptation
    actions (case example),
    295–296
United Kingdom, climate change
    initiatives, 20–21
United Nations Framework
    Convention on Climate
    Change (UNFCCC), 14–15

United States, climate change
    initiatives, 21–22

V
Value Stream Mapping (VSM), 96–99
Variable Control Charts,
    construction, 129t
Vestas Wind Systems, Lean Six Sigma
    Initiatives (usage, case
    example), 230

W
Waste
    elimination, 45
    types, mudas, 44
Wind farms, quality
    improvement (case
    example), 231
Wind power, output, 225t

Y
Yield conversion table, 351–352